"As a longtime law professor and American Civil Liberties Union leader, I have intensely studied the issues surrounding free speech and higher education. But in *Free Speech and Liberal Education,* Donald Downs has provided me with invaluable, thought-provoking new insights, including by drawing upon classic works of political thought to illuminate the deeper significance of free speech jurisprudence and academic freedom for liberal democracy. In this engaging work, Downs also presents in-depth empirical analysis of the nature and extent of the threats to intellectual freedom on campus and in our society at large, as well as practical advice for constructive action gleaned from his extensive leadership in campus free speech politics. He balances due concern with appropriate hope."

—Nadine Strossen, John Marshall Harlan II Professor of Law, New York Law School; former president of the American Civil Liberties Union; and author of *HATE: Why We Should Resist It with Free Speech, Not Censorship*

"For decades, Donald Downs has fought in the trenches as one of our most compelling voices for freedom of inquiry and expression, on and off campus. In *Free Speech and Liberal Education,* he brings a lifetime of wisdom and passion to the task of understanding the spread of intolerance in American academic life—and a wealth of practical and humane suggestions for righting the ship. Along the way, he leads us on a journey from free speech theory to yesterday's newspaper. Best of all, his love for the academy radiates from every line. As I turned the pages of *Free Speech and Liberal Education,* I kept thinking, 'This is the book I've been waiting for.'"

—Jonathan Rauch, senior fellow, Brookings Institution, and author of *Kindly Inquisitors: The New Attacks on Free Thought*

FREE SPEECH

and

LIBERAL EDUCATION

FREE
SPEECH

 and

LIBERAL
EDUCATION

DONALD ALEXANDER DOWNS

Print ISBN: 978-1-948647-64-9
eBook ISBN: 978-1-948647-65-6

Library of Congress Cataloging-in-Publication Data

Downs, Donald Alexander, author.
   Free speech and liberal education : a plea for diversity and tolerance /
   Donald Alexander Downs.
      pages   cm
   Includes bibliographical references and index.
   ISBN 9781948647649 (hardback) | ISBN 9781948647656 (ebook)
   1. Academic freedom--United States. 2. Freedom of speech--United States.
   3. Education, Higher--Political aspects--United States. 4. Education,
   Higher--Aims and objectives--United States.
   LC72.2 .D689 2020
   378.1/213--dc23   2019051359

Jacket design: Faceout Studio
Jacket imagery: Shutterstock

Printed in the United States of America.

CATO INSTITUTE
1000 Massachusetts Avenue NW
Washington, DC 20001
www.cato.org

I dedicate this book to four entities. First, to the members of my family: Susan, Jacqueline, Alexander, Matthew, Megan, Madeline, Jolie, and Jackson. Second, to my colleagues on the late Committee for Academic Freedom and Rights at Wisconsin. Third, to my students at Wisconsin, with a special nod to those who supported our free speech and academic freedom movement in different ways that mattered. Finally, to the University of Wisconsin–Madison, my institutional home.

To live is to find ourselves fatally obliged to exercise our liberty, to decide what we are going to be in this world. Not for a single moment is our activity of decision allowed to rest. Even when in desperation we abandon ourselves to whatever may happen, we have decided not to decide.

It is, then, false to say that in life "circumstances decide." On the contrary, circumstances are the dilemma, constantly renewed, in presence of which we have to make our decision; what actually decides is our character.

—José Ortega y Gasset, *The Revolt of the Masses*

CONTENTS

A FREE SPEECH CRISIS IN HIGHER EDUCATION?

The main task we face is preserving the university not merely as a free political community but primarily as an institution that is privileged to be an intellectual sanctuary within a society that is now in political flux.

After all, the university's primary mission resides not in political activity but in the cultivation of the intellectual freedoms. . . . [I]t is imperative that no one facet of the university's activities, certainly not the political, should dominate its overall responsibilities for cultivation of the intellect. . . . [A]ny conflict between the intellectual and the political way of life must be resolved in favor of the intellectual over the political.

—*Berkeley Professor Albert Lepawsky,*
speaking during the Berkeley Free Speech Movement, 1964[1]

The question of the status of free speech and academic freedom in higher education today has captured national attention. Reports of violations of and affronts to academic free speech have spread across the land in recent years, as has debate about the nature of the problem and how extensive it is.[2] On the pessimistic side, the title of a March 3, 2017, op-ed in the *Chronicle of Higher Education* by former Stanford provost John Etchemendy featured foreboding words: "The Threat from Within: Intellectual Intolerance Poses an Existential Danger to the University." Etchemendy focused on intellectual echo chambers created by a lack of intellectual diversity and standards in some fields and campus arenas, as well as by the mistreatment of many speakers deemed contrary to campus orthodoxy.

Other examples of intellectual intolerance cited by various critics in our day have included disinvitations of qualified speakers for ideological reasons, illegitimate attacks on professors for things they have said or written, application of censorious speech codes, and bureaucratic proliferation of new policies and programs that can readily inhibit and smother the open and honest exchange of ideas that make a campus come intellectually alive. Such measures encompass trigger warnings, microaggression lists, designation of expansive "safe spaces" that shelter students from unwelcome ideas, mandatory sensitivity sessions that can become overbearing and intolerant of disagreement, and intrusive "bias reporting" systems that can engender a climate of Orwellian informing and accusation.

Though many of those policies originated in the commendable desire to foster equal respect for students and other campus citizens, they have too often morphed into politically progressive forms of censorship and bullying, thereby vindicating the observation that affronts to individual liberty are wrong regardless of the motives or political direction from which they emanate.[3] "Progressive censorship" can be every bit as detrimental to a free society as "conservative" or "traditional" censorship, as pessimists have noted.

On the more sanguine side, Arianne Shahvisi, a lecturer in ethics and medical humanities at Brighton and Sussex Medical School in Britain writes, "Free speech is widely declared to be endangered, and we are told that students and sympathetic academics are responsible for its demise. Yet on the ground, things feel much the same as ever. Lively debates *do* continue to happen. . . ."[4] This observation is also valid in many venues, as numerous academic observers will acknowledge. We hear a lot about the disruptions and inhibitions—which are all too real and condemnable when they arise—but less about the countless encounters where repression does not occur. Bad news grabs more notice than does good news.

The disagreement between Etchemendy and Shahvisi is emblematic of the larger debate in the national arena, which is not surprising. Higher education, after all, is a vast domain, and the status of intellectual freedom varies with each institution and sometimes even within the same institution. It also varies over time. What "ground" one stands on or observes can color one's assessment. In addressing the question of the status of academic free speech, we must avoid becoming either Chicken Little or the proverbial ostrich with its head in the sand.

When all the dust clears, however, experience and available evidence counsel us to take the problem seriously while also striving to be objective and fair. The best way to think about the status of intellectual freedom in higher education today is as *embattled*. This assessment means that its fate hangs in the balance and that what we do now and in the future matters. *Free Speech and Liberal Education* is meant to encourage what I consider constructive action.

For reasons depicted in this book, we do appear to have ventured further down the road toward repression, though there are reasons to believe that we can turn the cart around, depending on the choices we make. The number of reported anti-freedom incidents and the accounts of many professors, students, and commentators, plus the results of recent surveys, present reason for legitimate apprehension, especially when we note that suppression often takes place beneath the radar screen of public notice, as I will elaborate.

In addition, even if higher education happened to be free in most contexts, this fact does not mean that the anti-freedom incidents that do occur are somehow acceptable, except in certain limited areas that I will discuss at different points in this book. (Private schools, for example, have the right to choose their own destinies—ironically, the principles of freedom require no less—even if the path they choose for themselves is illiberal.) More universally, history reveals that intellectual freedom is always at risk. Some ideas will always be unwelcome and disturbing to entrenched interests and conventional wisdom however true they ultimately prove to be. Like conflict itself, the struggle for free speech is woven into the very fabric of human nature, human relations, and organized society.[5]

How we resolve the academic free speech problem matters because what happens in higher education influences the thinking and attitudes of our nation's future leaders and citizens. Furthermore, respect for intellectual freedom and the willingness to defend it make up the heart and soul of America's experiment in democratic self-government. If intellectual freedom in higher education falters, the prospects for liberal democracy itself diminish in an increasingly hostile world. As the noted free speech and educational philosopher Alexander Meiklejohn wrote in the midst of the McCarthy era in the United States, "To be afraid of ideas, any idea, is to be unfit for self-government."[6]

As this book will relate, however, upholding higher education's responsibility to nourish and defend intellectual freedom requires four essential tasks or obligations: *knowledge* of the principles and requisites of intellectual freedom, a knowledge that includes grasping the proper limits of freedom; *commitment* to those principles and basics; the *will* to act in their defense in the face of the pressures that arise in an imperfect world; and, finally, giving *priority* to those obligations, which is of central importance to higher education because its distinctive task is the pursuit of truth.

Honoring this responsibility lies at the core of the social contract—explicit or implicit—by which higher education possesses the institutional rights, privileges, and status that it enjoys. Prioritization is essential not only for the normative reason just accentuated, but also for strategic purposes. The landscape of higher education today is fraught with a host of competing tasks and commitments, making it difficult to see the forest amid the proliferating trees. Some of the alternative missions are confusing distractions, whereas others are antithetical to the central mission—at least in the shapes they now take.

The combination of knowledge, commitment, will, and prioritization points to the existential dimension of the problem at hand. Freedom is not manna from heaven. It has to be defended when it comes under attack, and doing so often requires accepting the trouble of standing up and taking heat in the face of counterclaims, which are often compelling in their own ways. Recent survey evidence that I examine in Chapters 1 and 6 indicate widespread belief—or lip service—to academic free speech principles among both faculty members and the heads of the nation's colleges and universities. (Another survey of lower-level administrators is notably less sanguine.) But such verbal commitment amounts to little or nothing if leaders are not willing to take difficult stances to protect intellectual freedom when it comes under attack by campus groups, especially if that threat comes from groups with whom one might otherwise sympathize or agree.

Given the different dimensions of the problem at stake, this book combines theory, practice, and empiricism. My own background might be helpful in answering the questions. I am an emeritus professor of political science at the University of Wisconsin–Madison and an emeritus affiliate professor of its schools of law and journalism. My writings and teaching have dealt with, among other matters, free speech, academic freedom, academic politics, the First Amendment, and political and legal thought. And I added practice to theory by serving as a leader of a distinctive, independent, and nonpartisan academic freedom group with some national connections at Madison from 1996 to 2016.

The Committee for Academic Freedom and Rights (CAFAR) was a nonpartisan group of 15 or so faculty members hailing from a wide diversity of fields and backgrounds. We also had many staunch student allies. During our tenure, UW–Madison confronted as many major free speech and academic freedom conflicts as any institution in the country, some of which I will discuss throughout this book. We achieved many policy successes at Madison, including abolishing and revising speech codes and related policies, as well as providing successful legal assistance to two dozen faculty members and students whose rights had been violated or jeopardized at Madison or other schools in the state.[7] The UW–Madison case presents evidence of both hope and challenge, and we often drew on the distinguished academic freedom heritage of the institution in our activism, thereby gaining further allies in the process.

My academic, practical, and political experience throughout the years reveals to me that the battle over free speech is a subset of a broader contest over the meaning of the university, a contest that was renewed in the 1960s and that was intensified in more recent decades. Three ideal-type models of the university are before us as we consider free speech in the American university. First is the traditional proprietary institution, in which the primary mission is to pursue a largely conservative or a substantive moral or religious vision.

Second is the modern, more secular research university that arose over the course of the 19th century and that prioritizes the open-ended pursuit of truth, accompanied by strong academic freedom. This model is liberal because it is predicated on the classical liberal notions of individual freedom, tolerance, and equal rights. Though it is liberal, trends today make this model seem conservative to many eyes, and many traditional liberals and conservatives have joined hands in defending it. And third is what I would call the progressive "social justice proprietary" university, which either prioritizes things such as social justice, diversity, and the pursuit of equality or gives those missions equal or close to equal standing in the hierarchy of ends.

The fundamental difference between the classical liberal and the social justice models is one of mission. The former prioritizes liberty of mind; the latter, the pursuit of equality of condition, which is a tension that Tocqueville also analyzed at length in *Democracy in America*. Tocqueville understood how equality and liberty coexist in a dynamic and productive tension in American liberal democracy, but he warned how the unqualified pursuit of equality of condition over liberty has a dark side that would lead to loss of individual and political freedom in favor of a tyranny of opinion and disrespect for individual rights and individual opinions. Historically, progressivism also hitched its wagon to enhancing bureaucratic power and administrative governance over democratic input, a phenomenon that Tocqueville disparaged and that we see in the expansion of administrative power on campus. This move challenges free speech, because free speech is intimately related to the raucous and unpredictable pursuit of truth.

The move also has implications for the self-governing interactions of "We the People," which take place outside the scope of top-down bureaucratic control. In the words of Michael Kent Curtis, free speech is "the people's darling privilege," as it was termed during debates over the Sedition Act in the early republic. (Nowadays we would call it "the people's darling right"—for rights are universal—and so we shall do here.) An efficient and principled bureaucracy is necessary to a viable modern political regime; the problem arises when administrative governance grows beyond its proper grounds and usurps the freedom of citizens in civil society.[8]

Equal rights matter, of course. Wrongful discrimination is part of our nation's history, and its effects and legacies remain with us. It is essential that activists remind us of our history. The drive for diversity that is such a preoccupation in higher education today can be productive if it broadens intellectual and moral horizons by exposing students to things such as the cultural and economic pluralism of the United States and the world and such concerns as the pros and cons of the tentatively established order. Problems arise when this drive becomes narrowly defined and bureaucratically dogmatic in content and application, as is sadly too often the case today.

In a famous 1963 speech about teaching, race, and intellectual horizons, Ralph Ellison called for a liberal education that not only expands the horizons of class and identity but also enriches the imagination. "But we are here, and since we are, let us try to see American society in all of its diversity. One of the things that has been left out in our discussion is imagination. But imagination exists even in the backwoods of Alabama, and here too is to be found a forthright attitude toward what it is possible to achieve and to become in this country."[9] Ellison called for the mixing of people from very different backgrounds, from the privileged to the less privileged, to engage in a common pursuit of citizenship and humanity. And the type of imagination he had in mind is nourished by respect for equality and freedom of the mind.

But sometime after the 1960s, the progressive drive for equality on campus decoupled itself to varying extents from the liberal principle of individual freedom, thus creating a tension between the liberal and the progressive models of the university. Before the 1960s, liberty of speech, equality, and social progress were veritable partners. Their separation today means that the fate of campus free speech hangs in the balance. For reasons of pluralism and liberty of conscience and choice, the United States should make room for all three models of higher education, as I will explain in Chapter 2. But it must do so in ways that do not marginalize the liberal freedom that is so important to a nation that, as Lincoln observed, is "conceived in liberty" as well as dedicated to "the proposition that all men are created equal." Social justice without liberal rights is oxymoronic.

I set the stage for our discussion in Chapter 1 by presenting the different dimensions of the threats to academic free speech that we face, while also introducing a few constructive examples of counter-actions. I also provide a lens by which to ascertain and assess what is taking place. A major concern is what transpires in the "shadow university" of bureaucratic pressure.

Chapters 2 and 3 treat different aspects of what a university is, thus furnishing a foundation for thinking about the connections between intellectual freedom and the mission of higher education. Chapter 2 defends the central "truth" mission and the concomitant intellectual virtues of the university. Human understanding is undeniably fallible, and the world is subtle and complex, as well as full of tensions and contradictions. In terms of both theory and practice, what works in one context can fail in another. So the pursuit of truth must respect dissent and conflict—aspects of Socratic virtue.[10] I also depict the university as a special type of community or "intellectual *polis*" that involves different roads to knowledge.

Chapter 3 takes a further step by delineating the important connections and differences between "academic freedom" and "freedom of speech," a distinction that requires its own chapter. Academic freedom demands more competence-based limits than does general free speech. When true to their distinctive intellectual missions, institutions of higher education cultivate both of those freedoms dialectically. Academic free speech is dynamic and multileveled, and learning is intellectual, emotional, personal, and interpersonal. These are reasons free speech should prevail not only in the classroom, but also in the far reaches of the *polis*, and they are why some of the new campus policies and programs can be so detrimental to liberal education and personal growth.

The model of liberal education that I portray in Chapters 2 and 3 is admittedly ideal in many respects. Recent works chronicle the ways in which student workloads, achievement, and enthusiasm have declined in inverse relation to the escalating costs and "corporatization" of higher education. I do not deny those findings.[11] Furthermore, some of the smartest and most insightful people whom I have known are not college graduates. Come to think of it, Lincoln barely went to primary school.

What I portray is how a liberal education can contribute to students' growth and curiosity when it does its job; in the process, I show what is lost when things go awry. What George Bernard Shaw called the "spark of divine fire" still lights up many students' minds when things go right.

In Chapters 4–6, I address different threats to academic freedom and free speech today. A host of forces and trends both inside and outside academia have made it more difficult for colleges and universities to give the priority to academic freedom and free speech that is so necessary for the institutions to live up to their obligations under the social contract. I also look at recent survey research that attempts to discern empirically the status of free speech on campus today and at how attitudes might influence this status.

In Chapter 7, I discuss why the status of academic free speech and free speech in general matters to us all. As the late Charles Krauthammer once wrote, "you betray your whole life if you don't say what you think and if you don't say it honestly and bluntly."[12] And free expression is indispensable to the success of liberal democracy as a social and political system. In addressing why it matters, I will draw on classic free speech and First Amendment theory, accompanied by some practical, empirical, and experiential findings that support this theory.

Respecting free speech protects individuals' rights and helps to secure social benefits. It can also foster a type of *character* that is open to and able to handle the challenges that the pursuit of truth and life in a democratic republic present. Sometimes the virtues of free speech are taken for granted in commentary. We no longer have this luxury in higher education today. It is important to remind ourselves of what is at stake and why it matters.

Finally, in Chapter 8, I explore practical remedies to the problem of academic free speech, and I look at bottom-up mobilization on campus, outside resources, and broader institutional policymaking. I will also address the appropriate limits to free speech. This particular discussion is important for two reasons. First, no right is absolute or without limits necessary to preserve proper order and to protect other important interests. Second, one of the virtues a university should foster is the ability to abide by proper limits, thereby developing the self-control that is essential to citizenship in a constitutional democracy. Freedom is a paradox that is nourished by the proper mix of self-control, discipline, respect for others' rights, and a spirit of self-reliance and assertion that can take the form of intellectual rebellion and even transgression. We must accept uncomfortable yet viable established truths at the same time that we challenge those existing beliefs that need correction.

CHAPTER 1

FRAMING THE PROBLEM

What happened to me is being repeated at colleges and universities throughout the country. Unfortunately, a growing number of university students equate being made uncomfortable in the classroom with being "harmed." And in this they are encouraged by a growing number of faculty and administrators who view the mission of the university as more about shielding students from such "harm" (for the sake of "inclusivity") and less about meaningful education. In the "surveillance university," students are encouraged to report on the transgressions of faculty, and in what has been called an impulse of "vindictive protectiveness," faculty are judged guilty and harshly punished.

—Evan Charney, Duke University associate professor on being fired from Duke as a result of sensitivity complaints by a few students[1]

This chapter sets the stage for the subsequent analysis in three ways. First, I discuss some campus speech disruptions, which are the most conspicuous displays of intellectual intolerance. Second, I use the case of Laura Kipnis at Northwestern as a vehicle for thinking about the role that the university's bureaucratic shadow can play in the politics of academic free speech. Speech disruptions are often symptomatic of the anti-speech aspects of campus culture that are abetted by the ever-growing campus administrative state and other forces. In interesting ways, student reliance on this new apparatus represents a retreat from the abolition of *in loco parentis* policies that student activists successfully exiled from campus life in the 1960s and 1970s. That abolition was driven by the aspiration of students to be treated as adults with the wherewithal to handle the rights, responsibilities, and rigors attendant upon citizenship in a constitutional polity that is based on self-government.

Today, a new alliance of students and administrators appears willing to give back some of this hard-earned ground in a campaign accompanied by claims of student emotional vulnerability that new bureaucracies accommodate.[2] How many students are complicit in this effort remains to be seen, but I will report instances throughout this book.

Third, building upon Kipnis's observations, I offer a lens on how to think about the nature and scope of speech restrictions and on how to build potential resistance and countermovements. During the middle of the first decade of the 2000s, higher education appeared to have taken a breather from the widespread investigations and campus prosecutions that had taken place in the later 1980s and the 1990s under the aegis of new forms of identity politics, new speech codes, and expanded harassment codes that had extended their reach into new domains of censorship.

It was as if the so-called "era of speech codes and political correctness" had run out of steam after too much exertion. But a colleague of mine at Madison tendered what proved to be a prescient observation. "Political correctness might not have died," he observed. "It just might have metastasized." By this he meant that it was now instituting itself within the sinews of campus bureaucracy and culture, in what Alan Charles Kors and Harvey A. Silverglate have called the "shadow university."[3]

And sure enough, sometime around 2015, we began to hear about the widespread institutionalization of seemingly less overt but potentially more intrusive policies dealing with matters such as trigger warnings, safe spaces, micro-aggressions, bias reporting, intensified forms of sensitivity training, and an even more recent drive to include questions about things such as sensitivity and inclusiveness in course evaluation forms. Those policies thereby provide yet another vehicle for students to attack instructors for political or ideological reasons. It is to this realm that we must look to gain a full picture of academic free speech suppression.

One of the ideas behind the new policies has been to avoid the overt forms of censorship that had grabbed so much national attention and opprobrium during the heyday of the speech code era. The fate of politics is often affected by who wins the rhetoric game, and free speech advocates in this previous era often won in the court of public and judicial opinion by being able to label the new codes "*speech* codes." But the harms of policies such as bias reporting are less evident on the surface. After all, bias is wrong, so what is improper with reporting it? One must look deeper to see what might be harmful here, which is one of this book's purposes. Here I lay the groundwork for that discussion.

SPEECH DISRUPTIONS

Alas, the advent of the new bureaucratic measures has not meant that speech codes and speech disruptions have gone the way of the horse and buggy. Indeed, campus diversity and sensitivity bureaucrats, along with some faculty members, have often worked or interacted with students to nourish anti–free speech thinking and activism, and the new administrative policies have often provided vehicles for such efforts. Seek and ye shall find.

Accordingly, a new wave of speaker disruptions in campus forums and the classroom started breaking out around 2015, and they were highlighted by confrontations that sometimes involved mob actions, physical intimidation, and anger. The cases I mention here represent actual disruptions, which means that the speaker had to be stopped or was prevented from fulfilling his or her objective. The new state bills designed to protect speech on campus (see Chapter 8) borrow a standard from the Supreme Court case *Tinker v. Des Moines School District*: counter-speech that "materially and substantially interferes" with the speaker crosses the line that separates legitimate protests and disruptions.[4] Simple heckling and comments from the audience during a speech do not transgress the line unless they pass into the realm of substantial interference. As with the application of many legal standards, when that line is violated is a matter of informed judgment.

A small sampling of the most notorious episodes includes cases at the University of Pennsylvania (speaker CIA director John Brennan, 2016), California State University–Los Angeles (speaker Ben Shapiro, 2016),

Middlebury College (speaker Charles Murray and moderator Allison Stanger, 2017), Evergreen State (professor Bret Weinstein, 2017, driven from class), Claremont McKenna (speaker Heather Mac Donald, 2017), and Philadelphia University of the Arts (professor and speaker Camille Paglia, 2019). Those and several other cases documented by the Foundation for Individual Rights in Education (FIRE) and other sources typically have involved social justice or progressive activists who claim that the speaker's views not only go beyond the pale of moral acceptability, but also threaten students' sense of well-being and safety. But right-wing groups have also joined the parade. In October 2017, for example, an aggressive pro-Trump group substantially interfered with an event at Whittier College that featured California attorney general Xavier Becerra, a Democrat, and Ian Calderon, majority leader of the California State Assembly.[5] The Whittier disrupters were led by outsiders, a situation found in other cases as well. For instance, the mob violence directed against Milo Yiannopoulos at Berkeley in 2017 was instigated by anti-fascist, anarchistic outsiders. The resistance to this provocateur *par excellence* included physical attacks and the setting of fires.

One way to look at speaker disruptions is to compare numbers: given the existence of 3,000 or more institutions of higher learning in the United States, should we make a big deal out of the dozen or few dozen episodes that make the news each year? Yes and no. Higher education is a huge empire. Not surprisingly, after Charles Murray was forced off the stage at Middlebury, he was able to speak at other schools, such as Notre Dame and Columbia. And much depends on how institutions react to the disruptions and on the messages they send to people who are considering inviting a controversial speaker or speaking out themselves in a way that might provoke unjustified anger.

When bad incident meets weak response, the message can be inhibiting to those who are reluctant to experience the wrath of disrupters in the future. The attack on Murray at Middlebury—a speech disruption heard around the academic world—highlights the harm that can take place. Student "social justice" activists there ran the controversial political scientist off the stage through bullying and threatening tactics that included assaulting the event's moderator Allison Stanger, professor of political science. Stanger had to be temporarily hospitalized with a concussion she received from physical mishandling by what she described as a frenzied mob. In a *New York Times* op-ed written soon after the melee, Stanger expressed disbelief and shock at what she confronted:

> Most of the hatred was focused on Dr. Murray, but when I took his right arm to shield him and to make sure we stayed together, the crowd turned on me. Someone pulled my hair, while others were shoving me. I feared for my life. Once we got into the car, protesters climbed on it, hitting the windows and rocking the vehicle whenever we stopped to avoid harming them. I am still wearing a neck brace, and spent a week in a dark room to recover from a concussion caused by the whiplash.[6]

In the aftermath of this embarrassing incident, a pro–academic free speech group of Middlebury faculty members wrote a statement defending free speech and the open university, and they presented it at an emotional faculty meeting. However, a majority of the faculty at this prestigious academic institution refused to accept the statement. As Stanger wrote in another *New York Times* op-ed, a majority of faculty members were reluctant—or afraid—to challenge the claims of an aggressive form of identity politics. She pinpointed the anti-intellectual campus culture that was nourishing the support of the disruptive students. "The moderate middle at Middlebury currently feels it cannot speak out on the side of free inquiry without fear of being socially ostracized as racist. Most alarming, I have heard some students and faculty denounce reason and logic as manifestations of white supremacy. This is not a productive learning environment for anyone. This is not what the life of the mind is supposed to provide."[7]

Another issue that is associated with the disruption issue is the disinvitation of a speaker, the sibling of which is not inviting someone in the first place out of fear of encountering trouble. (In the parlance of free speech jurisprudence, this concern is a form of "chilling effect.") Not inviting a desirable speaker for nonintellectual reasons is a problem the extent of which cannot be fully determined. But disinviting a speaker raises the specter of censorship even more because the act of disinvitation often takes place as a result of overt pressure exerted by people who disagree with the speaker's message. A rebuttable presumption of viewpoint discrimination is present.[8] A classic example is Williams College, which in 2015 disinvited Susan Venker, a feminist writer who is critical of mainstream feminism. Ironically, the Venker speech was part of the new "Uncomfortable Learning" speakers' series at Williams, a special student-run program supported by alumni funding that was created for the express purpose of challenging students with views not always present on campus.[9]

Other, noncensorious, reasons obviously can prompt a disinvitation, so one needs to consider the facts at hand. That said, one has to wonder how many speakers who could contribute to and perhaps even revitalize the intellectual vitality and diversity of a campus are not invited in the first place because of the chilling effect of campus intolerance and orthodoxy. When one examines my experience and that of numerous colleagues I have spoken with across the land, the answer is virtually universal: of course most campus citizens think about the reaction, for better or worse. The courage to invite is related to the courage to speak out as a dissenter. The issues of disinvitation and noninvitation speak to the broader issues of intellectual diversity and of the culture of a campus.

On the encouraging side, FIRE's web page on disinvitations shows improvement in recent years as the blowback from campus censorship has gained some steam. And sometimes a disinvited speaker is re-invited later, as happened to me at Cornell University in 1999 when the panel to which I was invited was temporarily disbanded because of controversy. (I was also permanently disinvited from a forum at the University of Michigan Law School in 1995.) In 2018, the number of *recorded* disinvitation *attempts and successes* reached a 10-year low (9) after peaking in 2016 (43) and 2017 (37).[10] Note that those are only the recorded actions; no doubt more exist though we can never know how many. But the decline of recorded cases is encouraging in two respects. It suggests that the cycle of tolerance and intolerance is perhaps swinging back to a saner position, at least for now. And it likely reflects the effects of the constructive blowback that I discuss in Chapter 8 and more briefly later in this chapter.

This and other upbeat trends led Jeffrey Sachs to conclude in an early 2019 essay that "The Campus 'Free Speech Crisis' Ended Last Year."

Sachs acknowledges that the jury is still out on this question, so the title of the essay exaggerated his position, probably for presentation purposes. But he does point to positive campus cultural trends favoring free speech, some of which I touch on in Chapters 6 and 8. And he notes FIRE's latest report on the legal status of campus speech codes, which shows continued, though incremental, improvement in that category over time.[11]

In addition, 2019 has featured some reversals on the free speech front that erupted around the time Sachs published his essay. For example, toward the end of 2018, a host of faculty members at Williams College began pressuring the administration to reconsider the school's decision to adopt a pro–free speech campus policy modeled on the famous University of Chicago Statement on the Principles of Free Expression. As of this writing, the debate over free speech has put this elite institution "in meltdown," in the words of Luana S. Maroja, a biology professor who helped write the original pro–free speech proposal. Now 400 faculty members have signed a petition to reconsider the college's free speech policy. At an emotional yet inconclusive faculty meeting in November 2018, student activists showed up in resistance. Maroja reported that they shouted "free speech harms" and that they alleged that pro–free speech faculty members "were trying to kill them."[12]

Sachs also raises doubts about self-censorship and silencing. The question of self-censorship is always tricky, similar to assuming things such as Freudian "repression" or "unconscious bias" and motivation. But reports of students and faculty self-censoring are widespread and are consistent with what numerous students have told me and my colleagues.

In a recent interview with C-SPAN's Brian Lamb, Yale's distinguished professor of international politics and strategy, John Gaddis, shared this concern and lamented that it is nigh impossible to have an honest and open discussion of national politics and the 2016 election at Yale. Robotic thinking about a matter of crucial national interest takes over at one of the world's leading academic institutions.

[It] can't really be done on a rational basis most of the time within the university—a university like Yale, the feelings are so visceral, it's hard to have any conversation that does not say predictable things. . . . Anybody who tries to say something less than predictable is apt to be disregarded. People do not try. . . . [A new domestic outreach program at Yale for students in Gaddis's Grand Strategy program] is just our small effort to try to break down some of the isolation that somehow the elite universities have locked themselves into, the bubbles into which they have placed themselves."[13]

As accentuated in this book's introduction, the best way to think about academic free speech in higher education today is that it is embattled. Sachs agrees, though he is more sanguine than many critics are about the positive trends. The Williams College case just discussed appears to support the embattlement model, because it pits earnest pro–free speech faculty forces against those who consider free speech to be threatening and dangerous. Of course, one response to the embattlement model is "why should a right and practice so foundationally essential to liberal education and liberal democracy be embattled at all? Or at least as embattled as it is, replete with attacks that derogate the very value of free speech?" Arguments about the proper limits to free speech are universal, and the courts are always busy with cases in which the sides battle over where to draw the line. But reasoned censorship is different from the claim that "free speech is killing us." In the end, what matters is how Williams resolves the dispute.

One area Sachs does not address much is the shadow university, where self-censorship is encouraged by a plethora of new policies. Let us now look at the Laura Kipnis case.

LAURA KIPNIS AND THE "NETHERWORLD" OF THE SHADOW UNIVERSITY

An adequate reckoning of what is going on requires looking beyond speech codes, speech disruptions, and other more manifest aspects of censorship. Laura Kipnis's case at Northwestern University and what she learned from her experience are educational in this respect.

In 2015, Kipnis was targeted with a harrowing federal Title IX sexual harassment investigation, which was backed by full university cooperation. Her offense? Writing an opinion piece critiquing campus "sexual paranoia" in the *Chronicle of Higher Education*.[14] The Title IX investigation was a product of new mandates for the handling of sexual misconduct and harassment cases handed down by the Obama administration's Department of Education (DOE). Among other things, the DOE required schools receiving federal funds to investigate and prosecute cases more aggressively; to lower the standard of proof of guilt to a "preponderance of evidence," the lowest standard of culpability in legal doctrine; and to disallow meaningful cross-examination of accusers. Given the mixture of the changes and campus politics and pressure, the new regimes often boiled down to turning the long-standing presumption of innocence inside out, assuming the guilt of the accused unless proven otherwise.[15]

In the past, higher education did not do enough to deal with the genuine harms of sexual assault and harassment, so reform was called for. Institutions even failed to make evidence of sex crimes public, thereby opening the door to outside, sometimes federal, intervention. (The failure to protect academic free speech is now opening the same door.) But new problems arise when reforms undermine classic rights such as due process and the presumption of innocence and when reforms stretch the conception of harassment to include simply writing an opinion piece about a controversial matter. Justice without due process and free thought is not justice. Indeed, when I first read about Kipnis being investigated for writing an opinion piece, I thought I was reading *The Onion*—the proud satirical newspaper founded by UW–Madison students—not the *Chronicle of Higher Education*.

Kipnis's troubles began when students accused her of harassment for having written the *Chronicle* essay—a classic example of the conflation of speech and action that is a major feature of many new attacks on freedom of speech. She did not dismiss the problem of campus sexual assault and the culpability of perpetrators, but she argued that many claims were murky and that too many women had fallen prey to an infantilizing victimhood mentality that was overblown and detrimental to their independence and mature sexual relations. Her position was a matter of honest opinion, and some responsible men and women have made similar points, while others have disagreed.

Kipnis ultimately prevailed in the investigation. But rather than simply retreating into a cellar and waiting for the exposure and ordeal to pass—a common route for many wrongly accused individuals—she fought back and wrote about the accusation in another *Chronicle* article. In addition, she began looking into other cases at Northwestern and elsewhere, ultimately becoming a lightning rod for individuals nationwide who felt wrongly accused of sexual misconduct.

She also wrote *Unwanted Advances.* In this 2017 book, she postulated that new forces sweeping higher education have left it "so radically transformed that the place is almost unrecognizable." In addition, she reported how learning about the activities of campus bureaucracy opened her eyes to miscarriages of justice that she had not previously imagined could exist. Her observation of this discovery is worth quoting at some length:[16]

> It turns out that rampant accusation is the new norm on today's campus; the place is a secret *cornucopia* of accusation, especially when it comes to sex. My in-box became a clearinghouse for depressing and infuriating tales of overblown charges, capricious verdicts, and frightening bureaucratic excess. I was introduced to an astonishing netherworld of accused professors and students, rigged investigations, and closed-door hearings, and Title IX officers run amok. *This was a world I'd previously known nothing about, because no one on campus knows anything about it.* . . . And those in the know are terrified to speak out.[17]

I can attest to the validity of Kipnis's observation. Over the 20 years of its existence, CAFAR dealt with many cases at UW–Madison and other Wisconsin institutions that took place in this netherworld. If one thinks about the magnitude and different dimensions of campus censorship, it is not enough to just consider reported speech disruptions and prominent applications of improper speech codes, however important those problems are in themselves. Cultural inhibitions and nonpublic bureaucratic actions matter too. CAFAR usually kept such incidents out of the limelight to protect the reputations and interests of our clients, so our opportunity to shine much light into the shadows was limited—though we did activate our flashlights whenever we felt justified in doing so. On the positive side, we achieved our objectives in all our cases as we demonstrated the potential effectiveness of appropriate resistance and drew on the historic academic freedom principles of the institution, which were still alive.

But even here a caveat is in order. Over the years, CAFAR often worked with administrators at UW–Madison who were willing to work with us and to make concessions because of the mutual respect we developed, and they shared some concerns with us. In 2018, the legal office, led by Vice Chancellor for Legal Affairs Raymond Taffora, in cooperation with CAFAR, a FIRE representative (Azhar Majeed), and the dean of students, revised four campus codes relating to speech to earn "green lights" from FIRE, which means that the codes as written pose no First Amendment problem. All UW–Madison rules related to speech are now green-lighted. There are no "yellow" (potential problem) or "red" lights (definite problem as written). Unfortunately, a yellow-lighted UW System rule about internet use remains in effect as of this writing, and it is being reconsidered by the state government beyond the aegis of UW–Madison, which has challenged the rule.

After I began writing about higher education and became more known regarding academic free speech cases in different capacities, I had my own Kipnis-like experience: I started to hear from previous students and faculty members who had encountered difficulties that I and others had never heard about. This acknowledgment does not afford a license to assume abuse where it is not demonstrated. But it does mean that we need to broaden our lens in looking for abuse while avoiding unwarranted assumptions. Presuming guilt is wrong, regardless of the target.

Nonetheless, examples of bureaucratic pressures abound. For example, the University of Michigan has recently adopted a remarkably vague and overbroad bias reporting system that encourages students to report incidents of bias that can include speech considered "hurtful" or even "bothersome." And by the highly subjective and relativistic standards that prevail in many quarters today—see Chapter 4—those concepts can have quite expansive application. A new student free speech group is presently suing Michigan on First Amendment chilling effect grounds. One wonders: where was the faculty when this and allied programs at Michigan were instituted?

In recent years, Michigan has hired 100 administrators to work in its diversity offices.[18] Yale has followed suit, adding scores of new administrative offices and training sessions to promote diversity "related to race and other aspects of identity and difference." According to Heather Mac Donald, "These new positions come on top of Yale's existing diversity bureaucracy," which is already very extensive. Mac Donald's recent work on campus culture entails an updating of what Frederick R. Lynch called the bureaucratic "diversity machine" 20 years ago.[19]

Less overtly bullying forms of persuasion also take place in the administrative realm. Alexis de Tocqueville, history's keenest eye on the strengths and pathologies of democracy in America, would have considered such programs species of "soft despotism," by which he meant omnipresent cultural and bureaucratic impositions that smother the spirit of individual and intellectual freedom in subtle and less-subtle ways.[20] For example, Georgetown University's Office of Institutional Diversity, Equity, and Affirmative Action has recently and relentlessly badgered faculty members to complete online training that deals with discrimination, harassment, and sexual misconduct. Faculty members need to know the rules against such acts, which merit punishment when committed. No argument there.

The problem is that the program came across as preachy, intellectually dogmatic, sophomoric, and insulting according to faculty members who reached out to me for advice. They considered their mandatory participation, which included signing off to affirm that they had completed the course, to be similar to signing an ideologically laden loyalty oath and an affront to academic freedom in spirit, if not its law. As a form of soft despotism, the program did not overtly or substantially interfere with their intellectual freedom, but it gnawed at their intellectual consciences, especially because it coexisted with kindred programs in an evolving campus culture. This kind of badgering goes on all the time in higher education, thus harming the climate for intellectual honesty and freedom.[21]

Understanding the intensity of the drive for diversity that is based on identity politics categories is essential to grasping the powerful campus forces behind many programs that can affect academic free speech in different, meaningful ways. This force has grown along with the burgeoning of campus administrative bureaucracy, which has far outpaced the growth in the ranks of faculty members and which has grown in power as faculty power has waned. Those forces come from inside and outside the campus. Like many institutions, Yale hired a diversity specialist from the corporate world to reenergize its programs. Many faculty members who disparage the "corporatization" of higher education too often look away when it comes to the origins of many concrete diversity programs.

CONSTRUCTIVE COUNTERMEASURES AND A MODEL OF MOBILIZATION

Despite the problems touched on in this chapter, at least three sources of free speech hope lie before us. First, as Sachs and others have pointed out, trends regarding codes, reported disinvitations, and the like appear to be improving for now. Sachs draws much of his analysis and conjecture from FIRE itself, the least likely organization in America to play the Pollyanna of academic free speech. Second, recent survey research about the attitudes of faculty members, college and university heads, and students shows significantly broader support for free speech than for censorship, though some key exceptions also exist. A new survey about administrators is much less encouraging.[22]

Third is the growing influence of mobilization of pro–free speech activism both inside and outside colleges and universities. For now, let me concentrate on inside mobilization. Resistance is possible inside higher education institutions for a lot of reasons, one of which is that respect for free speech and academic freedom apparently still live in the breasts of most students and faculty members regardless of political persuasion. Action must follow belief in order to matter. But sometimes a free speech crisis can compel mobilization or at least resistance.

Backing intellectual freedom with the requisite institutional power is especially important for another reason: most previous eras of censorship on campus withered after the causes for repression waned over time. But the new threats to liberty of discourse have persisted now for more than three decades, beginning with the Speech Code Movement launched in the late 1980s. This is a crucial point. Some commentators claim that the present problem will eventually fade. But we are now witnessing the start of the fourth decade of campus censorship. A major reason is that whereas earlier eras of censorship passed when the offending external forces dissipated, the new forces are more internal and intimately connected to ideological pressures, cultural trends and movements, and career incentives inside the academy. Any adequate assessment of the campus scene must account for this culture and the threats it poses. Culture matters.

Evergreen State, the prototypical social justice school, provides one surprising example of potential resistance following abusive actions. In the spring of 2017, a hostile and threatening mob of students drove liberal professor Bret Weinstein out of his biology class. His offense was refusing to abide by student calls for all white people to stay off campus for a day in honor of the Day of Absence, an annual event intended to highlight the significance of racial diversity and justice. Weinstein considered the call to be racist in its own right because it singled out whites. Previous years did not feature such exclusion.

In the wake of the Weinstein disruption, the university was overrun for several days by intolerant mobs that intimidated others with threatening statements and made non-negotiable demands to the stunned and compliant administration. Many instructors and students stayed away from campus simply to ensure their physical safety. But rather than gaining support for their tactics, the bullying tactics of the activists and their fellow travelers ultimately alienated erstwhile supporters, as well as much of the nation. Weinstein and his wife, Heather Heying, a successful evolutionary biologist, were compelled to resign from the school after working out a legal settlement. They have since joined the pro–academic free speech movement on a national scale.[23]

But something interesting happened the next academic year as campus stakeholders, including alumni, pushed back. For starters, applications for admission to Evergreen the following year dropped 20 percent. In the fall of 2017, a professor interviewed 50 students in his statistics class, almost all of whom were self-designated progressives. He found enormous backlash, with more than a third saying "academic mobbing" was a leading concern. "They now feel they can't speak their mind without getting attacked."[24] In 2018, the school did not hold Absence Day. A similar student reaction took place at Reed College in 2017, when students fought back against activists who disrupted classes in the name of stopping white privilege, another agenda central to identity politics today.[25]

The resistance at Evergreen was based on a norm that we will encounter often in this book: well-intentioned citizens who are in a free society and who rebel against being bullied and treated disrespectfully as means to other people's ends. The spirit of freedom also rebels against orthodoxies that press for dogmatic conformity regardless of their political pedigree. Along this line, Heying and Weinstein also write for what the *New York Times* calls the "Renegade Intellectual Dark Web," another pro–free speech vehicle for liberal and conservative writers who challenge many of the assumptions and pieties that reign in higher education today.[26]

Middlebury also experienced a similar resistance in April 2019, though the scenario is still evolving, with strikes and counterstrikes. The administration—which apparently had not learned the lesson of 2017—cancelled a speech at the last moment by professor Ryszard Legutko, a Polish member of the European Parliament and author of a book titled *The Demon in Democracy: Totalitarian Tendencies in Free Societies*. Legutko had been invited by the Alexander Hamilton Forum, a group led by Keegan Callanan, who had helped to lead the pro–free speech group at the 2017 faculty meeting described earlier. The forum is a response to the free speech crisis at Middlebury.

The administration feared disruption after some students complained that Legutko promoted "homophobic, xenophobic, racist, misogynistic discourse" because of his conservative eastern European views, and students called for a counterprotest. According to an account in the *Wall Street Journal*, the protesters planned to meet elsewhere on campus and made it clear in their Facebook announcement that Ryszard's speech should proceed as planned. In a separate action, political science professor Matthew Dickinson allowed Ryszard to speak in his class of nine after a unanimous student vote, and 36 other students joined the session after word got out on social media. What we could call Middlebury II appears to have entailed a constructive student and faculty resistance in support of free speech in the face of pressure and in spite of less courageous administrators.

A subsequent report by a Middlebury student in *Quillette* has painted a less encouraging picture for free speech advocates, however. An emergency session was held in the immediate wake of Ryszard's appearance; it featured a large number of students and three highly sympathetic administrators. "The whole thing resembled a modern-day Struggle Session, with kids literally weeping over the 'violence' that supposedly had been brought to campus through the vessel of Legutko. The response of the administrators was an endless expression of sympathy and guilt, as well as pledges to make things right." Many of those students had participated in a "standing-room-only" meeting earlier in the semester in which the meeting organizer demanded "the need to eliminate racial violence from the Middlebury curriculum," which needed "decolonization" because "the violence we experience in the classrooms is truly across disciplines."[27]

How the Middlebury battle turns out will depend on what faculty members, students, and key administrators do in the face of the virulent attacks on free speech that have arisen and on when they have to choose which principle or value to support in the face of pressure. For freedom of speech and open inquiry to prevail, those core rights must take *priority* and be backed by *power* from meaningful sources. Pro–free speech alumni have also added their voices to the fray.

In addition to some organized resistance to censorship, many campuses at the urging of disgruntled alumni, trustees, regents, or—as at UW–Madison—coalitions of faculty activists and sympathetic administrators have initiated programs to teach the principles of academic free speech and to broaden intellectual pluralism on campus. For example, several colleges, including The American University in Washington, DC, are starting to engage in civil discourse programs that teach students how to deal advantageously and civilly with different views. Though promising, such programs also must avoid overemphasizing politeness or falling into political correctness themselves. In one such program, a student posed the right question: "How are we going to create these conversations if we're conversing within a single ideological band or spectrum?"[28]

Preachments without action are mere words. Even a child knows that a parent's actions speak louder than his or her words. Similarly, when campus leaders—administrators or faculty—go wobbly in the face of pressure, students notice. Today, the answers to the empirical questions I pose hang in the balance. The key is to engage in the struggle lest free speech and open inquiry vanish from campus culture. In *The Closing of the American Mind*, Allan Bloom wrote, "Freedom of the mind requires not only, or not even specially, the absence of legal constraints but the presence of alternative thoughts. The most successful tyranny is not the one that uses force to assure uniformity but the one that removes the awareness of other possibilities."[29]

In *Private Truths, Public Lies*, economist and sociologist Timur Kuran picks up where Bloom left off by analyzing the political, social, and psychological processes by which an authoritarian regime can hang on to power despite the fact that a majority of citizens strongly oppose it. This ostensibly stable situation can hold so long as many citizens fail to mobilize and speak out because the consequences of doing so are too severe for them.[30] But this state of affairs can unexpectedly crumble if a crisis erupts and a critical mass begins speaking out, thereby triggering a bandwagon effect that provides cover for others and galvanizes regime change. The fall of the Soviet Union in 1991 is a classic example of this process.

Kuran also applies a model for remedying troubling yet less dangerous or oppressive situations, such as public normative consensus in higher education that hides underlying dissent. (He mentions dissent regarding affirmative action and speech codes as examples.) What CAFAR did at UW–Madison was similar.[31] Though the circumstances on America's thousands of campuses vary case by case, it is plausible that a Kuran-like problem can exist in an institution, rendering even majority support for a principle inoperative if the circumstances and characters involved are inauspicious. Facts on the ground matter.

I now turn to two questions that animate the entire discussion in this book. Just what is the fundamental purpose or mission of the university and higher education? And what places do free speech and academic freedom have in the achievement of this mission?

CHAPTER 2

WHAT IS THE UNIVERSITY?
TRUTH, THE INTELLECTUAL *POLIS*,
AND HISTORICAL CHANGE

In a university, knowledge is its own end, not merely a means to an end. A university ceases to be true to its own nature if it becomes the tool of Church or State or any sectional interest. A university is characterized by the spirit of free inquiry, its ideal being the ideal of Socrates—"to follow the argument where it leads.". . . Dogma and hypothesis are incompatible, and the concept of an immutable doctrine is repugnant.

—Justice Felix Frankfurter,
Sweezy v. New Hampshire *(1957), concurring opinion*

THE TREES HIDING THE FOREST

Each institution has a distinctive function, purpose, and set of obligations that define it and serve to justify the rights and privileges that society bestows on it in a kind of social contract, explicit or implicit. If it does not live up to the obligations inherent in this covenant, it jeopardizes its claim to special status and its legitimacy. Some scholars have depicted universities as quintessential "First Amendment institutions," which means that free speech and open inquiry are essential to their character.[1] They do so for a good reason: the modern university's distinctive purpose—*its raison d'être*—is the pursuit and teaching of truth and knowledge, plus the fostering of intellectual virtues that make this task possible, which must include the support of intellectual freedom. An important side effect of this mission is helping to create the qualities of character and mind conducive to citizenship in a constitutional republic. Not all educational institutions fit this model, as we will see at the end of this chapter. But it is the predominant official mission, competing missions notwithstanding.

Universities and colleges have several secondary missions above and beyond the pursuit of truth and intellectual freedom. In 1964, University of California president Clark Kerr declared that the modern university had grown into a "multiversity" that houses many functions and purposes. Today, the multiversity hosts things such as academics and the pursuit of truth; teaching and numerous pedagogical programs; job training and clinics; various types of research from the practical to the purely intellectual or theoretical; socialization programs; a plethora of student groups organized for various purposes; entertainments, sports, clubs, internships, and extracurricular activities; media offices and television deals; jobs to help pay tuition and fees; and a growing number of administrative units dedicated to matters other than intellectual attainment. And the egalitarian social justice mission now vies for ascendency. Not surprisingly, it has become progressively easier for the core mission of higher education to fade into the background among all the trees in the thickening forest—especially if administrative and other stakeholders back the competing missions.[2]

Consider two examples of different priorities that compete with intellectual inquiry, one of which is social justice oriented. First, according to a 2018 report in the *Chronicle of Higher Education*, in recent years, Auburn University has allowed its athletic department to commandeer academic and curricular authority by allowing the department to oversee its own public administration program that provides athletes—primarily football players—with an easy major that props up their eligibility.[3] We have maybe all heard or made jokes about "a football team with a university," but here is the real thing—or close to it.

Second, in 2018, San Diego and other University of California campuses began requiring faculty job applicants to write essays on how their hiring would "contribute to diversity." The guidelines state, among other things, "Departments and search committees should consider a candidate's statement as part of a comprehensive and transparent evaluation of their qualifications." Academic freedom is not stressed along with this emphasis. The point here is that new missions are now competing for attention and resources on campus, potentially crowding out scholarly excellence per se and academic freedom.[4]

THE SOCRATIC PURSUIT OF TRUTH

In his noteworthy 2018 book, *Speak Freely*, Princeton's Keith Whittington defends the primary intellectual mission of the university as "the production and dissemination of knowledge."[5] I have no real quarrel with this definition, which is a sister to my own. But I choose to give priority to the pursuit of *truth*, which is slightly different from the pursuit of *knowledge*. Knowledge is what scholars produce out of the pursuit of truth, but it is often incomplete and fallible, subject to being challenged. Hence, the necessity of protecting freedom of inquiry and criticism. In the worst situations, undue conformity to the consensus of knowledge in a field hinders the pursuit of truth—hence the "echo chamber" problem. One of my best students, who highly valued her Wisconsin undergraduate education, nonetheless confided to me, "Downs, I treasure the education I have received. But in some ways, the discipline resembles following the latest fashion."

Philosophers of knowledge distinguish between "ontology" (what *is*, what *is* true) and "epistemology" (the means by which we interpret or know truth, or *how* we know).[6] Our perception of truth is affected by our instruments of inquiry and by the structures of our minds, but facts and natural laws also exist independent of us and of our desires.[7] We seek the *truth*, but what we tentatively settle on is better termed *knowledge*. It remains the case that only by prioritizing truth can we have a standard by which to critically assess the knowledge that we produce.

Green Bay Packer Hall of Fame quarterback Bart Starr related what legendary Packer coach Vince Lombardi said to the team when he became coach in 1959: "Gentlemen, we will chase perfection," Lombardi declared, "and we will chase it relentlessly, knowing all the while we can never attain it. But along the way, we shall catch excellence." Similarly, in higher education, we seek truth relentlessly, but we often settle on knowledge. This position is consistent with the skepticism regarding virtue and human comprehension that is embedded in the U.S. Constitution itself, at the same time that the position acknowledges the importance of striving toward improvement.

Note that the Framers promulgated the Constitution "in order to form a *more perfect* union"—not a "perfect union." [Emphasis added.] The constitutional system of checks and balances is predicated on this realization.[8] Progress in knowledge arises from those who challenge the consensus in fields in the name of new truths that become apparent. To distinguish between knowledge and truth is not relativism; relativism arises when we give up the assumption that truth exists.

Truth and knowledge are both found in many contexts—of which the academy is only one in our pluralist polity. Regardless, the scholarly pursuit of this purpose is of central importance to higher education, which consists of faculty members who have undergone extensive training and evaluation in order to achieve their positions. In his book *Versions of Academic Freedom*, Stanley Fish delineates a conception of *academic* freedom that distinguishes it from political freedom and from freedom of expression more generally. Academic freedom boils down to the freedom of professional scholars (which includes students under the guidance of competent faculty members) to pursue truth and knowledge that are germane to their fields and that are subject to the considered and trained judgment of their academic peers.[9] Things they say or write in other contexts are not matters of academic freedom per se, but rather of personal opinion, however well informed. Fish's professional and more technical understanding of *academic freedom* distinguishes it from the principle of *freedom of speech* more generally. I will explore this distinction more fully in the next chapter.

For now it is important to note that this distinction matters to the question of prioritization and the mission of the university. Pure free speech principles allow one to affirm even plainly false assertions. Such assertions, however, do not generally survive long under free academic criticism and evaluation. Thus, although free speech is indeed an essential principle in higher education and is indispensable in certain contexts, it is less important than are academic freedom and academic excellence when we are talking about higher education as a distinct institutional enterprise. (In addition, I prefer using the term "freedom of *speech*" over "freedom of *expression*" because the concept of "expression" tends to imply less intellectual content. But I defer elaborating on this point to another occasion.)

Fish's critics maintain that he reduces his concept of truth to the scholarly consensus that determines knowledge, thereby downplaying the distinction between truth and knowledge that provides an independent basis by which to criticize academic convention. I agree with this critique. The responsible pursuit of truth accepts the existence of truth at the same time that it harbors due doubt of our ability to grasp it. (I will discuss this seemingly paradoxical stance and its relationship to the First Amendment in Chapter 7.) There is an intrinsic link between respect for truth that exists independent of our desires and liberal democracies that respect rights and provide checks on power and absolutist claims. But Fish's distinction between academic freedom and free speech and his understanding of distinctive institutional mission are both directly pertinent to the prioritization problem at the heart of this book because they point to higher education as first and foremost an *academic*, intellectual enterprise.[10]

If one had to select a person who epitomizes the university's primary mission, that person would be Socrates, though it is hard, even absurd, to think of Socrates as an "academic." But Socrates represents the painstaking pursuit of truth through probing questions and honest, critical examination. Socratic discourse is about the intellectual process—a state of mind—as well as the conclusions this quest might reach. To carry out the Socratic mission, higher education must foster the type of *character* that is conducive to the pursuit of truth and thoughtfulness. It must teach the *intellectual virtues*.

The Socratic virtues of the university entail four essential principles, or virtues: (a) reason and intellectual standards in the pursuit of truth, (b) intellectual honesty, (c) intellectual and academic freedom, and (d) due respect for the limits of reason and what we know.[11]

Regarding the first three virtues, intellectual freedom is a necessary condition for the pursuit of truth, and reason's relationship to truth is self-evident. Commentators do not often underscore intellectual *honesty*, but it is essential. That virtue means more than avoiding plagiarism or fraud, though those proscriptions are imperative. It also demands speaking and writing honestly about one's conclusions, as well as defending them through the exercise of intellectual standards, evidence, and reasoning. Such virtues require strength of character and courage in the face of pressures to conform.

If one shades the truth he or she has found in order to avoid controversy, to please his or her colleagues, or to achieve political ends, is this not an intellectual fraud of a different kind? I know of cases in which well-known professors have requested at the last moment that publishers abstain from publishing their critical reviews of a book because they got cold feet and feared offending certain communities of scholars. One faint-hearted reviewer confided that his request meant that a book he considered intellectually irresponsible would receive only flattering reviews for wrong reasons.

The fourth virtue, due respect for the limits of reason and what we know, is less discussed and more nuanced. It is embodied by Socratic irony or paradox. Socrates strove for truth but also maintained that his wisdom lay in recognizing what he did not know. Knowledge is inherently incomplete for several reasons, some of which are pretty straightforward and some of which are less so. One straightforward aspect of incompletion or error is human nature itself, which I discuss in Chapter 5. Another aspect of the limit of knowledge pertains to what Crane Brinton has called the unending quest for "cumulative" knowledge, which is empirical knowledge that builds on established knowledge and theory as new discoveries are made. The cumulative knowledge model is most pertinent to inquiry in natural science and in empirical inquiries in the social sciences and humanities such as political science and history. As we learn new facts and connections, we expand our knowledge, which was previously incomplete. And as Thomas Kuhn articulated, new theories or "paradigms" can arise from this process.[12]

What Brinton labeled "noncumulative" knowledge is found in works of literature, poetry, art, music, political theory, and certain types of philosophy, among others. The writings and works of luminaries such as Plato, Friedrich Nietzsche, Leonardo da Vinci, Niccolò Machiavelli, Fyodor Dostoyevsky, Emily Dickinson, George Eliot, T. S. Eliot, and Hannah Arendt draw from and relate to the works of others, but in a different way from the testing of propositions and hypotheses that are more characteristic of cumulative knowledge. Their works stand on their own as unique insights into life by brilliant minds, and the works are as profound today as when written. Yet the works are not part of a process that might eventually cover an entire field of inquiry, in the way that empirical knowledge proposes to do. And like cumulative knowledge, such works are unavoidably incomplete or contain errors of assessment and judgment, however brilliant and insightful.

Noncumulative knowledge often wrestles with questions and matters that perplex reason itself, such as the meaning of love, power, justice, life, and death; the eternal question of why evil exists in the world; the extent to which our will is free or not; and the concern about whether God or something similar exists in the universe. Asking the right questions can be the most important element of teaching. Such questions are about meaning and other normative matters, and they open the door to mystery, wonder, imagination, and tragic consciousness. (Wonder and imagination are also important to cumulative scientific breakthrough, as Einstein and other great scientific minds understood.)

As Hamlet informed Horatio, "There are more things in heaven and earth, Horatio, / Than are dreamt of in your philosophy." And as Kenneth Clark wrote of Leonardo's greatest paintings, which embodied both extraordinary artistic sensibility and scientific knowledge, "Mystery to Leonardo was a shadow, a smile, and a finger pointing into darkness." Beyond all this is what Nietzsche christened the tension between the Apollonian and the Dionysian, the latter of which points to a darker and more mysterious joy than does the former—and to an aesthetic-tragic sensibility in dialectical tension with its more reasoned partner.[13] Human truth encompasses both sources of knowledge.

As the house of reason, the university has a relationship to aesthetic and Dionysian inquiry that is understandably ambiguous. But the

humanities and some of the social sciences do teach worthy noncumulative works, and rightly so, because they comprise important aspects
of knowledge, as well as *understanding*. And both forms of knowledge
defy being limited by the confining strictures of political correctness and
other forms of intellectual rectitude. Given the interests and tensions in
any polity, the honest pursuit of truth will always entail at least a measure
of what Nietzsche called being "beyond good and evil."[14] Appreciating
the subtle connections between cumulative and noncumulative knowledge raises a broader question about the relationship between reason,
emotion, and politics. Perhaps surprisingly, this relationship is relevant
to understanding the university as an intellectual *polis*.

I use the term *polis* because the university is a type of interactive
community that attempts to abide by its own principles, rules, commitments, and missions. There is such a thing as university *citizenship*, which
denotes responsibility for upholding the institutional mission and working with others to make this happen. (Indeed, I will argue later that the
decline of such citizenship is one reason for the distortion of institutional
mission that I critique.) In this sense, the university and higher education resemble the Greek *polis*, especially Athens because of the way that
Athens combined political duties and respect for intellectual achievement, at least when it was at its best. I am aware that Greek *poleis* also
restricted citizenship to free males, excluding it from women and slaves.
In no way is my use of this term meant to support such restrictions on
campus, as I hope the thrust of this book makes clear. The type of *polis*
I have in mind is one consistent with the democracy, freedom, equality,
rights, diversity, and rule of law that are the essential principles of liberal
democracy and is conducive to the intellectual freedom, standards, and
intellectual diversity and tolerance befitting liberal education.

REASON, EMOTION, POLITICS, AND THE UNIVERSITY: THE RIGHT BALANCE

Universities and colleges are institutions that comprise scholars, students,
and supporting staffs. Consequently, the pursuit of truth and knowledge
in those institutions is both individual and collective. The university is
an intellectual *polis*, which means that learning and the pursuit of truth

involve stepping back and thinking for oneself with self-reliance, as well as interacting with others in a communal process that is both intellectual and interpersonal. The model of the university I present here and in the next chapter is centered on "book learning" as well as on interpersonal relations and exchanges. One learns from at least three sources: (a) from books and related data, (b) from people and the quality of their minds and characters, and (c) from the findings of one's own mind.

The ivory tower includes aspects of the real world at the same time that it is detached from that world. Interpersonal life goes on inside it as in the real world, while the distinctive preoccupation is intellectual. Free speech philosopher Alexander Meiklejohn expressed a similar understanding when he wrote, "The First Amendment is not, primarily, a device for the winning of new truth, though that is very important. It is a device for sharing whatever truth has been won."[15] Though winning truth, contra Meiklejohn, *is* the primary purpose of a university, the sharing aspect is of great importance in the university as a liberal *polis*.

Although the inculcation of reason is an integral component of the mission of higher education, the interactive *polis*-oriented model I present in this and the next chapter does not exclude emotion, but rather it pays due respect to emotion, passion, and relations with others as vital aspects of life while striving to assimilate those phenomena to reason. Emotion fuels life for better or worse depending on how it is used. In psychological terms, the process of molding emotion to serve reason is a form of sublimation, as is the channeling of basic desires into more civilized and disciplined pursuits. This is one aspect of higher education's traditional civilizing mission.

In Daniel Kahneman's famous terminology, human beings engage in two different levels of "thinking": fast and slow. Fast thinking is quicker, more subject to intuition and emotion—and mistakes—whereas slow thinking is more rigorous and analytical. Fast thinking exists in a kind of twilight world between emotion and reason. Most of us think fast most of the time when we endeavor to think. But learning how to think in slower terms is necessary for certain tasks, and we hope learning how to engage in it can influence the quality of our faster thinking, making us more thoughtful citizens. (Alas, slower thinking is hardly immune from making mistakes, either. Human fallibility runs deep.) If reason serves as our candle in the darkness, learning how to think more seriously and slowly can provide us with a brighter, longer-lasting candle.[16] The university's task is to create brighter candles.

I situate reason and passion in this way for several reasons. First, psychiatry teaches us that maturing, understanding, and appreciating truth and others' views require that reason be properly infused with affect. Reason without affect and appreciation is pathological, not human understanding. We think truth, but we also need to feel it.

Second, relations with others, including those that take place on campus, necessarily involve emotional as well as rational engagement. Estimable teachers convey not only rational learning to their students, but also certain emotional respect that helps to nourish the pedagogical enterprise. This fact can lead to emotional entanglements that are irresponsible, but responsible teachers know how to channel emotions in the direction of constructive and legitimate ends.

Third, the best students and scholars are those who come to love what they do. Though Plato elevated reason above the passions in his philosophy of knowledge (see Jonathan Haidt's take on Plato later herein), he also taught us in *The Republic* and *The Symposium* that philosophers should be driven by love for the truth. My students who thrived in class were those who had at least a sufficient affection for the subject matter and the class. Thus, emotion is itself part of reason and understanding. But the arrangement of the relationship matters. Reason must not be distorted by emotion, and emotion must direct its force toward the right intellectual objects, which means loving or caring about truth.

Commitment to truth is an element of maturity because it takes one outside oneself. In a post-truth world or polity, one's focus too easily regresses to such narrower ends as self-interest, materialism, pleasure seeking, immature subjectivity, or narrowly defined loyalty to a group. Regression makes one more fearful and less able to deal with the complexities, nuances, and challenges of reality. Freud properly considered the retreat from the reality principle to be a form of emotional and mental regression.

My fourth reason for this integration is due to simple realism in respect to human nature. For this point, I turn to Jonathan Haidt. Haidt's research in *The Righteous Mind* supports David Hume's classic realistic view that reason is usually the servant of inclination and emotional preference rather than the other way around. Both Plato's elevation of reason and Thomas Jefferson's equivalence of the heart and the mind get it wrong, Haidt claims.[17] Emotion is neither secondary nor equal as a motivator for most human belief and action. Nietzsche put the matter graphically: reason is our frailest faculty because it is our most recent from an evolutionary perspective. In neuroscience language, the cortical modules of the brain are more primitive than the subcortical.[18] Not even the best colleges and universities can change this fundamental human reality.

What universities can do is first to give reason and thoughtfulness a stronger hand in what is an unequal partnership with emotion, self-interest, and various tribal inclinations that we all feel and then to make reason foremost in certain contexts, however precariously. This task includes the intellectual standards and frame of mind that are necessary to evaluate and assess truth claims. There are many important situations in which we demand reason to prevail, such as in the jury room, in building bridges, in evaluating and making public policy, and in countless other responsible activities. By being especially tasked to teach the intellectual virtues—respect for truth and evidence, reason, critical thinking, and freedom of the mind—universities and colleges have a duty to give reason more meaningful presence in our lives, thereby checking the human tendency to rush to judgment. But colleges and universities cannot perform this task unless, as institutions, they prioritize intellectual virtues over the emotional and the tribal in their own domains, especially given the other temptations that press on higher education today.

Indeed, thinking about the human drama that plays out between reason and passion—both within each soul and in the polity—is itself an integral part of liberal education, which should open windows to understanding our lives. Reflecting on the tensions, conflicts, and tragedies embodied in human nature is a universal theme of literature and many of the social sciences, making it a major topic of liberal education.

Thus, the relationship between reason and emotion lies at the center of the inquiry. Emotion consists of many forces, including love, hate, passion, fear, likes and dislikes, awe, and wonder—to name a few.[19]

Haidt writes about the tribal and centripetal nature of morality and emotion. Tribal commitment, or commitment to a group or community, is paradoxical, thereby creating a basis for moral commitment and belonging that people need and that plants the seeds for broader moral development. But it can also thwart morality, individuality, and justice if it makes a person blind or indifferent to people and claims outside of that individual's more limited horizon. Organized political orders naturally harbor both local and national loyalties and legal commitments, such as the principle and practice of federalism in the United States. The tension between narrower and broader loyalty is a classic theme, extending at least as far back as the ancient Greeks, as seen in Aeschylus's *Antigone* and Aristotle's defense of personal loyalties to family and friends versus Plato's more universalistic approach.

The identity politics that is so prevalent in higher education today revisits this tension in its own way and is an important cultural aspect of the disputes over academic free speech. Critics maintain that identity politics as practiced today has exacerbated the balkanization of campus citizenship and politics, with academic free speech—which is an institutional principle applicable to all campus citizens as a community—being a major casualty. The pervasive special programs and space that administrators have created or facilitated exclusively for minority students also intensify the divisive effects of identity politics. There is merit to this claim. Taken too far, identity politics can threaten the institutional appreciation and application of common intellectual standards and rights. Identity groups, as well as the new academic programs and departments they spawn, often strive for solidarity, recognition, and affirmation, whereas criticism and critical reasoning are the lifeblood of free speech and academic freedom.

Of course, such programs can also provide points of view and knowledge that established programs and fields have ignored or wrongly downplayed. (See Chapters 5 and 7 herein.) People with different concerns and backgrounds, including historically marginalized groups, often have the incentive and need to make us aware of new truths, and such truths often need requisite power to give them a place at the intellectual table. But such programs and truth seekers must, in turn, be as subject to criticism and probing inquiry as anyone else in a university community. All ideas and perspectives are fair game for Socratic criticism.

As a colleague of mine once observed, "Identity politics is not consistent with John Stuart Mill." In *On Liberty*, Mill said that everything should be challenged and questioned; the book you are reading is replete with examples of how campus identity politics has harmed free speech, as we have already witnessed in Chapter 1.[20]

In a related sense and in unchecked forms, identity politics can undermine commitment to the broader, more universalist loyalties that sustain a polity or the university as an institution. As Columbia scholar Mark Lilla recently lamented, today's version of identity politics "has left [students] unprepared to think about the common good and what must be done practically to secure it—especially the hard and unglamorous task of persuading people very different from themselves to join a common effort."[21]

In venues other than *The Righteous Mind*, Haidt has critiqued the new forms of identity politics as troubling departures from more constructive visions.

> The identity politics taught on campus today is entirely different from that of Martin Luther King [Jr.]. It rejects America and American values. It does not speak of forgiveness or reconciliation. It is a massive centrifugal force, which is now seeping down into high schools, especially progressive private schools. . . . Today's identity politics has another interesting feature: it teaches students to think in a way antithetical to what a liberal arts education should do.[22]

This said, the question of identity politics is more subtle and complex than some critics allege. Identity politics is a part of life and is predicated in meaningful ways upon the drive for recognition and respect, which Hegel and others have posited as a universal human need. In its own way, it is normative, political, and psychological.[23] Identity can provide a sense of self-respect through solidarity in a hostile world and can be a basis for resistance and for fighting back against discrimination and injustice. King, a student of Hegel and resistance movements, understood the importance of racial pride to the civil rights movement, and the subsequent women's movement and gay rights movement built on such thinking. Emphasizing identity can be an important step in the process of achieving equal respect. Such movements can further the pursuit of truth by compelling the dominant culture to recognize the injustice that exists in society—a phenomenon I will explore in Chapter 7.

However, the emphasis on "ascriptive" aspects of identity such as race, gender, and sex can be confining and detrimental to justice, individual development, and pursuit of truth. The greater the oppression at stake, the more intense solidarity makes sense. But what should happen when oppression is less intense and when common ground is more present? King and others dealt with truly dangerous and repressive situations. It is almost certainly a vast exaggeration of the truth to claim that the protesters at Williams College or Middlebury depicted in Chapter 1 suffer similar oppression, despite their claim that free speech on campus is "killing" them. Sadly, such students appear to be forsaking the intellectual and emotional growth that a top-notch education can give them. Note also that King was a formidable champion of free speech and knew that the enforcement of free speech principles and law helped to pave the way for his movement to succeed.[24]

As we will see in later chapters, the rise of the civil rights movement was intimately entangled with the Supreme Court's expansion of the right of free speech and association in the 1960s and 1970s. And King knew that excessive identity solidarity also undervalues the individual differences that exist within each identity community. Students with the full array of ascriptive orientations played major roles in our free speech movement at UW–Madison, and each one of them deeply resented the fact that many of our opponents assumed that one's positions and beliefs should be dictated by his or her gender, race, or sexual orientation.[25] Such stories are commonplace. Each student was proud of his or her ascriptive identity and willing to stand up for it but took even more pride in his or her abilities and intellectual and moral conscience as an individual; the students felt loyalties beyond their ascriptive selves, such as to the principles of academic free speech and the heritage of the university. As social philosopher Anthony Giddens has maintained, identity is naturally a fluid, evolving aspect of individual lives, and most of us move in and out of different personas.[26] In addition, the liberal arts present insight into the universality of human nature at the same time that they reveal differences that are based on nature, nurture, circumstance, and power.

So we need to think about the ways in which identity politics furthers the intellectual responsibilities of the university and about the ways in which it cuts in the other direction. The task of liberal education and liberal democracy is to expand the scope of one's thinking and commitment to the wider sphere of the regime or even humanity while not squelching the more personal commitments to individuals and associations that are so vital to a community. (A healthy polity nourishes associations in civil society.) The success of the experiments of higher education and liberal democracy depend on a delicate balancing act that can go astray if emotion and tribalism go too far. It is here that the prioritization of the principles of academic free speech comes into play. Such emphasis can influence the practice of identity politics to be more appreciative of the larger institutional principles that a university has to offer.

One of the best ways to effectuate a nontribal form of community and emotional commitment that also promotes equality and diversity is to bring individuals from different backgrounds and identities into common endeavors. Shared purpose and responsibility encourage participants to focus on the task at hand beyond their own personal needs and identities, and they provide the most solid basis for engendering mutual respect, creating a sense of community, and overcoming wrongful prejudices. This process of uniting through diversity takes place all the time in activities such as dramatic performances, business and political projects, sports, and the like. And it happens in a good class, which features bringing students of different backgrounds into a common intellectual objective of learning, interaction, debate, and intellectual conflict. I have witnessed many examples of students forming strong friendships in the class, often with those whose views differed from their own, sometimes dramatically so. Enemies in campus politics even emerged as friends from the class. A good class builds the bridges that are becoming an endangered species in our polity today because it encourages students to buy into the common intellectual purpose of the class, which is a kind of intellectual *polis*.

THE "CIVILITY" QUESTION IN HIGHER EDUCATION

The call for civility is heard often in higher education today, and some schools have passed measures to either encourage it or enforce it. Properly understood, civility is a function of active citizenship, which is a First Amendment ideal. And it substantively connects to the model of the university under discussion as an intellectual *polis* because it involves not the repression of emotion, but rather its sublimation, which entails the kind of distancing from emotion that is necessary for reason to do its job. The debate over civility is an extension of the foregoing discussion about reason and emotion.[27]

In a 2016 book, Sigal R. Ben-Porath, a professor who is at the University of Pennsylvania and who has been deeply involved with student activist groups, criticizes the call for civility on campus because she claims it downplays passion and is dismissive of the intensity with which students, especially minority students, deal with issues of marginalization. She is right about the relationship between passion and speech, as free speech theory, law, and lore amply display.[28] We want students to be passionate about their ideas and claims at the same time that we want them to be thoughtful and respectful of the rights of others. There is a reason that Dante, in *The Divine Comedy*, reserves a special realm in hell for the indifferent.

Furthermore, codes that punish incivility are an open invitation to abuse because of the practical elusiveness of the term—if a student raises his or her voice too much or does not smile enough, is that uncivil?—and because such codes can be pretexts for idea-based censorship. (Similarly, the American Association of University Professors [AAUP] opposes using collegiality as a standalone criterion for tenure or professional standing for those reasons.)[29] So Ben-Porath is onto something, and civility is not a thing that can be coded. At the same time, her understanding of civility as primarily unemotional politeness is misleading, thereby raising a key question in higher education politics and policy today: just how should we conceive of the concept of civility? Though elusive to define, we can conceptualize it in a more constructive way.

In many respects, modern conceptions of civility have diminished a more robust and propitious traditional understanding of the term that we should revive. The *English Oxford Living Dictionary* describes the origin of civility as follows: "Late Middle English: from Old French *civilité*, from Latin *civilitas*, from *civilis* 'relating to citizens' (see civil). In early use the term denoted the state of being a citizen and hence good citizenship or orderly behaviour. The sense of 'politeness' arose in the mid-16th century."[30] More traditionally understood, civility pertains to the attributes of *citizens* who share common concern for the polity with fellow citizens despite their differences, and who relate to each other from the vantage point of their *roles* or *duties* as citizens rather than as individuals or groups defined by their emotions and needs.

The sharing of common concerns in this respect should also entail assuming at least fundamental good will on the part of those with whom one disagrees, though this assumption is rebuttable at some point. Many students and secondary school and college educators whom I have spoken with in recent times have bemoaned the proliferation of what they call discussion or conversation "stoppers" in their institutions. By this term they mean unmerited personal attacks and accusations that a discussant harbors discriminatory or hateful intent simply because he or she disagrees with a point of view on intellectual or normative grounds. Such stoppers signify a closed mind on the part of the accuser and undermine the possibility of the mutual due respect that allows discussion and debate to flourish. They should be deployed only with much caution and consideration. This proviso is especially important because of forces I discuss in Chapter 4 and elsewhere that include the unreasonable expansion of concepts such as "harm" and "hate." One also wonders what institutional and social forces are implicated in fostering the stopper mentality.

This notion of civility does not disparage intellectual conflict; rather, it makes constructive conflict more possible by *depersonalizing* disagreement in a manner that focuses on ideas, policies, and claims rather than on the personal qualities and vulnerabilities of one's opponent. Except in extreme cases, we should attack ideas and positions, not persons. Taking on the formal role of a citizen in one's professional role provides a *mask* that protects an interlocutor from feeling personally attacked, thereby facilitating the mental posture that allows genuine intellectual engagement and conflict to take place. Think of how members of Congress go after each other after first addressing each other in terms of their professional roles, as "the Senator from X" or "the Congresswoman from Y."

Consider also a pedagogical example. Students typically rebel against professors who wear their personal and emotional needs on their sleeves when they teach. What students want is an instructor who takes on the role with the competence expected of the job and who applies his or her passion to illuminating the subject matter. Emotional teaching can be excellent, but only if the teacher's emotion is sublimated into the intellectual standards of the job, which are distinct from the personal needs of the instructor. This sublimation and distancing are also things we demand of people when they take on other jobs. Do the job; don't spend your time putting your feelings on display. Doing a job right requires rising up to the standards for which the job calls. Achieving respect in this sense constitutes a kind of transcendence of the self in the name of duty to the *polis* or to others—getting outside oneself. The most effective leaders in cases of struggle often combine the personal and the transcendent, and their personal commitment adds fuel to the higher cause for which they strive. But their effectiveness comes from keeping their eyes on the prize and not wallowing in their psychological need or personalities.

Today we find ourselves increasingly prone to personalize differences of opinion and to rush to judgment in public and interactive life. Concurrently, our skins are thinner in a society that is increasingly governed by the "triumph of the therapeutic" and the hypersensitivities of aggressive identity politics.[31] Therapeutic politics is antithetical to virtues such as courage because it is obsessed with psychological vulnerability (victimhood), which is inconsistent with courage and the republican virtue model of free speech touted in First Amendment jurisprudence. Excellence in the public realm of citizenship requires courage, which both Hannah Arendt—the leading modern theorist of the qualities of the public realm—and the ancients considered the "political virtue *par excellence.*"[32] Civility and courage are partners, not foes.

The process of distancing and sublimation from one's personal needs is similar to what Simone de Beauvoir called "transcendence" in her path-breaking book on gender equality, *The Second Sex.* Transcendence entails a form of self-control over the emotions but in a manner that transfers emotion into reason, ability, and responsibility. Such transcendence is necessary to maturation and the fulfillment of duties and to the regime of self-government itself. As Alexander Meiklejohn has written, "Political freedom does not mean freedom from control. It means self-control."[33] If we do not control ourselves, the modern state will do it for us. But such transcendence or sublimation requires training and effort that is first taught in the institutions and arrangements of civil society. Higher education should further this educational process.

This conception of civility is also related to the pursuit of truth, higher education's *raison d'être.* To fulfill their obligation, universities must teach students how to be able to accept truths that they find disagreeable and emotionally upsetting for whatever reasons. This acceptance is both an intellectual and an ethical demand that bespeaks what we could call *intellectual character.* In Haidt's terms, acceptance of uncomfortable truths calls for education of both the emotions and the mind. Teaching civility, rightly understood, furthers this call.

HISTORICAL CHANGE AND THE UNIVERSITY

The main question is whether higher education will *prioritize* its intellectual mission or rather give priority to or equal weight to concerns such as feelings, diversity, social justice, and the like. "Equal weight" might make sense on paper; but in the real world of pressure and campus politics, giving equal weight to other agendas often means that the other priorities will prevail at freedom's expense. Before the 1960s, the Supreme Court often applied a so-called ad hoc balancing test in free speech cases involving governmental claims against speech. Given the governmental and societal pressures at stake, free speech often lost in the bargain. Meaningful protection for controversial dissent arose only when, in the 1960s, the Court abandoned this arbitrary test by replacing it with a strong presumption or priority in favor of free speech, henceforth placing a higher burden of proof on the state to justify suppression by satisfying the test of strict scrutiny.[34]

The Court's doctrinal shift was a product of both experience and logic, of practical jurisprudence in the aid of deeper constitutional principle. It had tried the balancing of interests, and the effort failed to protect controversial speech in a time of protest. For example, during World War I, the Supreme Court and federal courts upheld criminal punishment for citizens who simply advocated anti-war ideas and commentary that fell far short of actually inciting illegal action against the draft or the war. A mere bad tendency to cause illegal action in the eye of the beholder was sufficient to constitute a crime against the state.[35]

The same task confronts higher education today. The intellectual function of the university must be given special weight in the face of conflict, or it will succumb to other principles, values, and agendas in pressure situations. In his book on the important 1992 Supreme Court decision, *R.A.V. v. St. Paul,* which was legally relevant to college speech codes (see Chapter 4), Edward Cleary wrote about Justice Hugo Black's legacy in free speech jurisprudence in words that are germane to the task at hand. Black "inherited the mantle of Holmes and Brandeis" because he "displays the requisite passion" for the First Amendment, which requires "that the judge respond to the fact that this is not just another rule or principle of law."[36]

That said, universities are naturally subject to historical change, and the relatively recent commitment to diversity and inclusion is a valid part of this adjustment, unless those terms are dogmatically and narrowly defined in a manner that disserves common purpose and respect for dissent. The trick is to acknowledge necessary and legitimate change without losing the commitment that makes you what you are. Given the inescapable reality of history, our task is to take account of historical change while preserving the essential character of the institution whose purpose is to influence that same history in an intellectual fashion. How much can higher education institutions adapt without losing hold of their distinctive missions? This is the $64,000 question.

Higher education's historical task is similar to the process that takes place in constitutional jurisprudence, a subject about which universities, not coincidentally, have had much to say over the centuries.[37] Whereas the U.S. Constitution, or indeed any constitution, cannot ignore new facts on the ground, the whole idea of constitutional governance is that unavoidable historical change must be guided by constitutional principles, not vice versa. As Justice John Marshall averred in *McCulloch v. Maryland*, a case in which he famously declared that the Constitution was not a mere "legal code" but rather a document written to endure for the ages: "[W]e must never forget that it is *a Constitution* we are expounding."[38] Translation: though flexible within reason, the Constitution's job is to shape historical change in its own image.

Higher education cannot help being influenced by historical change, and it is obligated to acknowledge and face historical needs and realities. For example, in World Wars I and II, higher education institutions became veritable armed camps preparing young men to fight, and much research was dedicated to assisting in the war effort.[39] That said, their normal distinctive purpose is to influence historical change in a manner that makes such change more knowledgeable, thoughtful, and respectful of intellectual freedom—in other words, in a manner that bears the institution's distinctive image. Marginalizing free speech, due process, and kindred rights is detrimental to this task. *As an independent force in the world, a university must mold history as well as reflect it.* And some trends in history simply need to be resisted, such as those that dumb down the citizenry or compromise intellectual freedom and virtue.

Students come to higher education because the institutions have something special to offer them, not vice versa. Of course, our duty is to serve the educational needs of students and society, and good teachers rightly revel in the dialogical interaction with students, learning from such engagements: yet teachers do so not by catering in an unreflective way to students' demands or whims, but rather by providing students with an intellectual product that challenges them and enhances their minds and their ability to function in a demanding and competitive polity.

Back in the early 2000s, an administrator at UW–Madison proclaimed that the university had as much to learn from students as they had to learn from us. This observation turned the proper relationship between the institution and students upside down. One manifestation of the aggrandizement of administrative power on campus has been the introduction into campus governance of many individuals who lack the advanced academic background in research and teaching that tends (a) to make one more committed to intellectual standards and necessities and (b) to appreciate how some agendas disserve this priority of the institution.

In its path-breaking 1915 Report on Academic Freedom and Tenure, the AAUP compared the modern university's mission to the older proprietary conception of the university. The modern conception of the university is composed of what I called the liberal model of higher education in this book's introduction. The AAUP defined the primary purpose of the premodern proprietary institutions as "not to advance knowledge by the unrestricted research and unfettered discussion of impartial investigators, but rather to subsidize the promotion of opinions held by the persons, usually not of the scholar's calling, who provide the funds for their maintenance."[40] Back then, proprietary missions were predominantly conservative or religious in nature. In many respects, those today who call for elevating other missions to equal status with truth—or to greater status—open the door to returning to a proprietary model, only this time in a progressive or social justice form rather than the more conservative identity of the traditional proprietary institution. And some proprietary institutions combine religious dimensions along with progressivism; religion in America has many political faces, some of which are progressive.

The progressive vision of the university today amounts to the return of a student-protective *in loco parentis* standard, one that the nation's courts have long since backed away from. It is just one example of recent trends in higher education that sociologist Frank Furedi and others have observed.[41] As briefly outlined in the introduction, three ideal type models of higher education appear to be vying for acceptance today: liberal, conservative proprietary, and progressive proprietary.

In many respects, the seeds of the progressive social justice university were planted in the liberal era, as reflected by the fact that many great liberal universities are struggling today with the tension between liberal and progressive values and goals. Equality is an essential attribute of justice and liberal democracy. But much depends on how equality is defined and how it is achieved. Liberty and individual justice suffer when the drive for equality marginalizes respect for individual rights and freedom, thereby leading to a stifling orthodoxy of opinion that Alexis de Tocqueville famously feared.[42] The contemporary burgeoning of campus bureaucracy and administration has not coincidentally accompanied this decoupling. The administrative state inherently distrusts the pluralistic and cacophonous nature of free speech as "the people's darling" right.[43] The administrative state's counterpart in the university is the administration, and it is often little different in this respect.

The progressive university's ambiguous position on free speech betrays the historical way in which free speech has been championed and used by oppressed groups to push their claims in the public arena, thus leading to progressive change consistent with liberal values. Free speech has consistently empowered the causes of civil rights groups, gay activists, feminists, and other minority groups throughout U.S. history.[44] Today, however, the progressive social justice university is calling into question the historical relationship among free speech, justice, and progress.

The AAUP report emphasized something else: it praised the *type of character* faculty members should possess, which also serves as a model for students to follow. This part of the report echoes the character traits discussed in the section on civility earlier. The report's section on "The Nature of the Academic Calling" declares: "If education is the cornerstone of the structure of society and if progress in scientific knowledge is essential to civilization, few things can be more important than to enhance the dignity of the scholar's profession, with a view to attracting into its ranks men of the highest ability, of sound learning, and of strong and independent character."

Three goods are linked here: the good of the polity as a whole, intellectual advance, and individual and institutional character. A self-reliant character is destiny for both knowledge production and for republican democracy. This logic leaps out of the pages of the concurring opinion by Justice Louis Brandeis in *Whitney v. California*, in which Brandeis rooted First Amendment jurisprudence in virtues such as self-reliance, intellectual discovery, and courage.

> Those who won our independence by revolution were not cowards. They did not fear political change. They did not exalt order at the cost of liberty. To courageous, self-reliant men, with confidence in the power of free and fearless reasoning applied through the processes of popular government, no danger flowing from speech can be deemed clear and present unless the incidence of the evil apprehended is so imminent that it may befall before there is opportunity for full discussion."[45]

PRIVATE SCHOOLS: INTELLECTUAL DIVERSITY AND CULTURAL PLURALISM

We have talked about the importance of intellectual and cultural diversity in the U.S. polity and about how it should coexist with a commitment to the regime of common citizenship. A question naturally emerges: why should only one model of higher education, such as the liberal intellectual freedom model classically championed by the AAUP, be worthy of our respect? Given the commitment of this book to the liberal intellectual freedom model, my answer to this question might seem paradoxical, but it is nonetheless clear: it is good also to have a meaningful portion of schools that are premised on substantive proprietary missions as defined by the AAUP. This tolerance is a paradoxical part of the common U.S. regime: we are one country living under the self-evident truths of the Declaration of Independence; therefore, we tolerate individuals and groups who live by their own lights.

Some more conservative critics of liberalism lament the modern research university for lacking soul or spirit because of its dedication to the endless pursuit of elusive truth, whereas more progressive types chide the same institutions for being irrelevant to the substantive social ends to which they aspire. A truly pluralistic constitutional regime characterized by exit, voice, and loyalty legitimately tolerates proprietary educational institutions as a remedy to those criticisms.[46]

One of our nation's historical gifts is its commitment to freedom of association and to the private visions of the good that composes the heart of such visions. Ironically, the liberal freedoms embedded in the constitutional regime also honor the right of individuals and groups to harbor anti-liberal beliefs and to form associations dedicated to such beliefs, so long as they abide by valid general laws that include not coercing their members. This principle is similar to the constitutional and political principles of federalism and of checks and balances. A major reason for both principles is to guard against the stifling uniformity of opinion that the Framers were dedicated to preventing. The coexistence of nonliberal and liberal institutions of higher learning serves to further this objective, and it can add a dynamic and creative tension to higher education and the polity writ large.[47]

This appreciation of the coexistence of proprietary institutions comes with some caveats. First, public schools should not be proprietary in this sense because they are partly funded—however decreasingly—by the taxpayers, and their histories and trademarks are stamped with "state" association; thus the liberal principle prohibiting viewpoint discrimination should apply to them. If they become proprietary, they violate public trust.

Second, whereas regimes in liberal democracy properly support the right to establish anti-liberal educational associations, liberal institutions and practices are most likely to prevail overall. Though we may imagine them as wholly static, private religious colleges and universities have often been keenly attentive to developments in secular knowledge and education in order to maintain intellectual credibility while simultaneously striving to preserve their religious proprietary visions. Religious conviction and secular knowledge are not necessarily exclusive and can coexist in a productive and dynamic tension.[48]

Critics of liberalism such as political theorist Patrick Deneen point out that the excessive individualism and autonomy of unalloyed liberalism may fall into anomie and social breakdown if they are not buttressed by nonliberal institutions such as community, family, and intermediate associations in civil society. Tocqueville—whom Deneen cites frequently—foresaw a bleak future for liberal democracy in the absence of such institutions. Deneen is deeply pessimistic about the fate of liberal democracy, and there are reasons to take his concerns seriously, especially if you believe that liberal democracy remains the best regime in an imperfect world.[49] If we want liberal democracy to succeed, we need to foster intermediary institutions that support its prospects while encouraging those nonliberal inputs that make liberal principles viable. Maintaining due respect for certain proprietary institutions is one step in this direction.

One of my most influential college teachers, the late Walter Berns at Cornell University, was a conservative who defended liberal democracy as the best practical regime. Like Deneen and Tocqueville, he advocated the strengthening of civil institutions to remedy the defects of liberalism. He argued that the university should strive to be one such institution by teaching intellectual virtues and the responsibilities that help to sustain freedom.[50] Liberalism cannot do its task alone. Even liberal academic institutions need to foster a sense of community and mutual respect in order to assist students in developing the wherewithal to deal propitiously with provocative discourse and the challenges of constitutional citizenship. Teaching the intellectual virtues is itself a proprietary mission, in a sense, albeit a crucial one for the larger polity.

Third, we need to remain aware of just how problematic proprietary forces can be if they are not tempered by liberal principles. Even Deneen concludes that any new type of political regime that might succeed liberalism must maintain core liberal principles of freedom in order to be legitimate and just. (The question of just how different this polity would be from liberalism itself is an open question, especially because liberalism has historically coexisted with nonliberal communities and practices outside the context of pure liberal theory.)[51] An excessive proliferation of nonliberal institutions in a liberal democracy could be very problematic because liberalism's checks against state domination depend on some generally shared liberal norms.

We must remember that the meaning of "social justice" is itself highly contested in the history of political thought, just as religion is on another column of the proprietary ledger. The ultimate question in political theory is "How should we live?" And the history of political theory from Socrates to modern times teaches us that *there are different legitimate views regarding this fundamental question.* One is left to ask: just what kind of social justice is it that can be achieved in the absence of due process and respect for individual differences of mind?

With these caveats in mind, if a private school wishes to experiment with a social justice or religious mission or both, more power to it. In championing the rights of the states to be laboratories of democracy, Justice Louis Brandeis wrote that a "state may, if its citizens choose, serve as a laboratory; and try novel social and economic experiments without risk to the rest of the country."[52] Proprietary institutions can serve similar functions, but they must be honest, open, and consistent about what they are up to.

As Georgetown law professor John Hasnas points out in a recent essay about private schools and academic freedom, although private institutions are not bound by First Amendment strictures, many or most of them nonetheless promise similar free speech and academic freedom rights to students and faculty members by virtue of their contracts and campus policies. Unfortunately, many schools violate those institutionally promised rights in the name of competing proprietary values. In July 2018, the Wisconsin Supreme Court ruled that Marquette University had violated its own rules in this sense.[53] One exception to the widespread hypocrisy is Liberty University, which openly announces that students and faculty members should act and speak in ways consistent with the traditional Christian proprietary mission of the school. It is incumbent on private institutions to avoid hypocrisy and falsity in advertising if they wish to legitimately practice their proprietary missions, and this commitment falls outside the scope of the First Amendment in any case.[54]

Now, a key question we need to address concerns the relationship between the principles of *academic freedom* and *free speech* in higher education. How are they related? Which concept should have priority and in which situations? Addressing those questions facilitates thinking about the university as a *polis* and the dynamic ways it can practice and encourage free speech. We will turn to this question in the next chapter.

CHAPTER 3
FREE SPEECH AND ACADEMIC FREEDOM

Academic freedom . . . is of transcendent value to all of us and not merely to the teachers concerned. That freedom is therefore a special concern of the First Amendment, which does not tolerate laws that cast a pall of orthodoxy over the classroom. . . . The classroom is peculiarly the marketplace of ideas. The Nation's future depends upon leaders trained through wide exposure to that robust exchange of ideas which discovers truth out of a multitude of tongues, [rather] than through any kind of authoritative selection.
   —*Justice William Brennan,* Keyishian v. Board of Regents,
   385 U.S. 589 (1967), p. 603

"Academic freedom" and the more general right of "freedom of speech" are, in fact, distinct concepts. Much confusion is generated by the failure to acknowledge this distinction, and I have found that a surprising number of activists and scholars in the field do not pay it sufficient heed. But working through the implications of the distinction helps us to more fully grasp the nature of the university at its best, which involves a dialectical relationship between the two forms of freedom. This chapter will give some idea of that relationship as I understand it.

   One of the most perspicacious analyses of academic freedom and the freedom of speech is that of Yale law professor Robert Post, a former dean of that school as well as a previous legal adviser to the AAUP's Academic Freedom Committee. Post addressed the distinction in a keynote address that he delivered at a conference about "Free Speech and Intellectual Diversity in Higher Education" at Arizona State University (ASU) in February 2018, which I attended along with several other scholars, administrators, organization leaders, and students. Post's speech was titled "The Classic First Amendment Under Stress: Freedom of Speech and the University."[1] Here I want to lay out the fundamentals of Post's presentation at this conference and discuss why I agree with the distinction while drawing different conclusions regarding its application to all of the domains of an institution. In so doing, I will also present more thoughts about free speech and liberal education.

Post articulated the ways in which the fundamental doctrinal principles of First Amendment and free speech jurisprudence are inappropriate when applied to the specialized context of academic life. The distinction speaks to the special fiduciary obligations of colleges and universities in our constitutional polity—their *raison d'être*—and is a major topic in current debate over the meaning of academic free speech today.[2]

The truth-seeking mission of the university requires not only the strong protections of intellectual freedom, but also the ability and willingness to sift truth from half-truth and falsehood. The earth is not flat; astrology is not scientifically verified; the Holocaust happened even if debate exists over its scope and other empirical aspects of it. Academic freedom entails respect for freedom along with commitment to intellectual standards of proof, evidence, and reason. In his speech, Post referred to Cardinal John Henry Newman's concept of the university's mission: "A university training . . . aims at raising the intellectual tone of society, at cultivating the public mind, at purifying the national taste"—something we are in dire need of today.[3] While accepting this point, I will argue that the principles of classic First Amendment theory should play more of a role in colleges and universities *as intellectual communities* than Post's position entails. And to the extent that the law does not support this proposition, practical action by campus citizens should be undertaken to fill the gap.

TENSIONS BETWEEN FIRST AMENDMENT THEORY AND ACADEMIC SPEECH

At the risk of oversimplification, I will first boil Post's position down to his three most basic points. Then I will add two of my own. Those points will be familiar to anyone conversant with First Amendment law and jurisprudence, and they are very accessible to nonexperts. Though scholars have posited many different justifications or purposes for freedom of speech, Post premised his depiction of classic free speech doctrine on the self-government philosophy of democratic theory, which is a widely respected principal justification.[4] Here are the key assumptions that Post posits as the linchpins of general First Amendment jurisprudence outside the context of academia:

1. Under our system of government, the ultimate truth and strength of ideas are to be determined by We the People in the marketplace of ideas, in the public forum, or in our own minds and not by the state or other authority in their different guises.[5] Accordingly, in regulating speech except in narrow situations of necessity, the state may not engage in *content discrimination* or, especially, *viewpoint discrimination*. Beyond Post, I would add that this rule entails an *anti-paternalism principle* when it comes to the speaking and reception of ideas. Except in limited and distinct circumstances, the state may not treat adults like children who need the state to protect them from exposure to controversial or potentially harmful ideas. The anti-paternalism principle is directly relevant to the campus free speech debate today because many of the calls for restricting free speech on campus are related to claims that college students today need paternal or maternal protection from unsettling ideas and influences. As Frank Furedi puts the matter, the line between college and lower education is being eviscerated in this era of subjective feelings and emotional vulnerability.[6]

2. *All ideas are equal* under the First Amendment. As the Supreme Court declared in an important libel case (*Gertz v. Robert Welch*) to which Post alluded, "We begin with the common ground. Under the First Amendment, there is no such thing as a false idea. However pernicious an opinion may seem, we depend for its correction not on the conscience of judges and juries, but on the competition of other ideas."[7] Post mentioned a related

condition in John Rawls's theory of equality and liberty that is pertinent to this core operating assumption: "In justice as fairness, there are no philosophic experts. Heaven forbid!"[8]

3. Except in very limited circumstances, a state *may not compel* a person to speak, especially when the speech embodies ideas or beliefs. This is the rule against "compelled speech" or "compelled association." Though Post did not mention it, the most famous case based on this principle is probably *West Virginia Board of Education v. Barnette*, in which the Supreme Court ruled that a school could not compel a student, who was a Jehovah's Witness, to stand and pledge allegiance to the U.S. flag. In so holding, Justice Robert Jackson spoke among the most famous words in First Amendment lore: "If there is any fixed star in our constitutional constellation, it is that no official, high or petty, can prescribe what shall be orthodox in politics, nationalism, religion, or other matters of opinion, or force citizens to confess by word or act their faith therein. If there are any circumstances which permit an exception, they do not now occur to us."[9]

I add a fourth important principle that Post did not mention: *lack of trust* in government to make the decision regarding what people should be allowed to hear or say. Lack of trust in government ("who decides?") is perhaps the most convincing justification for protecting free speech from government control.[10]

Now consider the ways in which academic principles and practice deviate from classic free speech and First Amendment doctrine and theory, as Post presented them.

1. Content and viewpoint discrimination *properly* permeate higher education. For example, the academic freedom of faculty members and students in the classroom is limited to speech that is "germane" or "relevant" to the subject matter at hand. To be sure, what passes as relevant or germane should be generously construed because learning is enhanced by showing how a particular subject or topic is related to or connected with other

aspects of knowledge, and instructors should be given due discretion to determine such relevance. (In another work, Post and Matthew Finkin denote this exercise as "heuristic.")[11] More generally, giving breathing space to the valid discretion of instructors is necessary to protect academic freedom. But this discretion must be within reason. A physics teacher must not spend inordinate time discussing the latest election. In addition, the kind of willful and obvious hate speech that is protected in a general public forum may be restricted in classroom situations. In a classroom, a basic distinction between gratuitous offense—substantial offense uttered simply for its own sake—and incidental offense that is based on the presentation of ideas is operative and is subject to appropriate safeguards for intellectual freedom. In his book *The Harm in Hate Speech*, for example, law professor Jeremy Waldron—also a participant at the ASU conference—defines *hate speech* as views "that express profound disrespect, hatred, and vilification for the members of minority groups."[12] (His address at the conference was about heckling, not hate speech, however.) Waldron's position has engendered much debate, and he would apply the standard to the general public forum as well to the domains of academic speech, so as to exclude hate speech from them both. Some scholars contend that Waldron's standard would be subject to administrative abuse in higher education.[13] But the point here is simply that some such restriction is more acceptable in classroom contexts than in the general free speech realm because of the special obligations of the classroom. Those obligations include acting with due respect for all participants. And Waldron affirms that his definition of hate speech should not pertain to the presentation of *ideas* that have racially unsettling or offensive implications, as well as that the "dignitary" harm he is talking about is not the same thing as "offensiveness."

2. In contradistinction to the general standard for admissible free speech articulated in *Gertz v. Robert Welch*, the pursuit of academic truth means *precisely* distinguishing truth from falsehood.

Some ideas are better than others, even if we concede, as we must, the imperative Millian principle about human fallibility. And students normally receive grades that reflect differences in the quality of their work. Sure, graders make mistakes, and grading has become inflated. But those fallibilities do not mean that we should abandon academic standards in grading. Furthermore, colleges and universities correctly strive to place experts in the roles of instructors, not charlatans. Rawls's maxim that there are no philosophic experts is patently and legitimately violated in academic settings.

3. Finally, Post points out that students are often *compelled* to speak or write. For example, in *Axson-Flynn v. Johnson*, which Post did not mention, a federal court ruled that a religiously conservative theater student could be compelled to use language she considered sacrilegious so long as the requirement was "reasonably related to pedagogical concerns."[14] The doctrine prohibiting compelled speech simply does not apply in such cases. And, of course, faculty members are compelled to do quality research in institutions that live by the publish–or–perish rule, as most such institutions do. I had to write reports for department meetings that I sometimes welcomed like pulling my own teeth.

4. As for my earlier additional point about trust, in higher education, a great deal of trust is delegated to the institution, departments, committees, individual scholars, or a combination of those to decide core academic matters, including authority over what Justice Felix Frankfurter considered the four essential pillars of academic freedom in *Sweezy v. New Hampshire*. To honor those pillars, the university must be allowed "to determine for itself on academic ground who may teach, what may be taught, how it shall be taught, and who may be admitted to study."[15] It is noteworthy that Frankfurter ultimately placed his emphasis on the freedom of *the institution* to decide such matters according to the deference that society grants to the expertise of academics to determine academic matters. This emphasis would prove to be problematic a few decades after Frankfurter wrote, as I explain

shortly. We should also note that this trust has been bequeathed to us not only by previous generations of students and their parents, but also by the earlier society as a whole. The institutional autonomy that is a hallmark of academic freedom was bestowed as part of an (at least) implicit social contract, which includes a responsibility that the AAUP has declared to be attached to the right of academic freedom: *the affirmative duty to do what is necessary to defend academic freedom itself*—the duty to protect the right at stake.[16]

In sum, maintaining a fundamental distinction between academic freedom and free speech is necessary to the distinctive mission of the university. The distinction applies most readily to the professional academic realms of teaching and research and to professional and scholarly activities such as decisions regarding curricula, hiring, tenure, and professional meetings on campus. What about speech outside those contexts, particularly that type of speech that is more pertinent to classic contexts of free speech, such as the public forum on campus, student advocacy and free speech groups, and invited speakers? Like some other writers who have underscored the special nature of the university, Post contends that classic First Amendment doctrine is not fully applicable to those realms either.

In a 2017 essay in *Vox*, Post wrote, "No university, public or private, could perform its mission were it not permitted to evaluate the merit of ideas" even in those realms.[17] Post was thinking about the right of inflammatory and racist speakers such as white nationalist Richard Spencer to speak on campus. In October 2017, for example, Spencer's appearance at the University of Florida–Gainesville generated heated controversy. Post is certainly correct that no one has a right to be invited to a campus to speak. Beyond the question of a right to be invited, Post goes further and argues that even public universities should be able to limit the speech of outside speakers in two contexts: (a) speakers invited by students and even faculty members if the university appropriately deems the speech clearly inconsistent with the intellectual missions of the institution, and (b) uninvited speakers who show up in open public forums on campus if their speech is plainly contrary to the institutional values and pedagogical mission. Post is clear to maintain, however, that decisions to limit the campus forum should be based on intellectual grounds, not on political, ideological, or similar forms of bias.

The general counsel and president of the University of Florida concluded that the school had a First Amendment obligation to allow Spencer to speak, given the nature of the place in which he chose to appear—a campus public forum that the university was not required by constitutional law to maintain. But the university chose to keep the place open because it considered such a forum an important part of students' educational experience—broadly understood. In First Amendment parlance, such an optional forum is a limited public forum, which means that the school is free to shut it down at its discretion. However, the school must abide by standard First Amendment requirements so long as it keeps the forum open.[18] Even if we agree with Post for the sake of argument that the standard First Amendment doctrine of the limited public forum should not be applied to campus public forums even at public universities, a normative nonlegal case could be made that schools should nonetheless abide by this doctrine on a voluntary basis. However, as I argued in Chapter 2, it is advisable to allow private schools to deviate from this norm at their considered and honest discretion.

Four justifications are credible. First, like Florida, a school might decide that allowing Spencer is the price it has to pay if it is to maintain the limited public forum for its broader educational value. (Of course, this argument assumes that First Amendment standards should apply to such forums in the first place—the claim that Post contests.) Second, one could accept Post's position that the school should have the legal discretion to deny certain speakers in such forums. However, the school might not want to give itself the power to make such decisions because of concerns about mistakes, slippery slopes, paternalism against students, and the like. We could call those two reasons negative arguments.

Third, there might be a more positive argument, though it is admittedly more controversial. The school could allow the speech of people like Richard Spencer, whom most people reasonably find morally reprehensible, because such a speech can still contribute to the wider education of students in a dynamic, perhaps counterintuitive sense. Exposure to such speakers can make us more genuinely aware of the harsh realities of political life and what is happening in the world, including the human capacity for injustice. In addition, as an African American civil rights leader once replied to me when I asked him if the First Amendment should protect racist, anti-black publications, he said that he would worry about the proverbial slippery slope of censorship, especially given his racial minority status, and that he wanted to know his enemy.[19]

The national director of the American Civil Liberties Union (ACLU) said something similar in defending the ACLU's defense of a small yet noxious Nazi group to demonstrate in Skokie, Illinois, in the late 1970s despite the presence of hundreds of Holocaust survivors there: it can be a good idea to know one's enemy. And if the rights of a highly unpopular and discredited Nazi group are secure under the Constitution, so are the rights of the rest of us, including Jews, *a fortiori*.[20]

Controversially, sometimes even morally reprehensible speakers can open the door to moral improvement, because they compel us to mobilize against their ideas and claims. More controversially yet, in some cases, what seems morally reprehensible today can become morally acceptable later.[21] This reversal has happened often in history, with homosexuality and interracial marriage among recent examples. (See Chapter 7 for more examples.)

It is well nigh impossible to believe that such a reversal of opinion will eventually vindicate racists like Spencer, but if we sanction censorship in his case on moral grounds per se, we set in place a principle of censorship that can then be applied to cases in which the potential for judgment reversal is more feasible even though we do not know so originally. Spencer gets a permit to speak in order to guard against this problem.

Concern about making mistakes in this manner is one reason that the Supreme Court typically limits permissible punishment for speech to situations in which concrete harm to society or individuals is clearly demonstrable, such as genuine threats and direct incitement to violence or law breaking. (See Chapters 4, 7, and 8.)

The exclusion of obscenity from First Amendment protection is one possible exception to this point, but the Court has concluded that the prurient nature of obscene material means it lacks the ideational content that brings First Amendment protection into play in the first place. But in a nod to those who disagree with this claim, the Court limits the obscenity exception to the most sexually explicit forms of hardcore pornography.

THE RELATIONSHIP BETWEEN FREE SPEECH AND ACADEMIC FREEDOM RECONSIDERED: THE UNIVERSITY AS AN INTELLECTUAL *POLIS*

I veer from Post's position in several respects, though I agree with his understanding of academic freedom as the *sine qua non* of higher education: that which makes it distinctive. If instructors were given green lights without qualification to teach things such as Holocaust denial and Ptolemy's astronomy as factual truth, the university as we know it would cease to exist.[22] But there are good reasons that most higher education institutions should adhere to classic First Amendment standards in other domains for at least normative, if not legal, reasons. An appropriate balance between the standards of academic freedom and free speech jurisprudence is truer to the mission of higher education than is upholding only the pillar of academic freedom. I arrive at this position because of the model of the university as an intellectual *polis*.

First, consider the argument of Erwin Chemerinsky and Howard Gillman in their 2017 book, *Free Speech on Campus*. They posit two realms of campus life in the wake of the Berkeley Free Speech Movement of 1964:

> Rather than view the university as a heavily regulated space of professional instruction and scholarly activity, the students [at Berkeley] demanded that it also be recognized as a public forum for free speech. . . . We should think of campuses as having two different zones of free expression: a professional zone, which protects the expression of ideas but imposes an obligation of responsible discourse and responsible conduct in formal educational and scholarly settings; and a larger free speech zone which exists outside scholarly and administrative settings where the only restrictions are those of society at large.[23]

Speech outside of professional settings matters.

This is one reason that so-called extramural speech by a faculty member—speech to the public in one's capacity as a citizen about a matter of public importance—should be considered part of protected free speech in the academy even if the speaker is talking about something not directly related to what he or she knows best. As Keith Whittington has pointed out, meaningful breathing space should be given in this realm because good universities and colleges should want to encourage widespread discourse in different domains; the punishment of extramural speech can have a harmful effect on the status of academic free speech in other campus domains.[24]

A key point arises here: what happens in one sphere of campus can have an effect on what happens elsewhere in the campus *polis*. Colleges and universities have distinctive realms, but they are also organic wholes. Accordingly, allowing a speaker to be shouted down in a forum can have a chilling effect on honest and challenging speech in the classroom and elsewhere. Faculty members who shy away from publicly criticizing the shouting down of speakers on their campuses because "it doesn't affect me or my class" need to heed this fact.

In speaking extramurally, faculty members should make it clear that they are speaking for themselves and not for the institution and that they are subject to the standard limits of free speech. But the Supreme Court created further problems for extramural faculty speech when it ruled in 2006 that state employees are not entitled to First Amendment protection when they speak about matters relating to their "official duties," a term several lower federal courts have interpreted quite broadly.[25] The Court left open the application of this test to the academy because of special concerns relating to academic freedom, and lower courts have been divided in their decisions dealing with faculty extramural speech. But my point regarding such speech is normative regardless of how courts ultimately resolve the question.

In 1974, Yale published a famous report on free speech and higher education. The *Report of the Committee on Free Expression at Yale* (also known as the *Woodward Report* in honor of the committee's distinguished chair, historian C. Vann Woodward) proclaimed that free speech is foundational to the institution. In its section "Of Values and Priorities," the report proclaimed:

> The primary function of a university is to discover and disseminate knowledge by means of research and teaching. *To fulfill this function a free interchange of ideas is necessary not only within its walls but with the world beyond as well.* [Emphasis added.] It follows that the university must do everything possible to ensure within it the fullest degree of intellectual freedom. The history of intellectual growth and discovery clearly demonstrates the need for unfettered freedom, the right to think the unthinkable, discuss the unmentionable, and challenge the unchallengeable. To curtail free expression strikes twice at intellectual freedom, for whoever deprives another of the right to state unpopular views necessarily also deprives others of the right to listen to those views.[26]

In the spirit of the Woodward Committee, I would go further than Chemerinsky and Gillman. There is *a third dimension* beyond the public forum: the countless interactions that campus citizens have in the numerous nooks, crannies, and venues outside of libraries, classrooms, and speaker forums. Colleges and universities should be alive with Socratic exchanges in many domains. The seminal 1968 Supreme Court case dealing with the First Amendment right of a high school student to wear a black armband to school to protest the Vietnam War championed the broad institutional aspect of student free speech that I have in mind; and the point is even more pertinent to higher education, where intellectual freedom properly reigns more supreme than in high school—as both pedagogical theory and numerous court decisions have acknowledged:

> That [schools] are educating the young for citizenship is reason for scrupulous protection of Constitutional freedoms of the individual, if we are not to strangle the free mind at its source and teach youth to discount important principles of our government as mere platitudes. . . .
>
> The principle of these cases is not confined to the supervised and ordained discussion which [*sic*] takes place in the classroom. . . . *Among those activities is personal intercommunication among the students. This is not*

only an inevitable part of the process of attending school; it is also an import-ant part of the educational process. [Emphasis added.] A student's rights, therefore, do not embrace merely the classroom hours. When he is in the cafeteria, or on the playing field, or on the campus during the authorized hours, he may express his opinions, even on controversial subjects like the conflict in Vietnam, if he does so without "materially and substantially interfer[ing] with the requirements of appropriate discipline in the operation of the school" and without colliding with the rights of others.[27]

Protecting free speech in all three domains is important for both practical and normative reasons. It is practical simply because it acknowl-edges that a vital college or university is an institutional community or *polis*. If we deny this reality, we blind ourselves to the ways in which free thought can flourish in different spheres, as well as how the suppression of speech in the informal realms can readily spill over to the formal realms—and vice versa. Controversial views should not be relegated to the bathroom or subway walls or to the sounds of silence, as has some-times been the case.[28]

And it is normative because so much learning and intellectual growth occur outside the formal settings. When I taught, I considered my classes to be springboards for student discussions in different campus domains, and I always relished the countless intellectual interchanges I had with students in the various spaces of the campus. I considered it a moral victory when I learned of discussions and debates students had about ideas from my class in their dorm rooms and apartments, in the Memorial Union, or in the watering holes that line State Street. Often the discussions spread to other subjects, evincing the interconnectedness of truths and knowledge.

But the formal learning that takes place also elevates and gives more substance to the exchanges and engagements that transpire in the informal spheres. And informal learning performs another important function: it can motivate students who are less engaged with what goes on in class. I know of numerous cases in which students became more interested or involved in the class not because of me, but because of interactions with friends or acquaintances from the class in other venues.

Each realm nourishes the other. The flourishing of knowledge and truth is often very personal. Socrates had an intellectual and an emotional effect on Plato; students today often take courses not simply because of the subject matter, but because of the qualities of the instructor and students.

This dynamic is why undue bureaucratic oversight or intrusion into this interpersonal realm can be so damaging to the heart and soul of a campus, whether it emanates from Washington, DC, or the local sensitivity office. When (as shown in Chapter 1) Laura Kipnis spoke about improper extension of Title IX investigations, she was talking not only about due process, but also about the intellectual vitality and honesty of everyday encounters. At one point, she observes that a Title IX administrator possessed "the psychological acuity of a mollusk"—not exactly the intellectual sophistication one normally associates with Northwestern University.[29] Harassment and sexual misconduct are obviously not proper parts of this process, and they need to be dealt with authoritatively. But legitimate free speech needs to be protected. Higher education must be conscientious in drawing the proper line.

In 2008, students at Rhodes College, an otherwise excellent liberal arts school in Memphis, told me that student affairs administrators had initiated an Orwellian policy of *requiring* students to inform on others who, in *private conversations,* said things considered insensitive about the identity politics grounds of race, gender, sex, and the like. Conscientious and impressive student leaders in student government brought me to campus to give them and the student government advice on how to remedy the problem, as well as to give a public lecture about student freedom. They wore the sincerity and depth of their dismay on their faces and sleeves—they felt betrayed by the institution that had promised them liberal education and that charged them considerable fees for it.

In the end, the students did not pursue the strategies I proposed, perhaps because I considered more pressing resistance as the only way out because the administration had dismissed their concerns up and down the administrative chain. During this visit, I thought of

Boris Pasternak's portrayal in *Doctor Zhivago* of how the private aspects of mind, conscience, and civil society are essential to a free society and of how the Soviet state dedicated itself to commandeering this realm.[30] As we will see in Chapter 4, Rhodes was a harbinger of things to come.

There is even a fourth realm of campus speech activity: the realm of independent student associations and groups, which can involve rights of privacy and association that are independent of public engagement. Such groups are "a way of telling the world who you are, and for aligning yourself with like-minded people."[31] The First Amendment and our constitutional scheme in general protect the right to establish your own community of meaning and truth in opposition to state and community truths, so long as you accept legitimate general laws that do not unnecessarily infringe on this right. Constitutional and communal meanings are forged by the constant struggle of groups to define their own understandings and to "maintain the independence and authority of their own *nomos*."[32] The First Amendment has both a public and a private face.

It is useful to think of the connections among the four realms in terms of the relationship between formal activities and play, which is an aspect of the interplay between emotion and reason that I discussed in Chapter 2. (As we will see in Chapter 4, those connections provide a qualified case for safe spaces.) Whereas formal situations and presentations constitute specialized contexts for the achievement of excellence, play is the realm where we can be more experimental and spread our wings. It is also the domain in which we can be more transgressive and rebellious and can challenge the restraints of formality.

This domain is especially important for young adults, who are experimenting and feeling their way in a trial-and-error respect, a process that also entails defining themselves vis-à-vis authority. (The authoritarian trend in higher education today is not its best feature.) As Hans-Georg Gadamer has discerned, truth about human qualities and nature is often disclosed in the acts of play, commitment, and creation. As Shakespeare also knew: "The play's the thing wherein I'll catch the conscience of the king."[33] The highest form of excellence is when we combine the two forms into seemingly effortless effort: making official performance itself a form of play, or elevating play itself to a higher level.

HECKLERS' VETOES, HYDE PARK, AND THE UNIVERSITY

Given the normative importance of free speech forums to campus life as heralded by the Woodward Report, hecklers' vetoes of protected speech are deeply problematic, as the Supreme Court came to appreciate when it crafted the so-called "heckler's veto doctrine" in the 1960s in order to protect the rights of civil rights protesters against their censorious enemies. The basic idea is as simple as it is profound: if you allow hecklers to disrupt or prevent (to veto) constitutionally protected speech because they threaten disorder, you surrender the free speech rights of rightful speakers to those who not only disagree with the speaker, but also are willing to use coercion or force in order to achieve their own political or normative ends. When police play along with hecklers by standing down or telling speakers to cease, they become complicit in privately sponsored censorship. In the South in the 1960s, the state often positively endorsed such censorship, using that endorsement as a pretext for its own racist ends. Police would typically arrest *legitimate* speakers for disorderly conduct or for disobeying the police order to stop speaking, as if the lawful speakers were the ones responsible for the disorder.

By heeding the advice of the distinguished civil liberty scholar Harry Kalven Jr., whose scholarship pioneered the concept, the Court developed the heckler's veto doctrine: the rights of legitimate speakers must not be placed in the hands of their enemies.[34] The First Amendment law regarding the heckler's veto has coalesced around the following rules, which sometimes call for discerning judgment on the part of the police or other authorities: (a) when someone threatens disorder or disruption if the speaker is not shut down, the first duty of police is to protect the rights of the speaker if at all possible; (b) lawful speakers are not properly arrested if they refuse to obey an unlawful police order to cease speaking;[35] (c) police must make reasonable efforts to control the unruly hecklers; and (d) only when police reasonably ascertain that they cannot protect both the speakers' rights and public order may they order the speaker to step down. I should add that in such cases the hecklers should be arrested for violating the rights of the speaker and for threatening imminent violence themselves.[36]

When hecklers disrupt a speech on campus, they violate several rights: (a) the right of the speaker, (b) the right of any group or sponsor that brought the speaker in, and (c) the right of listeners to hear the speech. This last right includes those listeners who oppose the speaker but who for various reasons still want to hear what the speaker has to say. Meiklejohn has argued that the right of listeners is the most important part of the freedom of speech clause of the First Amendment. In the academic setting we should add another right: (d) the right of the university community to be a place where freedom of speech flourishes. In the university context, the disruption of speakers harms the very civilizing mission of the campus by replacing persuasion with force.

So the successful practice of free speech calls on official power to protect the rights of speakers, listeners, *and* counterspeakers. First Amendment scholar Thomas Emerson taught that free speech is a "system" of interlocking rights and duties. Speakers have a right to speak but a duty not to violate legitimate laws demarking the legal limits of free speech; listeners have the right to disagree and even protest, but they may not disrupt the rights of speakers or create disorder; and legal authorities must secure the rights of lawful speakers while also protecting general order. It is this very system that is under attack when hostile audiences do not honor the rights of speakers and when campus officials and local police stand down to let hecklers have their way. It is no wonder that many of the publicized disruptions of legitimate speakers in higher education present echoes of authoritarianism. Such disruptions tear at the fabric of ordered liberty, a matter that is of central constitutional concern. Liberty cannot prevail in the face of lawlessness.[37]

A further question deals with higher education institutions having to bear the costs, which can be substantial, of police protection for controversial or provocative speakers. The law on this question is fairly clear: lawful speakers must not be charged fees to enter the public forum that prevent them from being able to speak; but what is not clear is how sustainable this law is, given the increase of intentionally provocative speakers and their hostile receptions on campus, as well as the extreme expense of providing protections when the two come together. Recently, Berkeley has promulgated a policy designed to balance the rights and interests at stake. (I discuss this policy at some length in Chapter 8.) One remedy is to restrict controversial speakers to less public parts of the campus where their views are quarantined, as it were.[38] But courts have properly ruled against mandating such "Hyde Parks" because the First Amendment entails the right to take your message to where the issue is most pertinent and potent.

Similarly, campuses may not restrict free speech to limited free speech zones. Martin Luther King Jr. took his message to the most racist places in America, including Cicero, Illinois, at a time when he and his forces—along with Dan Rather of CBS, who was covering the event—were met with bricks hurled by hostile crowds. One function of free speech is to challenge social and individual defense mechanisms that buttress systemic injustice.

FOUR OTHER CONSIDERATIONS

Let me advance four additional and related reasons for giving free speech jurisprudence more, yet appropriately balanced, influence in higher education. First, though the realms of academic freedom and free speech are distinct for the reasons we have articulated earlier, they also share an essential common ground: the commitment to the pursuit of truth and the intellectual freedom that is essential to that end. (See the observation of the Woodward Committee earlier.) This is one reason that efforts to define free speech and academic freedom often overlap and are conceptually complex. An example might be the University of Chicago's famous "Statement on Principles of Free Expression," which focuses on free expression—a general term—but which is meant to have meaningful application to academic freedom.[39] Accordingly, courts have upheld student and student group free speech rights in the face of improper speech codes and other campus restrictions at public institutions, such as restrictive free speech zones and improper viewpoint-based funding of groups.[40] I always thought that restrictive free speech zones imply that the institution feels the need to quarantine free speech on campus, as if free speech were some kind of disease. It is not surprising that courts have been skeptical of this practice.

Second, the best universities have historically been places where academic principles and vibrant free speech have coexisted. In this respect, I am reminded of Spanish philosopher José Ortega y Gasset's vision of the university in his classic book titled *Mission of the University*. On the one hand, Ortega makes it clear that the foundation of the university is the cultivation of the mind through an emphasis on science. Ortega's concept of science is similar to the German concept of *Wissenschaft*, which is more expansive than the term "science" in English. It means "any systematic form of inquiry into nature, history, literature, or society marked by rigorous methods that secure the reliability or truth of its findings."[41]

On the other hand, Ortega praises the concept of an open university that faces the pressing issues and controversies of the day. Although his emphasis is similar to that of the Woodward Report, it is somewhat different, deriving from Ortega's general philosophy of historical vitality, struggle, and phenomenology:

> Not only does [the university] need perpetual contact with science, on pain of atrophy, it needs contact, likewise, with public life, with historical reality, with the present, which is essentially a whole to be dealt with only in its totality. . . . The university must be in the midst of life, and saturated with it.[42]

Some of the best teaching combines aspects of the purely academic realm and what Ortega calls "public life," which is the sphere of energy and engagement with the wider world, including political and social life. Most of the theorists we study in political science and philosophy were deeply committed to engaging the pressing public issues of their time in one form or another. The theorists draw universal insights from their particular circumstances; thus, involvement with the life around the university gives students who simultaneously study the great thinkers, or who learn intellectual rigor in other respects, a taste of the actual intellectual and existential circumstances of those thinkers.

The great international relations theorist Hans Morgenthau called this combination of rigorous intellectual study and engagement with contemporary issues a form of "higher practicality." When properly conducted, the higher practicality makes the big questions of social and political existence come alive for students and shows them how historically notable political thought is often forged in conflict and pressure. Such education involves not only the intellect, but also the emotions, character, and commitment—universal themes one finds in the history and theory of free speech. This engagement broadens, deepens, and enlivens the inquiry. Taking the best works of political thought seriously adds depth and intellectual responsibility to the quest for relevance. Contra to Marx's critique of Hegel, the purpose of philosophy is to understand the world *before* trying to change it. Is not changing the world before understanding it a form of recklessness?[43]

Learning involves not only confronting and engaging with the different ideas and beliefs of others, but also interacting and struggling with persons themselves. Of course, sometimes the "other" is indeed a real threat, which is another lesson to learn. Learning to distinguish real threats from imaginary ones is both a necessary aspect of maturation and a central feature of First Amendment theory and jurisprudence. Interactions with others constitute part of learning because of the different ideas and interpretations that others bear, and because of the different characters and personalities they present to us, both engaging and conflicting with us. The process of growth has both an intellectual and an interpersonal aspect.

The best instructors motivate students for a variety of reasons, including the depth of their knowledge, their respect and love of the subject matter, the respect they have for students, and the often intangible nature of their individual characters. Perhaps most important, the best instructors often challenge students and make them feel uncomfortable. Students have a right to feel physically safe. They do not have a right to feel intellectually safe. The confusion of those two forms of safety is not the least of our pedagogical problems today.[44]

Maturation and higher learning entail learning how to deal responsibly and advantageously with conflict, which is an intrinsic part of living.

In *Speaking Freely*, Keith Whittington stresses repeatedly that the future of higher education depends on campus citizens learning how to deal with intellectual conflict more constructively.[45] Conflict chisels abilities and skills while compelling one to think seriously about what is worth fighting for. Constructive agonistic conflict can enhance understanding, increase legitimacy by opening the realm of discourse to all comers, and give meaning and vitality to fundamental principles. Ideas and truth "come alive," as it were. Mill's articulation of this reality in *On Liberty* is one of the best defenses of the need for intellectual challenge and debate. Mill understood the connection between the sustenance of truth and human emotion.

However much truth exists ontologically outside human acceptance, human beings must be committed to truth in order for it to have presence in the human world. Hence the need to educate and sustain commitment lest truth slide into oblivion. Even answering false ideas can lead to greater understanding because this obligation compels us to defend and sharpen our understanding. Mill argued that we should allow false opinions to be heard and be the subject of discussion lest we lose the opportunity of "the clearer perception and *livelier impression* of truth produced by its collision with error." [Emphasis added.][46] This position certainly applies to the academic realm when teaching is creative, so long as demonstrably false ideas are not treated as truth. But using demonstrably false ideas as discussion points or foils can be utterly consistent with the professional pursuit of truth.

A third reason for striving to maintain a proper balance of free speech and academic freedom is the way in which such a balance represents a further commitment to both intellectual standards and a healthy regard for human fallibility, which is a hallmark of free speech theory. Truths and interpretations espoused in the academic freedom domain of the classroom are naturally more authoritative than are those expressed in other realms of free speech, but they are not infallible. The campus forum can check or supplement the fallibilities or biases of the classroom. Respect for the fallibility principle is mandatory, which means maintaining due doubt about truth claims, however compelling they may be, and whoever voices them.

The Holocaust happened, but honest and fair debate continues regarding actual details and its consequences for various aspects of national and international politics. Ditto for climate change, over which fair and natural disagreement reigns regarding such matters as the validity of the computer models to study it, the weight to be given human input, our predictions of its future trajectory, its economic effects, the economic effects of fighting it, and how we should balance efforts to decrease it with efforts to accommodate to such climate change.

Healthy skepticism also lies at the heart of our constitutional system, which promotes checks and balances in order to guard against the imperfections—intellectual and moral—of those who govern us. At the same time, that system establishes requisite power for the government to constitutionally govern citizens in order to protect us from our own fallibilities and threats.

Maintaining a public forum for speakers on campus and delegating authority to student groups and faculty members to invite speakers constitutes a special kind of check against the more formal academic realm. It also contributes to the development of students' sense of responsibility. It can provide a domain for appropriate rebellion and challenge to authority, which a democratic republic needs. The popular and scholarly literature about higher education is replete with examples of students and faculty members bringing in speakers to challenge or to supplement prevailing truths and orthodoxies in the academy.

Political theorist Paul Eidelberg explains the intellectual and political rationale behind the Constitution's checks and balances: "[T]he first object of government is to prevent any attempt to bring about a massive uniformity of opinions, passions, and interests. . . . Madison wished to institute a system of checks and balances to preserve the republic from the leveling spirit. To guard against that spirit is to guard against the degradation of the republican form of government."[47]

For the fourth and final point, let us return to the question of *trust* that I added to Post's list of core free speech principles earlier. Lack of trust in government—and indeed in many other forms of authority—is a classic free speech value that is at odds with the institutional autonomy and trust that higher education's leaders have traditionally enjoyed in practice and in law. But given the threats to intellectual freedom on campus today, just how much is such trust merited? Surely a significant amount, for reasons I articulated earlier in this chapter. Only extremists want outside political powers to dictate academic judgments. But how much trust is warranted? As I mentioned earlier, academic freedom was originally conceived as an institutional right more than an individual right. And this is how courts have tended to treat it even to this day, though the relationship between individual and institutional autonomy is not crystal clear and is inherently in tension.[48]

There are different reasons for this emphasis, one of which is the fact that most of the historical threats to academic freedom hailed from outside the university's gates, largely from the right. Accordingly, individual and institutional interests in academic freedom within the academy coexisted more or less in harmony, at least compared with more recent times. But this arrangement has changed over the course of the past few decades. Though threats from the right continue, most threats today have come from the academic left and from *inside* higher education itself.

The main debate today is over the *extent* of the problem, not its reality. To the degree that this situation prevails, it is no longer as feasible as it once was to blithely trust the judgments of academic leaders to determine academic policy for themselves. The classic question of "Who decides?" is applicable here. No doubt it is much better to let a fallible academic body decide academic questions than to bow to members of the state legislature or political appointees on the boards of trustees and regents. But reasonable, duly respectful checks on academic judgments are consistent with core principles of liberal democracy. The situation should be one of "trust, but verify."[49] Maintaining a vibrant public forum on campus is one key way to check the academic authority that might otherwise overreach or become monolithic. In Chapter 5, I discuss issues related to the lack of intellectual diversity in domains of higher education today. One internal remedy to this problem is to foster a vibrant discussion and disagreement in the less formal realms of campus life. Because these realms include voices from inside the academy itself—or voices invited by campus citizens or allowed by institutional policy—they avoid the problems associated with remedies dictated from outside authorities.

In 2002, Brady Williamson, a prominent First Amendment attorney who is from Madison, Wisconsin, and who won the federal case against the University of Wisconsin's system student speech code in 1991, gave a guest lecture in my First Amendment class. He declared, "The two most important words in First Amendment theory and law are 'Who Decides.'" I agreed with him, though at one time I thought the "who decides" point was too simplistic. But as my experiences in pedagogy and free speech politics and policy deepened, I came to realize that this question is indeed foundational. By fostering a vibrant realm of discourse beyond the classroom and other formal campus settings, higher education provides its own check on formal authority and thinking that is consistent with institutional autonomy rightly understood.

CHAPTER 4

MAJOR THREATS TO ACADEMIC FREE SPEECH: CONTEMPORARY POLICIES AND RELATED ASPECTS

If we wish to preserve a free society, it is essential that we recognize that the desirability of a particular object is not sufficient justification for the use of coercion.

—*F. A. Hayek,* The Constitution of Liberty

In this chapter, we will look at more specific policies and contemporary threats to campus free speech and academic freedom, as well as how these phenomena detract from the obligation to properly prioritize the academic mission. The main focus will be the conflation of speech and action, which entails elevating subjective feeling and vulnerability over the reason and rigor that are so essential to the intellectual mission of the university.

NEW POLICIES OR PRACTICES THAT INHIBIT FREEDOM OF MIND AND SPEECH

In certain respects, the policies we will encounter in this chapter constitute end runs around the overt censorship that made formal speech codes so vulnerable to legal challenges in previous decades. Things such as trigger warnings, microaggression lists, safe space policies, and bias reporting systems are not necessarily blatant forms of censorship. But their omnipresent potential to be misapplied can make them Orwellian in nature, thus inhibiting and chilling the kind of interchange and discourse that are the lifeblood of the university as an intellectual *polis*.

What kind of honest and vibrant discourse can take place when a major institution such as the University of California officially declares that sentences such as "Where are you from?," "America is a melting pot," "America is the land of opportunity," and "I believe the most qualified person should get the job" are unacceptable microaggressions? As we will see, microaggressions are reportable to campus authorities at many institutions. Even questioning the legitimacy of affirmative action as a *policy* is considered a microaggression in some places.[1]

A common theme that emerges is the elevation of subjective claims over what law calls the position of the reasonable person, which is the model for what the law labels an objective standard: if a fear or emotion is subjectively felt, that reaction is considered sufficient for it to cause a harm that needs to be accommodated, however unreasonably. In 2013, for example, the Office for Civil Rights (OCR) in the DOE required schools receiving federal aid to enforce a subjective standard for determining sexual harassment, not an objective one.[2] However, under the aegis of its new secretary, Betsy DeVos, in February 2019 the DOE proposed a return to the older objective standard. The reform is being hotly contested, and the decision process is underway as of this writing.[3] But even if the move back toward an objective standard succeeds, the cultural and intellectual emphasis on subjective standards of offense and fear remains strong in higher education.

The reasonable-person standard is sufficient to punish perpetrators, and it is essential to protecting freedom of speech because the pursuit of truth is expected to be painful at times. And as we have seen, an intellectual community is premised on reason. To be sure, what constitutes a reasonable person is naturally open to dispute in a world subject to change and struggle. But claims that reason and judgment are simply constructions of power or merely arbitrary overshoot the mark and undermine the viability of an intellectual community. Without standards of reason applied to all, unreasonable claims of harm and hecklers' vetoes can hold legitimate free speech hostage.

In *Unwanted Advances*, Laura Kipnis portrays the different forces on campus—intellectual, psychological, political, and cultural—that have moved the needle toward the subjective end of the campus continuum:

> Irony doesn't sit very well in the current climate, especially when it comes to irony *about* the current climate. Critical distance itself is out of fashion—not exactly a plus when it comes to intellectual life (or education itself). Feelings are what's in fashion. I'm all for feelings; I'm a standard-issue female after all. But this cult of feeling has an authoritarian underbelly: feelings can't be questioned or probed, even while furnishing the rationale for sweeping new policies, which can't be questioned or probed, either. (I speak from experience here.) The result is that higher education has been so radically transformed that the place is almost unrecognizable.[4]

Let us now look at some concrete new policies that are manifestations of this culture.

TRIGGER WARNINGS

The idea of trigger warnings derives from the decades-old trauma movement in psychology and post-traumatic stress disorder studies. That movement holds that exposure to certain material may trigger memories and trauma on the basis of past stressful experience. Properly used and completely voluntary, triggers can be tools of decency and good pedagogy. I have used them on occasion in class, mainly in teaching cases involving violent crimes. I never would have tolerated administrative pressure to use them, however. The first concern is obviously practical: what should receive a warning, and how can one know who might be emotionally vulnerable in the class? And what if an instructor and student clash over this question? A bottomless pit of controversy impends.

Students have demanded triggers for classic works such as *The Great Gatsby* (Rutgers) and Ovid's *Metamorphoses* (Barnard).[5] Normative concerns compete with the practical. Psychiatrists and others caution that trigger warnings can send messages to even nontraumatized students that challenging subjects are dangerous, as Jonathan Haidt and Greg Lukianoff report in *The Coddling of the American Mind*.[6] A professor I met was investigated by his institution for simply assigning Haidt and Lukianoff's *Atlantic* article of the same title for his class to discuss.

One student complained, and her subjective feeling of offense was all the university needed to conduct an investigation.

As University of Pennsylvania professor Jonathan Zimmerman has written, triggers can also compel students to focus on the section of the reading that is triggered, thereby ignoring the larger context and literary or intellectual value of the work. Anna Karenina's suicide is an important part of Tolstoy's great book, but the rest of the work is essential to making it a literary masterpiece.[7] The AAUP and the National Coalition Against Censorship have called trigger warnings "infantilizing."[8] And accentuating trauma in this manner can discourage the stretching of the imagination that is so important to the adventure of learning and personal growth.

MICROAGGRESSION LISTS

Again, general politeness dictates that we at least consider avoiding certain expressions if they are rude or cause gratuitous offense; even good-willed individuals have something to learn in this respect. But what education historian Diane Ravitch calls the "Language Police" can enter the scene if we are not careful.[9] One common response to microaggressions is public shaming, which not only is a harm in its own right but also is counterproductive in relation to the policy's objectives. Rather than opening one's mind, shaming makes one defensive and resentful of the loss of respect. Such "shaming is often carried out by mobs with no mechanism to make the punishment proportionate to the offense. And public shaming targets some people who did nothing wrong (friendly criticism is better for fallible critics)."[10]

To the extent that the negative effects of microaggression programs seep into the sinews of campus life, they can seriously inhibit the kind of interpersonal relations that are so important to a dynamic liberal education in the *polis*.

AFFIRMATIVE CONSENT POLICIES

Another example is recent efforts by campus authorities and even state legislatures to limit sexual discourse in ways that treat students as children and that inhibit campus intellectual exchange. The laws do not pertain to class discussions relating to sex, but rather to the verbal interactions attendant upon the rise of sexual relations. For example, legal scholar Evan Gerstmann delineates the ways in which new affirmative consent laws and their like affect sexual relations in detrimental ways, including harming the right of sexual autonomy and of intellectual freedom on campus.

Such affirmative consent laws require affirmative verbal consent for each stage of sexual activity, assuming nonconsent unless express consent is given at each step. This logic ignores the many other ways that sexual consent can be given in normal human relations, especially in couples who have had long-standing relations, and the logic entails a dramatic expansion of the criminal law's definitions of nonconsent. Although rightly condemning unwanted sexual advances, Gerstmann critiques laws that, in words that echo Laura Kipnis, encourage the bureaucratization of sexual relations:

> It is important to understand that affirmative consent regimes go beyond merely requiring consent. They regulate how students express that consent and do so in a manner that is contrary to how most people actually engage in sexual activity. They turn many, if not most students, into expellable perpetrators of sexual assault. . . .
>
> The scope of these rules [is] often breathtaking. They make no exceptions for couples in long-term relationships, or even married couples who develop over time their own understandings of what rules of sexual conduct are.[11]

The new breed of affirmative consent rules differs from the new microaggression policies because it deals with sex per se and is directed at imperative concerns about sexual misconduct. But the rules' scope and vagueness threaten to criminalize much of the normal verbal interchange that typifies sexual interaction. Bureaucratic incentives to regulate add to this potential, especially given two factors: the way that the new rules expand the conception of consent, and the legal requirement in many jurisdictions for third parties to report sexual offenses when they hear about those actions. Wrongly applied, this new regime of rules would constitute yet another way in which the important human interactions on campus are inhibited.

BIAS REPORTING PROGRAMS

The mission and effect of bias reporting programs combine several of the different new policies under discussion into one package. Administratively, they are the products of national administrative networking. Bias reporting programs create bias response teams (BRTs) that strive to foster safe and inclusive campus climates by providing "advocacy and support to anyone on campus who has experienced, or been a witness of, an incident of bias or discrimination."[12] FIRE's 2017 *Bias Response Team Report* stated, "FIRE discovered and surveyed 231 Bias Response Teams at public and private institutions during 2016. The expression of at least 2.84 million American students is subject to review by Bias Response Teams. Although most students in higher education do not yet appear to be subject to bias reporting systems, we believe that the number of Bias Response Teams is growing rapidly."[13]

BRTs arose for reasons related to the other new policies we are discussing, including (a) the reports of overt acts of bias on many campuses, as well as more covert or implicit acts; (b) the felt need of many students and campus citizens to provide remedial action and education; and (c) it must be said, the administrative agendas of the diversity industry. Overt examples of bias have included racist letters sent to Ohio State students through campus mail in 2007 and several recent incidents of acts such as racist symbols being set up in prominent campus locations under cover of the night.[14]

Given valid concerns about student safety and well-being, campuses have reason to know about harassment that meets legal standards as well as about threatening actions and speech—and to respond accordingly. And, as we will see later, the First Amendment does not protect either harassment or true threats. Students are entitled to feel physically safe and free from wrongful discrimination. The problem arises when concern for *physical* safety expands into concern for *intellectual* safety.

The definitions of bias used in these programs typically focus on identity politics rather than on more universal concerns about threats. (What if someone threatens you but it doesn't involve race, gender, sexual orientation, or some other identity category? Threats are not limited to identity-based bias.) In an essay in *The New Republic*, professors Jeffrey Aaron Snyder and Amna Khalid point out several other problems. For example, definitions of bias are often not limited to threats and clear harms, which lie outside the First Amendment's protective umbrella. Instead, they encompass the growing list of vaguely defined microaggressions and impolite words. Snyder and Khalid provide some examples of suspect forms of expression: "objectifying women," "avoiding or excluding others," "I was joking; don't take things so seriously," and "making comments on social media about someone's political affiliations or beliefs." In other words, people are encouraged to report or inform on others for expressing constitutionally protected beliefs and attitudes that fall short of constituting harassment and threats as those terms are defined in law.

Students are often encouraged *to report* such expressions to administrative authorities and sometimes even to the *police*. The BRT website at Portland State University in Oregon, for example, includes—along with harassment and threats—"physical, spoken, or written acts of abuse, insensitivity, [and] lack of awareness." Across town, the University of Portland urged students to report "incidents of *discomfort*" to the police.[15] The nanny state and Orwellian implications of such inclusions are self-evident. Programs targeting such language can easily chill even sincere, kind, and potentially beneficial interchange. One false verbal step, and you are reported to the authorities.

According to Snyder and Khalid, a high percentage of complaints about insensitive or derogatory speech target the domain where intellectual honesty is most important: the classroom. In *Keyishian v. Board of Regents* (1967), the Supreme Court proclaimed, "The classroom is peculiarly the marketplace of ideas. The Nation's future depends upon leaders trained through wide exposure to that robust exchange of ideas which discovers truth out of a multitude of tongues, [rather] than through any kind of authoritative selection."[16] If this principle held true even for members of the Communist Party, then it should certainly hold true when we confront microaggressions today, which are commonly matters of mere thoughtlessness or insensitivity.

Numerous courses deal with controversial subject matter or historical truths that many people reasonably consider immoral or morally questionable today. But to fully understand such subject matter, one must open one's intellectual imagination and suspend certain intellectually stifling judgments for pedagogical purposes. At Dartmouth, for example, student activists confounded simply discussing a position with endorsing it and "demanded that the college ban from campus the use of 'any racially charged term' such as 'illegal immigrants.'"[17] Similarly, the BRT at the University of Oregon suggests that faculty members add the following classroom behavior statement to their syllabi: "No racist, ableist, transphobic, xenophobic, chauvinistic, or otherwise derogatory comments will be allowed."[18]

Imposing or fostering such intellectual straitjackets can seriously impede the intellectual curiosity and sense of adventure that promotes learning and discovery of the world and oneself. Students' minds are expanded by seeing how a subject matter connects to other fields and ideas in the seamless web of the world, a heuristic process that is necessary to good pedagogy.[19] In thinking about BRTs, one should bear in mind the survey evidence presented in Chapter 6 that shows a high percentage of students favoring the restriction of biased and offensive speech on campus, even if such speech is protected by the First Amendment. For example, a 2018 survey by the Knight Foundation found that 49 percent of the students surveyed favored restriction, as opposed to 51 percent who disfavored. Meanwhile, social psychologist Jean Twenge recently found that 28 percent of the most recent generation of college students believe that a professor should lose his or her job for simply making a racially insensitive remark in class on just one occasion.[20]

SAFE SPACES, SPEAKER SHOUTDOWNS, AND DISINVITATIONS

Most people have special places to which they retreat for privacy and for what Bob Dylan called "shelter from the storm." Sometimes obtaining a safe space is a truly serious matter, as during the civil rights battles of the 1950s and 1960s, when angry white racists were bent on harming demonstrators. Beyond this stark necessity, student groups have a right under freedom of association principles to form groups that are self-referential and reinforcing as opposed to being platforms for public discourse, as we saw in Chapter 3. And some students do feel uncomfortable or like outsiders or aliens on campus for a variety of reasons, so having places they can go to in order to feel that they belong is a good thing. Indeed, simply forming a ring of friends is a way of finding a safe space. We are communal creatures. Few college students spend their years on campus without having such refuge. Even a local bar can serve this purpose.

The problem arises when such retreats and the philosophies attached to them become invested in creating hostility toward and alienation from the rightful and productive public discourse that is so important to the campus as a *polis*.[21] Things get even worse under two circumstances. First, when the claim to safe space is applied to the entire *polis*, leading to campus-wide censorship and limits on speakers. Second, when safe space policy becomes a tool of the victim culture and is applied in a manner that weakens the psyches of students by appealing to their fears and vulnerabilities rather than to the inner strengths that they need to nourish in order to become successful citizens who are able to enjoy the fruits of constitutional liberty.

Civil rights groups sought shelter from the storm in order to renew their remarkable courage to confront their often dangerous enemies. Many advocates of safe spaces today harbor a quite different mentality. They settle for merely feeling threatened by speakers whose very ideas and presence anywhere on campus distress them. John McWhorter recently wrote that such claims are really often playacting in disguise.

> "You're hurting me," a black student earnestly objected when David Horowitz once spoke at UC–Berkeley. But Horowitz was simply arguing that reparations for slavery have already been granted in the form of affirmative action and the Great Society programs. One may disagree, but King, Malcolm X, DuBois, and Garvey would have been gobsmacked at the idea that Horowitz's statement qualified as a verbal punch in the gut. . . . In [professional] wrestling the payoff is entertainment; with the new protest movement, the payoff is that we all demonstrate our heightened sociopolitical awareness—our faith, as it were. These episodes are religious services of a sort, which is part of why they now occur so regularly.[22]

FIRE maintains a list of 340 speakers who have been disinvited since 2000. (Note, however, that several investigators have questioned the accuracy of some claims of disinvitation. According to FIRE's own reports, the number of recorded disinvites has receded over the course of the past couple of years.)[23] Disinvitees have included the likes of Janet Napolitano, Michael Bloomberg, George Will, and others. Even I was disinvited from a panel at the University of Michigan in 1995—before

FIRE began compiling its list—because another panelist did not like my position on a free speech question. I was disinvited from a campus-wide event at Cornell University in 2009 but re-invited a couple of months later after campus passions had settled down in the wake of the publication of my book, *Cornell '69*.[24]

Comedian Jerry Seinfeld eschews appearing on campus anymore because his jokes offend politically correct sensibilities.[25] It is worth noting that Seinfeld is well known for avoiding things such as politics and profanity in his comedy, while mentioning sex only occasionally. In a recent essay, Edward Johnson claims that the moral climate of higher education today is inhospitable to things such as ambiguity, irony, and humor. Such intolerance also shackles the pursuit of knowledge, which is often ambiguous and elusive. Johnson's take on humor and the ambiguity it evokes parallels the discussion of campus dialectical exchange in Chapters 2 and 3. "Hostility to ambiguity speaks to a pedagogic ethos that has become estranged from the open-ended pursuit of ideas. . . . In demanding that the outcome of learning should be stated in advance, this technique undermines the freedom that is required for intellectual exploration."[26]

Even some law students at major universities sought refuge from the storm ... of Donald Trump's election. For example, the University of Michigan Law School set up a special event for students that included "some stress-busting, self-care activities such as coloring sheets, play dough, positive card-making, Legos, and bubbles with your fellow law students."[27] Apparently, the school dropped the event in the face of public mockery.

More significantly, law student anxieties have cast a pall over some uncomfortable yet necessary classroom discussions about crime. Criminal law deals with thorny questions of *mens rea* (guilty mind) that often depend on confronting uncomfortable facts and wrestling with the best arguments of the prosecution and the defense. This obligation can be especially trying in cases of sexual assault, where the status of the perception of consent is pivotal. Becoming a lawyer requires the ability to understand both sides of a case, especially when the facts are blurry. But even at such an estimable institution as Harvard Law School, professors have noted students shying away from genuine discussion and debate regarding sexual cases, with activists encouraging such withdrawal in the name of protecting against trauma.[28]

THE SEVERING OF THE SPEECH-ACTION DISTINCTION

One of the most significant aspects of the new threats to free speech and academic freedom is the way in which many activists are now equating the speech they hate with actual physical or emotional harm—with what some even call existential threats. Like bias reporting programs, the issue of the conflation of speech and action serves as a kind of synecdoche that encapsulates a host of related threats to academic freedom and free speech, including the hyper-developed identity politics, the triumph of the therapeutic and victim ideology in society and higher education, and the increasing emphasis on subjectivity over objectivity.

Expansive interpretations of harassment are another example of this problem, as seen in the way Laura Kipnis was investigated for simply expressing an opinion on sexual due process in a national journal. As we have seen, Kipnis's case is but one of numerous examples of stretching of the harassment policy to include arguments about public policy that the First Amendment emphatically protects.[29]

A classic example of the expansion of the concept of threat took place at the University of Wisconsin–Stout in 2011 when the administration and local police sought to charge professor James Miller with a criminal threat for simply placing two posters on his door. The first poster depicted Nathan Fillion, who was a lead actor in the television series *Firefly* and was in costume, paired with a well-known quote from his character in that series, Malcolm Reynolds. When this poster was deemed unacceptable by the authorities, Miller put up a second poster that read "Warning: Fascism." It too was removed.

The authorities backed down only after local free speech activists and FIRE exposed the situation to national media attention.[30] Another telling example of the equation of speech and threatening action took place at Western Washington University in 2017 when students disrupted a speech by liberal free speech advocate Jonathan Zimmerman.

They shouted, "Your safe space is violent" and claimed that "the idea of complete free speech [is] 'violent.'"[31]

The politics of identity is part of the drive for recognition and equal respect, and traditional civil rights demonstrators took it seriously, as I stressed in Chapter 2. However, it can take an illiberal and unproductive turn when it morphs into an exclusionary form of politics with a therapeutic, anti-universalistic foundation that would deny the free speech of those whose views its acolytes find upsetting.[32] Frank Furedi adds that campus identity politics is now often linked to excessive claims of victimhood and the escalating emotional insecurity of students. He writes that "emotional correctness" has replaced political correctness in many domains of higher education. Furedi also highlights the ways in which therapeutic concerns have marginalized the prioritization of truth and intellectual freedom in his essay "Growing Up Disturbed," in *The Value and Limits of Academic Speech*:

> The call to immunize students from distress and pain underlines the call for trigger warnings and safe spaces. From this perspective, security and safety constitute first-order values, which clearly trump the value of free speech and academic freedom. This transformation of freedom into a second order value in campuses is the inexorable consequence of the psychological turn of socialization.[33]

HISTORICAL ASPECTS OF THE SPEECH–ACTION CONFLATION

Let us now look more directly at the trajectory of the conflation of speech and action in policy. This tendency threatens to undermine the modern doctrine of speech on campus and perhaps more broadly down the line. Activists in favor of this conflation seek to greatly expand the long-existing true threats exception to free speech that the Supreme Court carefully and narrowly fashioned over time. A true threat arises when a speaker's words constitute a serious intent to commit a violent or unlawful act. A true threat is subject to criminal punishment "if an objectively reasonable person would interpret the speech as a realistic expression of an intent to cause present or future harm" to that person.[34] Note that the emphasis is on the objectively reasonable person.

Objectivity in this context means the attempted ascertainment of a community standard that is independent of the subjective feelings of the individual and is based on what a reasonable person would consider a threat.

A related problem is the expansion of the concept of hate speech. Modern First Amendment doctrine protects hate speech unless it constitutes a threat, a direct incitement to imminent lawless action that is likely to occur, or an extreme form of fighting words, which the Supreme Court has limited to face-to-face encounters that a reasonable person would determine are likely to trigger an immediate violent response.[35]

As former ACLU president Nadine Strossen points out in her recent book *HATE*, activists are calling for those exceptions to be expanded. For example, in 2015, student leaders at the University of California–Irvine voted to ban the display of the American flag, stating that it "has been flown in instances of colonialism and imperialism, and can be interpreted as hate speech."[36] A crucial point emerges from Strossen's overall analysis, which probes the costs and benefits of expanding the present constitutional limits on hate speech and which shows why European countries' broader limits have been evidently counterproductive. Her point is the Supreme Court wrestled for decades with broader limits, yet through experience and careful thinking it came to realize that broader limits opened a Pandora's box of unintended consequences and adjudication difficulties. Present First Amendment doctrine did not emerge out of caprice or malice. It is there for a reason.

As seen in Chapter 3, Jeremy Waldron presents a prominent understanding of hate speech in his book titled *The Harm in Hate Speech*. In it, he argues for a return to the era in which the Supreme Court allowed the punishment of group libel, which involves speech that defames the reputation of groups by asserting that characteristics such as race, religion, nationality, and the like inherently cause members of the group to be defective and unequal to others. Outlawing group libel, which Waldron favors, would require the Court to resurrect the constitutional status of the 1952 group libel case *Beauharnais v. Illinois* (decided 5–4), which the Supreme Court and lower courts later painted into an inescapable corner in the wake of the growth of broader modern free speech jurisprudence.

Strossen presents convincing reasons to reject Waldron's call for expansion of the concept. However, it is worth noting that compared with, say, the UC–Irvine student leaders, Waldron provides a more principled and definitive definition of hate speech than many current expansions have managed. The actual *Beauharnais* case involved speech that overtly accused African Americans of being *inherently* criminal and morally inferior.[37] Waldron does not call for prosecution or censorship for causing *offense*, and he is clear about not punishing controversial and offensive *ideas* that do not constitute direct and intentional defamation on the basis of racial and similar characteristics. Waldron would protect strong arguments against, for example, affirmative action, out-of-wedlock births, counterproductive cultural practices, and presentation of statistical differences in crime rates for different races—speech that some activists on campus today consider forms of hate. But even Waldron's principled definition of hate speech could be subject to administrative or regulatory stretching and abuse in actual practice, especially in environments such as higher education today.[38]

Modern free speech doctrine could stand on its own only when the law began to treat speech and action as fundamentally distinct for matters of policy—when upsetting and provocative speech acts were no longer considered akin to criminal attempts.[39] To be sure, Hannah Arendt persuasively contended in *The Human Condition* that speech is often the highest form of political action. Václav Havel wrote an influential essay in the *New York Review of Books* three decades ago in which he noted that evil speech often planted seeds that eventually grew into evil deeds in history. But the broader causal connections between rhetorical speech and actual conduct are stubbornly complex. For example, France might have witnessed more anti–Semitic rhetoric in the 1920s than did Germany, but Hitler arose in Germany, not France. Political breakdown, disastrous inflation, weak enforcement of the law, cultural fear of compromise, and other factors also contributed to the ascension of Hitler.[40]

The conflation of speech with action or threats that we see today is a product of complex social, political, legal, and psychological developments that merit an entire book, so I can highlight only what I consider the most salient aspects. One major issue is debate over the meaning of *harm* itself. Conceptions of harm, both physical and emotional, can vary by culture, and they have changed over time. Individuals differ in terms of what is called the threshold for pain, and culture can influence one's assessment of what kind of pain is tolerable. More generally, the tolerance of suffering has softened with the rise of liberal culture and its emphasis on the pursuit of happiness.[41] Also, modern society has discovered or constructed new types of harms that were previously more tolerated, ignored, or not even conceived.

In *On Liberty*, Mill argued that liberty in general may be restricted only when its exercise constitutes a direct harm to the significant interests of society or another person. But our modern or postmodern age features less social consensus and a growing regard for subjective truths. The concept of harm has accordingly been expanded and "problematized," sometimes in credible ways but other times less so. Before recent decades, for example, society did not recognize things such as widespread environmental harm, discriminatory—as opposed to traditional moral—harms associated with pornography, harm caused by "micro-aggressions," and the like.[42] Four major speech-related questions loom regarding claims of harm today: Are they reasonable? Are they genuine? Are they political weapons in disguise? And what effect does their recognition have on the higher education mission?

The modern doctrine of speech requires that harm be demonstrable, substantial, and imminent in most cases before censorship is merited. (I am simplifying here for purposes of exegesis.) Except in limited circumstances, the modern doctrine holds that counterspeech and other forms of government response are sufficient to protect social order in the absence of harm that meets those criteria. We too often forget about the other forms, which can include legal forms of surveillance and scrutiny (even police or FBI infiltration of dangerous groups), education, aggressive counterspeech, and serious penalties for those whose thoughts eventuate in illegal actions or criminal attempt. Strossen presents those and other "non-censorial" methods to remedy the harms of hate speech in Chapter 8 of *Hate*—a chapter titled "Non-Censorial Methods Effectively Curb the Potential Harms of Constitutionally Protected 'Hate Speech.'"

The modern doctrine of speech attained its crown during the Supreme Court's reaction to the political dissent of the 1960s, most notably in relation to the civil rights and the anti–Vietnam War movements. Later, other dissenting and equal rights movements used free speech similarly. The Warren Court of the 1950s and 1960s was dedicated to the responsive law project of furthering legal and political equality across the constitutional board. The expansion of First Amendment rights was a key tool in this project. Rather than limiting speech considered harmful to the drive for equality, as the liberal democracies of Europe have been doing for decades, the Warren Court made a fateful decision that most free speech scholars and equality activists of the time supported: protecting the rights of all viewpoints—the anti–viewpoint discrimination doctrine—is the best and most consistent way to protect the legal and constitutional rights and equality of all.[43] Speech, liberty, and political-social equality are not antagonists, but allies. In a speech he gave on the evening before his assassination, Martin Luther King Jr. tipped his hat to the alliance between speech, liberty, and equality while denouncing a court injunction hurled his way.

But counterforces were already gathering over the horizon. In 1969, Herbert Marcuse, a leading German-American member of the Frankfurt School of critical theory, published "Repressive Tolerance." In it, he argued that in a polity in which repressive forces hold sway, free speech unjustly protects and furthers the power of the oppressors. What came to be known as *progressive censorship* was born—censorship in the name of promoting ostensibly progressive causes. In essence, Marcuse took Mill's clarion liberal call for free speech in the names of truth and progress and turned it on its head: truth and progress cannot be attained by wide-open freedom of speech in a society in which the deck is stacked in favor of repression and domination, even if that society espouses the liberal values of Mill.[44] Marcuse's was one of the first prominent academic attacks—this side of communism—on liberal intellectual freedom from the American left. Busy deploying free speech to further their controversial agendas, progressive forces largely ignored Marcuse's call for censorship at the time. The seeds that Marcuse planted awaited a catalytic event to sprout a few years later.

The famous Skokie case of the late 1970s presented the question of whether a small yet incendiary Chicago-based Nazi group possessed a First Amendment right to hold a "white power" demonstration in a classic public forum: in front of the Village Hall of Skokie, Illinois, a suburb just north of Chicago. Of Skokie's 70,000 citizens, about 30,000 were Jews, including 800 to 1,200 Holocaust survivors who had come to Skokie to seek refuge from the inhuman suffering to which they had been subjected back home in Europe. The case arose more than a decade after the court had put the finishing touches on the doctrine of viewpoint neutrality and its application to classic public forums such as the sidewalks outside government centers.[45]

The legal, social, political, and psychological aspects of the case are fascinating and complex. The bottom line for our present purposes is twofold: Skokie's town government made a concerted effort to keep the Nazis out, on the grounds that the speech amounted to a verbal form of *assault* rather than *free speech*; and state and federal courts, after a year of extensive and heated litigation and public debate, rejected this effort.[46]

The judicial decisions in favor of the Nazis stunned many liberals, progressives, and conservatives who were not yet up to speed on the full implications of the exceptionally permissive free speech doctrine the Supreme Court had fashioned in recent years. *"How could freedom of speech mean this?!"* many must have asked. Traditional conservatives objected to the liberal decisions on grounds that had long underpinned conservative free speech jurisprudence: morality, democratic norms, and social order. The ACLU, which provided free legal counsel to the Nazis, lost a third of its extensive membership for defending them, recovering only after a period of struggle and outreach. Despite the temporary setback, a former national president of the ACLU told me at a FIRE anniversary dinner in 2014 in New York that "[t]he ACLU would have been destroyed as an organization had we not supported the Nazis' rights at Skokie." Skokie was a challenge to the ACLU's very identity.[47]

In retrospect, Skokie was a watershed for at least five reasons. First, the case witnessed one of the first major splits on the left regarding the constitutional status of hate speech—a split that roils campus politics today, separating traditional speech liberals from what we could call the "progressive censorship left." Second, in ways that became more evident as time marched on, Skokie featured the tension between two types of allegiances (a) to one's ethnic group and (b) to the constitutional regime as symbolized by the First Amendment. On the one hand, a majority of Skokie's Jews who were not Holocaust survivors originally believed that the Nazis must be allowed to come and that they simply should be ignored rather than confronted. "Quarantine them" was the vernacular of the Anti-Defamation League's official position before Skokie occasioned a reconsideration of it.

The threat was objectively nonthreatening for the American-born Jews and others; the Nazis were in reality a small, isolated group of outcasts who lost members as the case dragged on. Most of the Holocaust survivors, on the other hand, were understandably emotionally assaulted; they seemed to be witnessing the nightmare reborn near Lake Michigan's shores. (Even survivor attitudes and positions were not uniform, however.) In the name of ethnic solidarity, they accused the First Amendment Jews of being disloyal to their people.

Survivor activists excoriated David Goldberger, the Jewish ACLU attorney who defended the Nazis' rights in the courts, but he never wavered in performing what he considered his professional and constitutional obligation. For a complicated set of interesting reasons, many American-born Jews eventually joined the survivors' resistance on legal grounds. The tensions in the Jewish community boiled down to which loyalty took precedence under the circumstances—*the classic question of prioritization that lies at the heart of this book.* (At many public meetings during the controversy, survivors were heard to shout, "Fuck the First Amendment!")

Third, the dissenting *legal* position at Skokie was premised on the claim that the Nazis' speech in the classic public forum would amount to an *assault* rather than free speech. It was a prominent example of the conflation of speech and action—of speech formerly protected by the First Amendment but now interpreted as an actual threat. (Understandable in the circumstances!)

Fourth, the case highlighted a severe tension between the emotional and cultural facts on the ground and the First Amendment doctrine.

And even though most Jews initially sided with the First Amendment, many reversed course out of understandable sympathy and the greater personal costs—in terms of friendships and community connections—of not changing position. Inside Skokie and the larger Jewish community, greater appeal and pressure was exerted by the anti–free speech position.

Truth in advertising: I, too, sided with the survivors' position in *Nazis in Skokie*, published in 1985. It was only after I experienced the harmful effects of censorship a few years later that I began the process of changing my mind about Skokie and the reasons that I once supported the survivors' position. My change did not take place overnight. I ineluctably came to fathom the longer-term consequences of allowing censorship at Skokie, and my teaching career had taught me to have more respect for the inner strengths of citizens and students, as well as how strong character is necessary to sustain a challenging liberal education and liberal democracy itself. And Skokie was an outlier, an extreme case that would have created problems had the arguments for censorship there been expanded to other cases—as we have seen in higher education today. It is said that "hard cases make bad law." Skokie had this potential.

The fifth watershed factor is the way that Skokie helped to set a normative, political, and legal precedent for future movements opposing or questioning the liberal modern doctrine of speech over the course of the next decades, thereby moving toward the progressive censorship of today. A few years later, for example, the feminist "civil rights anti-pornography" ordinance fashioned by radical feminists Catharine MacKinnon and Andrea Dworkin applied the logics of Marcuse and the Skokie dissenters along with other sources to call for the restriction of pornography in the name of countering pornography's effect on the equal treatment of and respect for women.

Though the effort failed in court while splitting the increasingly diverse feminist community—anti-censorship feminists prominently opposed the ordinance—the logic of the ordinance called attention to the notion of progressive censorship. The ordinance attempted to enthrone viewpoint discrimination by distinguishing pornography that is conducive to women's equality from pornography that is deemed detrimental to the cause. It considered nonegalitarian pornography to be *in itself an act of discrimination* regardless of its context or application, thereby further eviscerating the speech–action distinction.

The resisting survivors at Skokie focused largely on the Nazis' presence *in Skokie*, not their speech elsewhere. But the supporters of the MacKinnon–Dworkin ordinance deemed pornography's *presence anywhere* to amount to an assault or act of discrimination against women. In a speech delivered in the prestigious Oliver Wendell Holmes Jr. lecture series at Harvard Law School in the mid-1980s, MacKinnon observed that pornography constitutes a Skokie-type injury.[48]

The next stage in this legal tale is the introduction of college speech codes across America beginning in the late 1980s and the 1990s. Rather than applying to upsetting speech or "fighting words" on the limited grounds that the Supreme Court has allowed for censorship, the codes ventured into the emerging domains of identity politics and government-based categories that separated citizens along racial and other identity grounds. Those codes typically punish individuals or groups for saying or writing things that "disparage," "demean," "insult," or otherwise "offend" campus citizens on the grounds of race, gender, sexual orientation, religion, and the like.

Though often well intended as a means to make campuses more hospitable to minority students who were now entering higher education in greater numbers than before, the codes were often applied in heavy-handed and ideologically driven ways, resulting in viewpoint discrimination and the chilling of open and honest discourse surrounding the important issues of race, gender, sex, ethnicity, and religion.[49]

Like the Skokie resistance and MacKinnon's ordinance, the new college speech codes did not fare well at the hands of lower federal and state courts because of their breadth, vagueness, and viewpoint discrimination. A clash between First Amendment legal culture and campus political culture was becoming evident. In addition to lower court decisions involving higher education codes, the Supreme Court handed down a decision in 1992, *R.A.V. v. St. Paul*, that undercuts the constitutional viability of the new codes by ruling that a St. Paul ordinance that prohibited only "fighting words" that are based on race, religion, nationality, etc. crossed a constitutional line.

Fighting words are not in principle protected by the First Amendment if they are likely to directly provoke a reasonable person to respond with violence, thereby disturbing the peace. But Edward Cleary, R.A.V.'s attorney, argued before the Court that by limiting its application of fighting words to those identity categories, the city was allowing provocative speech on some subjects but not on others. Ergo: viewpoint discrimination. Cleary also pointed to the new college speech codes as examples of the abuse of such viewpoint-based rules. In an innovative decision that adopted Cleary's reasoning, the court agreed that prohibiting *only some* fighting words could constitute unconstitutional viewpoint discrimination under some circumstances. In words that had direct relevance to how college authorities were busy applying codes in viewpoint-discriminatory ways, Justice Antonin Scalia wrote:

> Displays containing some words—odious racial epithets, for example—would be prohibited to proponents of all views. But "fighting words" that do not themselves invoke race, color, creed, religion, or gender—aspersions upon a person's mother, for example—would seemingly be usable *ad libitum* in the placards of those arguing *in favor* of racial, color, etc., tolerance and equality, but could not be used by those speakers' opponents. . . . St. Paul has no such authority to license one side of a debate to fight freestyle, while requiring the other to follow Marquis of Queensberry rules.[50]

Tellingly, the number of identity-based codes on campus actually *increased* in the wake of the *R.A.V.* decision. The reason was the clash between campus culture and the law. Political and career incentives on campus favored the continuance of codes and related policies along with the culture that galvanized support for them, thereby rewarding ignoring the decision more than obeying it. This reaction presented another example of resistance against the implementation of court decisions, a phenomenon well documented in law and politics literature.[51]

The situation is also indicative of another threat to academic freedom and free thought: the willingness to downplay or disregard rights such as free speech, equal treatment, and due process in order to achieve what is considered a worthy end—in particular social justice. The cultural end of social justice trumped the proper means to its achievement, namely a free and open debate. This result distorted the proper mission of the university in the process.

Speech codes continue to populate college campuses, as seen in FIRE's annual reports. But to gain a measure of empirical insight, we need to consider two general contexts. The first pertains to the official rules and policies at institutions. The second deals with the attitudes of students and others regarding speech, which I will examine in Chapter 6. As seen, the absence of speech codes may matter or not, depending on the politics and culture of an institution.

Regarding the first context, the most definitive study is a 2017 report by FIRE. It reviewed a sample of 449 institutions, of which 345 were public schools; in that sample, 92 percent had policies that prohibited speech that the First Amendment protects.[52] FIRE did find the situation in 2017 to be an improvement over its 2016 report: the number of the worst policies (red lights) had modestly declined. So there has been some marginal movement in a more speech-friendly direction when it comes to official policies.

In addition, according to an op-ed in the *Wall Street Journal*, the National Science Foundation (NSF) discovered similar restrictions at 26 of the 30 institutions that receive the most federal research money. (The funding numbers were from the NSF, but the survey itself was conducted by FIRE.)[53] Sometimes schools adopt codes more for symbolic reasons than for enforcement purposes, but then administrators can take the codes off the shelf when needed. Of course, in recent times, colleges have adopted other policies that, at least in theory, strive to limit speech while eschewing the outright censorship posed by the codes. These policies include trigger warnings, microaggression policies, and others that we have discussed in this chapter.

CHAPTER 5

THE MAJOR THREATS: STRUCTURAL AND MORE UNIVERSAL ASPECTS

Any of us who have been in the trenches as long as I have know that freedom of speech and freedom of thought is a cause you can never relax about. For the entire rest of time, until the end of the galaxy, we will have to get up every morning of every new generation, and defend this idea because it's the most counterintuitive idea in the entire history of the human race: that people should be allowed to run around spouting wrongheaded, bigoted, misleading, offensive, seditious, heretical, etcetera, etcetera, etcetera, views.

—Jonathan Rauch, Brookings Institution, in Keynote Address at University of Wisconsin–Madison, Conference on Free Speech on Campus: Old Challenges, New Threats, *March 11, 2016*

TRUTH DECAY

Before looking at so-called structural problems that can harm free and open inquiry on campus, we should note a trend in both society and higher education that underlies everything under discussion: what appears to be a declining respect for truth. Truth is always an endangered species, given human and social realities; however, today it appears to be moving even more toward the precarious end of the continuum. We witness a lot of free speech in American society writ large, especially in the public square of the internet, social media, and numerous television and radio venues. But who can say that the *quality* of this speech has kept pace with its quantity? Reasoned discourse coexists with forms of speech that now enjoy worrisome new venues of expression, including rabid conspiracy theories and speech distorted by partisan tribalism. I need provide no examples because the instances are so omnipresent.

And the technological gods who control the internet are not exactly leading us to the Promised Land. Journalist Franklin Foer recently wrote about what happened when he asked Google to find the best thinkers on the ultimate question, "What is God?" Did Google lead him to the likes of "Augustine, Maimonides, Spinoza, Luther, Russell, or Dawkins?" Dream on. "Billy Graham is the closest that Google can manage to an important theologian or philosopher." Granted, Billy Graham is a worthy person to read. But to head the list? "For all its power and influence, it seems that Google can't really be bothered to care about the quality of knowledge it dispenses. It is our primary portal to the world, but has no opinion about what it offers."[1]

In 1967, Hannah Arendt wrote that at bottom truth and politics are "mortal enemies."[2] This universal truth will endure as long as we continue to reside east of Eden. But this maxim does not mean that there are not degrees of truthfulness and spin even in this realm. Unfortunately, the political scene in America today, both left and right, seems to have entered a twilight zone or netherworld for truthfulness. This trend makes the university's job all the harder; it also makes performing the job all the more imperative.

As seen in Chapter 2, higher education should be one of the institutions that resist the anti-intellectual forces besetting democracy in America. In Tocqueville's terms, it should be an intellectual remedy to forces compromising truth and the qualities of mind that a commitment to truth requires. But intellectual and political trends within higher education itself have thrown this obligation into question, including the following: the growing influence of postmodernism and relativistic cultural studies that downplay the possibility of objective truth or judgments; the reprioritization and concomitant politicization of certain domains of higher education, accompanied by echo chambers that are intolerant of dissent; and the rise of a therapeutic ethic that includes an overemphasis on subjective feeling and sensitivity over reason. These are among the forces that have led critical observers to descry what, in a recent major report, the RAND Corporation depicts as truth decay.

Historian John Sharpless, a leading CAFAR colleague and friend of mine at UW–Madison, once opined to me in a conversation, "postmodernism's marginalization of truth undercuts the very reason for the institution that employs postmodernists." To the extent that truth decay is happening on campus, it betokens the university's decline as an institution.[3]

STRUCTURAL PROBLEMS: TENURE, SHARED GOVERNANCE, AND RELATED PHENOMENA

The "multiversity" of today is characterized by a plurality of missions and regulatory mandates that have deprioritized the intellectual mission. In addition, several economic, social, and political forces exacerbate the situation, including the rising costs and tuition; the increasing mental health issues for students that, in turn, engender more bureaucracy and negative signaling to students regarding their mental and emotional potential; and the broader corporatization of higher education. Another problem is declining funding by states of their state universities. This trend, in turn, intensifies the problem of rising tuition to make up for the gap. In troubling ways, higher education is trapped in a downward spiral by a set of boa constrictor–like forces.

Public institutions have a special vulnerability because of their dependence on politicians. An act of public trust, the Morrill Act of 1862, provided land grants and funding and thus helped catapult many public institutions to equal research and pedagogical status with the best private institutions. According to historian Jeremi Suri and other scholars, the act was a landmark in furthering democratic citizenship, economic development, and state-education cooperation. This historic commitment of the public sector is now in decline.[4]

Beyond those trends, internal matters such as declining tenure, shared governance, and faculty power can affect the status of academic free speech on campus if those changes make it harder for faculty members to support such freedom with institutional power in the face of administrative suppression. This lack of support becomes an empirical question. Another empirical question is how marked those trends are.

According to a recent AAUP report, the number of full-time tenured faculty positions has declined by 26 percent over the past 40 years, whereas the number of part-time and adjunct faculty has increased 70 percent. Meanwhile, full-time positions on the tenure track—individuals who are on track but not tenured yet—have dropped by a half, presaging further decline of the tenured ranks. The lack of tenure cedes more power to administrators whose legions, unlike tenure-track professors, have mushroomed in recent decades. A DOE study found that the number of administrative positions increased 60 percent between 1993 and 2009, leading to increased costs—and in many cases, higher salaries for administrators. One consequence: escalating tuition costs for students.[5] And thus the balance of power on campus has shifted away from the intellectual faction of the university.

A good portion of this decline is due to trends outside the domains of long-established colleges and universities, such as the growth of nontraditional institutions like community colleges and for-profit schools. But less-prestigious established institutions are feeling pressures too. Many small liberal arts colleges are encountering significant financial headwinds, and second-tier public universities are downsizing or consolidating. Education researcher Michael B. Horn has reported on major public university consolidation in states such as Alabama, Georgia, Connecticut, Louisiana, Pennsylvania, and Wisconsin. He also writes, "According to Education Dive, of the 40 mergers that took place between 2010 and 2017, just under half involved at least one public college. And 36 public colleges have closed or consolidated since 2016."

Harvard economist Clayton Christensen recently predicted that 50 percent of colleges and universities will close or encounter bankruptcy in the coming decade. In 2013, Horn and Christensen as a team were more sanguine, foreseeing the disappearance by merger of 25 percent of the schools in each tier of educational reputation.[6]

Whatever the extent and causes of tenure decline, the status of adjunct faculty members who work off the tenure track can be very trying. Many live semester by semester with low pay, paltry resources and benefits, little power on campus, and little sense of security in the job. A recent book by Herb Childress titled *The Adjunct Underclass* details these sorry plights.[7] To be sure, adjunct faculty members often have jobs outside the education institution and add to students' education by exposing them to issues and experiences in the wider world. This contribution is especially the case for adjunct instructors in professional schools, but it also takes place in undergraduate programs. My point here is mainly about the balance of power in higher education; and the expansion of adjunct instructors further diminishes faculty power vis-à-vis administrators because tenured faculty typically enjoy more job security and concomitant power.

Tenure has its pros and cons. On the negative side, it can lead to "dead wood," or locked-in intellectual and ideological bias in a department, especially if tenured faculty members hire only those who fit their mold. But it is also a major protection in the other direction; I know many faculty members who dissent from campus orthodoxies and who credit tenure with shielding them from potential harm. Robert Maynard Hutchins, the late president of the University of Chicago and renowned champion of liberal education, argued during the 1930s that tenure is vital for securing faculty independence.[8] But tenure is a means to an end, not an end in itself. It is there to protect academic freedom, not academic sinecures. Those who have tenure have an obligation to fight for the academic and attendant freedoms that justify tenure in the first place, lest their voices ring hollow. Want to protect tenure? Start by making your support of academic freedom clear and convincing. Like democracy, tenure might be bad except for the alternatives.

Tenure can make opposition to institutional policy and action more feasible because it provides a stronger property interest in a job that is protected more adequately by constitutional due process. It is not an infallible shield, but it helps. In the many stances that CAFAR took in favor of individuals against UW–Madison and other schools between 1996 and 2016, we knew that two things protected us: (a) the historical UW–Madison institutional ethos of academic freedom that remained entrenched despite the actions we opposed, and (b) the brute fact of tenure, which itself reinforced and symbolized that ethos. Culture mattered, but tenure helped to anchor it.

The decline of shared governance, also chronicled by the AAUP, is related to the weakened state of tenure. Tenure and shared governance can erode in tandem, as they have in the University of Wisconsin System after legislative changes enacted in 2015 and 2016. Among other things, shared governance offers a vehicle for faculty members and other stakeholders to balance the power of administrators. Checks and balances can work in higher education as they do in government. By encouraging participation in campus affairs, shared governance can also enhance two important qualities of campus citizenship: (a) the sense of responsibility and common sense that come with being accountable for important decisions; and (b) commitment to the institution as a community, which should include support for intellectual freedom and for give and take so long as the institution makes freedom a priority. It also brings administrators into more personal contact with faculty members, thereby giving faculty obligations and concerns a more human face that adds to credibility and respect—in both directions.[9]

ADMINISTRATIVE AGGRANDIZEMENT

In *The Fall of the Faculty*, Johns Hopkins political scientist Benjamin Ginsberg chronicles the many ways in which the decline of faculty power and shared governance in the wake of administrative aggrandizement has harmed the intellectual and pedagogical missions of higher education in all manner of ways. He even provides examples of how administrators without meaningful teaching or scholarly experience or both have commandeered certain teaching programs and thereby weakened them. The central message of Ginsberg's book is that the rise of higher education's identity crisis—he does not use that particular term—is to a significant extent a byproduct of administrative and corporate encroachment. Many diversity programs, for example, are modeled on corporate programs that administrators then impose.

I would add another key question: *Why did faculty members allow this to happen?* Did they forsake the classic Madisonian norm for institutional actors? As Madison wrote in *Federalist No. 51*, "The interests of the man must be connected with the constitutional rights of the place."

Robert Hutchins also understood this point, affirming "that the faculty *was* the university. We have always said that the function of the administration was to minister to the needs of the faculty."[10]

Faculty members should have this institutional status not because they possess any special virtue, but because they are the ones with the training and knowledge that makes the university what it *is*. They should never be immune to the normal rules of behavior that govern university life, such as anti-harassment and anti-fraud rules. For example, in August 2018 nationally and internationally prominent scholars called for New York University to extend exceptional leniency toward a professor of comparative literature who had been accused of sexual harassment because of her distinguished international status. Those scholars were rightly mocked by most observers as practicing unjustifiable special pleading.[11] No one should want scholars to abandon rules like those.

Though often well intended, administrators can be misled by agendas. Sometimes the problem is obvious; sometimes, more latent. One meeting I attended late in my career at Wisconsin provides both an example and a counter-example of this problem. While I was discussing exams during a committee meeting about undergraduate pedagogical matters, an adviser informed me that the department's longstanding use of a multiple-choice test in some undergraduate courses was being frowned on by administrators who worried about students who were struggling academically. The clear implication was that we should adjust our exams to accommodate students whose styles of learning differed from the norm.

The multiple-choice test in my large lecture class that semester was one among three exams—the two others essay-like and more interpretive—and simply asked basic factual questions about points in my lecture and the readings, as well as some short hypothetical questions drawn directly from the class materials. Other faculty members and I objected to such potential administrative interference by individuals who had no idea of the nature of our courses, and the matter retreated for the time being. But it was made clear to us that this practice was now being watched.[12]

Another problem with excessive administrative government is that administrators can harbor ambitions that transcend commitment to the intellectual obligations of the institution, as do some faculty members. Some view their present stints as steppingstones to advancement, often at other institutions. (I should note that faculty members are no different in this regard.) A principal-agent problem can arise. In James Madison's language, such persons identify their interest not with the institution, but with themselves. Self-interest and ambition are natural, and they are values properly protected and encouraged in liberal democracy. But institutional and public goods require balancing or sublimating self-interest into broader interests.

A related problem is outside bureaucratic influence that has ruptured institutional governance. A leading example is how Title IX has been deployed from on high. The Obama administration essentially dictated to colleges and universities how Title IX should be enforced in the adjudication and investigation of sexual misconduct. As I mentioned in Chapters 1 and 4, higher education opened the door to outside intervention by not dealing rightly with sexual cases in the past—just as it has done with the free speech problem that coexists with the harassment and sexual assault problem today.[13]

But under the new interventions practiced by the DOE and its Office for Civil Rights (OCR) under the aegis of Title IX, due process has been sacrificed. Laura Kipnis has portrayed how this swing unleashed a "netherworld" of accusation that has often been Orwellian in nature. Political science professor R. Shep Melnick, an expert on law and administrative regulation, depicts how the DOE's Office for Civil Rights has distorted campus administrative procedure in this domain by surreptitiously instituting a new "sex bureaucracy" for each campus under the aegis of Title IX. Under the sway of leapfrogging OCR regulations, Title IX administrators ended up becoming, in Melnick's words, veritable "sex therapists like Dr. Ruth."[14]

The DOE has pushed its administrative will on higher education institutions through what amounts to administrative fiat, often without even going through the processes of accountability required by the Administrative Procedure Act and the due process clauses of the

Constitution. Overexpansion of the national administrative state has proved to be yet another threat to both the institutional autonomy of higher education and the freedoms within it.

CIVIC EDUCATION AND COMMITMENT TO THE INTELLECTUAL *POLIS*

Before we move on, we should briefly note that the decline of shared governance and the enlargement of administrative power are related to another problem that is also symptomatic of higher education's competing purposes and identity crisis: a perceived decline in commitment to the institution as an intellectual *polis*. I say "perceived" because I know of no specific empirical data about this problem, but many faculty members and commentators have alluded to it.

Ironically, the problem is perhaps inherent in the move to the modern conception of the research university that strives to balance entrepreneurial-like research with academic freedom (the AAUP model itself). The problem is that academic freedom does not automatically take care of itself unless it is nourished and protected by active engagement. The more faculty career advancement is furthered by research over teaching and taking time to engage in shared governance, the more faculty members will retreat from *polis* responsibilities. One motive that precipitated the student revolts of the 1960s was the student perception that faculty members were growing indifferent to the students' legitimate hunger for dedicated faculty pedagogical engagement.

Many bad policies and actions have taken place at leading research institutions because too many faculty members were busy looking elsewhere as regulatory "mission creep" took place. The 2018 lawsuit brought by a new free speech outfit against the University of Michigan's bias reporting system illustrates the problem. According to the suit, the program has cast a pall of orthodoxy over discourse, singling out speech subjectively considered "bothersome" or "hurtful."

Again one asks: just where was the faculty at this world leading research institution while this program got entrenched? In the 1989 case *Doe v. University of Michigan*, the federal court invalidated Michigan's old patently unconstitutional student speech code while going out of its way to scold the university for essentially not knowing what it was doing.[15]

In reading the case back then, I wondered: where were the faculty members? Today, the University of Michigan houses dozens of programs devoted to diversity, and in 2016 the institution pledged $85 million to enhance diversity on campus. The number of diversity officers at Michigan is as high as 100.[16] Has any money been devoted to securing academic free speech?

Meanwhile, many colleges and universities have forsaken the teaching of courses that convey critical understanding of the basic principles and institutions of liberal democracy, as presented in a recent report by the American Council of Trustees and Alumni (ACTA). ACTA's findings expose the growing dearth of courses about basic American history. Those findings parallel broader research on the weakening status of civic education in America.[17] A lack of constitutional knowledge naturally makes it easier to accept or advocate constitutional shortcuts to achieving one's ends. The landscape of higher education today features too many student groups and others attacking the Constitution as an outmoded impediment to the achievement of their social justice goals.

HUMAN NATURE: PASSION, FEAR, REASON, AND TRANSGRESSION

The value of free speech is universal, and threats against it cast their shadow on us all—and on human nature itself. The tolerance of views with which we disagree, let alone what Holmes described as "the expression of opinions that we loathe and believe to be fraught with death," is contrary to human nature. Established orders defend against challenge or transgression for two different reasons: first, some challenges are indeed morally or intellectually wrong and need to be resisted; second, some resistance to challenge is simply undertaken to defend the institutions' privilege and status against needed change. Pedophiles are wrongly transgressive. The civil rights movement was rightly so. We could call this the paradox of transgression. Sorting those two types of transgressors from one another is not always going to be easy for anyone. And often the two motives are inextricably mixed.

As Jonathan Haidt analyzed in *The Righteous Mind*, our capacity for morality has been forged in evolution through our emotional commitments to our tribe and communities: moral engagement is exclusionary at the same time as it leads us to commitments beyond our solitary selves. Accordingly, moral commitment widens our capacity for justice at the same time that it can be exclusionary and discriminatory unless it is ameliorated by reason and due doubt. As Haidt phrases the matter, morality "binds and blinds."[18]

Reason is one of the key attributes that has distinguished us as humans, and reason makes an orderly and just society possible. (Humor and the ability to laugh reflect another distinctively human attribute, as I used to tell my students.) But reason is relentlessly embattled. It is challenged not only by passion and self-interest, but also by certain aspects of our moral instinct itself. This is a tragic paradox of human existence: moral passion can give vent not only to what is best in us, but also to what is worst.

The late social theorist Paul Ricoeur provided one of the most tragic takes on the mixed nature of morality in his book *Freud and Philosophy*. One of Freud's great challenges to the Enlightenment was not only in showing how the moral instinct stands in conflict with the "aggressive instinct," but also in revealing how the moral instinct is actually *rooted in* the aggressive instinct, at least to some non-negligible extent.[19]

"Moral anger" is part of the phenomenology of justice; moral leaders such as Martin Luther King Jr. and post–World War II Nazi hunter Simon Wiesenthal were driven by it, to humanity's great advantage. Their quests were also committed to universally respected norms of justice.[20] Unmediated by self-control, reason, and communal agreement in the form of rule of law, moral anger can veer into vengeance and blind us to the rights of others. Among other things, social contract theory is premised on sublimating moral passion—what Aeschylus called the "moral furies"—into acceptance of the restraints of rule of law. In this sense, we may construe the principles of due process and free speech as the tributes that moral passion pays to reason.

Another primordial dimension of human nature is *fear*. Philosopher Francisco José Moreno writes about two types of fear. "Specific fear" is the fear that concrete events provoke in us, such as facing a pointed gun, having to speak before a hostile audience (or *any* audience for some of us), seeing an unexpected shadow in the hallway, and so forth ad infinitum.

"Basic fear" is the deeper form of fear and general dread that is woven into our DNA. Adding a further twist to our discussion, Moreno depicts basic fear as a primal condition *stemming in part from reason itself.* Reason tells us that we will die, but we can't know what lies beyond death. We cannot explain some of the most perplexing and troubling puzzles about existence. And our reason can conjure many things that threaten us. We could construe this phenomenon as the paradox of reason, thereby complementing the tension within morality just discussed.[21]

The question of fear is also a central First Amendment theme, which makes teaching it a contribution to liberal education on more than one level. "First Amendment jurisprudence requires us to distinguish rationally based fear from irrationally based fear when it comes to censorship," I used to tell students. This distinction makes sense on at least two levels. First, fear is not always detrimental. We *should* fear certain things, such as real threats and tornados on the horizon. This is the dilemma of fear: We know that some grounds for fear must necessarily exist, but we may not necessarily know whether we are confronted by any of them in the moment. As a second complication, we are prone to turning rationally based fear into irrational fear. A key lesson in life is learning how to distinguish rationally based fear from irrational fear—and to act accordingly.

Some things we fear are universally feared by humankind, whereas other objects of fear are historically shaped through social construction, such as the various forms of sexual panic that have periodically beset societies, including liberal democracies.[22] America has suffered spells of fearful zealotry periodically since Pilgrim times, from the Salem witch trials to financial panics, from the Red Scare during World War I and its aftermath to McCarthyism in the years after World War II, from the wave of false day care sex accusations in the 1980s and 1990s (and later) to campus zealotries of recent decades, which have come in different waves. Laura Kipnis's *Unwanted Advances* proceeds by connecting her experience under Title IX at Northwestern to this very history.[23]

Core First Amendment doctrine does not allow the state to suppress speech simply because of what the Court has called an "undifferentiated fear" of disorder or harm: it requires proof of distinct danger, which mandates the presence of reason in the face of fear or even moral panic.

By requiring the state to act with reason in the face of fear, First Amendment jurisprudence presents a first-order lesson in constitutional citizenship. I will discuss the First Amendment lessons regarding reason, fear, and citizenship at length in Chapter 7.

Ambivalence about censorship is also seen in the domain of sexual depictions, where the pornographic urge to transgress is universal, as is the urge to limit or punish such transgression. Richard S. Randall calls this tension "the paradox of eroticism." Erotic desire and curiosity are essential aspects of human nature, but for reasons of psycho-social (and psycho-familial) development, certain sexual desires must be repressed. The lure of the pornographic emerges out of this tension, as repressed desire seeks an outlet. "[W]e cannot be characteristically human without both the pornographic and the impulse to control it. . . . The matter is complicated in a liberal society, where beyond any freedom to act lies a presumably greater freedom to express oneself. . . ."[24]

The inner contradictions and conflicts discussed in this section are relevant to our inquiry in two respects. First, they denote aspects of the self that help to motivate the impulse to censor speech that otherwise merits protection in the responsible pursuit of truth. Second, the presence of the phenomena offers a more positive justification for maintaining a vibrant regime of free speech and open inquiry. Among other things, the mystery of the self consists of defense mechanisms and other forms of resistance that hide us from more complete knowledge of ourselves.

We are torn by inner contradictions (or "bi-formities") that can turn on a dime, including, to name but a few, expression versus repression, love versus hate, curiosity versus repulsion, reason versus unreason, loyalty versus betrayal, freedom versus "escape from freedom," and altruism versus self-interest. Criminals and saints dwell within each of us. Depth psychologists have written volumes about what Freud called the "emotional ambivalence" that adheres to many of our personal attachments. Mental health and self-knowledge require coming to terms with these tensions and integrating them into a more responsible and mature character. This quest is also the theme of classic literature, which often deals with the double aspect of the self and the epic struggle of protagonists to attain higher levels of understanding and integration of self and society.

On a broader, societal level, conflicts of interest, commitment, and understanding—what political theorist Isaiah Berlin called "discontinuities"—characterize all polities, and a viable democratic order duly integrates respect for the pluralism ensuing from such discontinuities with fundamental principles and the necessities of public authority.[25]

This discussion of human and societal pluralism sets the stage for thinking about the next problem we confront: the status of intellectual diversity on campus.

LACK OF INTELLECTUAL DIVERSITY

More and more critics of higher education today have pointed to the ways in which a lack of political and intellectual diversity has contributed to the travails of academic speech while shortchanging the education of students. But some caveats are in order. For starters, we need to distinguish political from intellectual diversity. It is quite imaginable that a department of 40 faculty members can be home to 40 Democrats or 40 Republicans or even 40 communists and still can present an intellectually responsible and diverse set of perspectives.

In my first semester in graduate school at Berkeley in the fall of 1975, I took a course on the history of economic theory from a noted self-proclaimed Marxist who was up front about his philosophical orientation in class. He was intellectually fair, thorough, and tolerant; he taught classical capitalist views with the same commitment as he taught the sections on Marxist aspects of economic theory. It was one of the best classes I took at Berkeley, and it has continued to educate me to this day.

We should note four caveats. First, the political persuasion of the faculty seems especially irrelevant in departments such as mathematics, the harder sciences, and some fields in the social sciences in which empirical facts and methodology trump or ameliorate ideology. As Joshua Dunn and Jon A. Shields write in *Passing on the Right*, who cares if an engineering department is top-heavy with leftists or rightists unless they somehow manage to sneak their ideology into their lessons? (And if they tried, I doubt engineering students would tolerate it.)

Second, even in more normative or interpretive fields where ideology is more likely to seep in, it is quite possible for faculty members (a) to keep their biases at bay when it comes to teaching and research or (b) to mitigate displays of their own views with appropriate openness and tolerance of dissent. Some of the best professors I had in college and grad school, as well as the great English teacher I had in high school, taught with a point of view—after all, they were men and women who "profess." But those instructors eschewed dogmatism, teaching in ways that engaged students and challenged them.

There is no single right way to teach well, and there are even more bad ways. In 2006, I served on a panel about intellectual diversity and campus politics at a conference in Washington, DC. A panelist remarked that when he was first hired in the history department at Harvard in the early 1960s, no colleague bothered to ask or even think about the political affiliation of others because "it just didn't matter." Alas, he went on to relate that this mentality vanished in ensuing decades.

Third, as Paul Horwitz points out in *First Amendment Institutions*, we need to be careful not to overrate the significance of intellectual diversity in higher education for a reason related to what we dealt with in Chapter 3: in an institution dedicated to the pursuit of truth, some ideas simply need to be discredited, sifted out, or marginalized in such academic settings.[26] It is not the lack of intellectual diversity per se that we should worry about, but the lack of *legitimate* intellectual diversity, broadly construed. We rightly do not give equal time to Holocaust deniers and other unhinged conspiracy theorists. But those examples are obvious. Many important topics and questions cry out for disagreements. The problem arises when members of echo chambers dismiss reasoned views that differ from their own for illegitimate reasons, including fear of not conforming, political bias, or simple lack of intellectual imagination.

A final caveat is the lack of systematic empirical information regarding the actual *presence* or *effects* of intellectual diversity in higher education's vast domains. No one to my knowledge has been able to fully fathom what transpires in actual classes day to day. We know of many anecdotal examples, and we have studies about faculty attitudes, political persuasions, many anecdotal accounts of faculty bias, and the one-sidedness of some important research. But we can probably never know in any truly systematic way just how classes are actually being conducted. In addition, a sometimes valid norm of professional courtesy can make one feel obligated to defer to the pedagogical judgments of colleagues even when one disagrees with those judgments. Such deference also represents the same kind of self-interested truce that underlies free speech practice: within limits, I agree to give you discretion to teach your class according to your lights so long as you promise to do so for me.[27]

Nonetheless, the research that exists is suggestive and allows one to at least provisionally conclude that the status of intellectual diversity matters for several reasons. Though an increasing number of liberal professors now appear to be the targets of campus activists for biased comments that are reported to the press or conservative watchdogs, it is conservatives or those who are less in tune with progressive politics who have evidently borne the brunt of suppression under the reign of speech codes and other internal policies. One cannot help but wonder if this would have been the case were ideological and political diversity on campus more prevalent. One of the things the history of free speech politics teaches is that many people are nonchalant or oblivious if their own ox is not being gored.[28]

Many observers have wondered why so many liberals allowed the persecution that took place under the aegis of the speech codes, and this conjecture is one possibility. A lack of intellectual and political diversity can affect the underlying culture of an institution in a manner that makes the neglect or censure of dissenting viewpoints seem less noticeable or troubling. As some commentators have noted, a lack of valid intellectual diversity has a way of making mere opinions or tentative conclusions appear as hard facts. Do you disagree with my view on the effects of colonialism? There must be something wrong with you.

A lack of intellectual diversity can harm the quality and thoroughness of knowledge in four senses. First, it can leave out perspectives that are needed to gain a full picture of a subject. Second, it can leave even truthful viewpoints less challenged, thereby causing them to lose the edge or thoroughness that comes with having to answer critics, as well as making them more prone to error and intellectual arrogance. In Haidt's terms, the human penchant for moralism and tribalism can take over.[29]

Third, according to some observers, a decline in opposing viewpoints opens the door to making dominant viewpoints less duly nuanced and more extreme, because there is less external check on extremism. Consider politics in cities and states where meaningful party competition is dormant; this phenomenon is not limited to explicitly political spaces.[30] Above and beyond the effect on a university education, recall the concluding point of the previous section of this chapter: intellectual pluralism is a constituent part of human freedom and flourishing. As Isaiah Berlin understood, the decline of pluralism is accompanied by the deterioration of freedom. They are connected at the hip.

Fourth and finally, students' educational experiences are less exciting and adventurous in a climate in which orthodoxy reigns supreme. An example is Berkeley's Boalt Hall Law School in the aftermath of the passage of California Proposition 209 in the late 1990s. Prop 209 outlawed affirmative action on the basis of race in public institutions. At Boalt, many students who either opposed or supported 209 were angered over how the overwhelmingly critical social justice or diversity reaction to 209 led to the stifling of open and honest discussions inside and outside class. It stifled virtually any issues involving race and social policy—the kind of social censorship that so concerned the likes of Mill and Tocqueville. One self-described liberal woman law student felt betrayed, as quoted in a book on what transpired. She felt betrayed at the same time that she simply felt bored:

> This lack of exchange is not only boring, it is antithetical to the educational mission of a university. Most of us at law school are relatively young, still trying out new ideas and testing the grounds of our beliefs. Yet this type of development requires a tolerant, forgiving atmosphere, one that allows for the full exploration of ideas, including directness, exaggeration, and even mistakes. But because no such atmosphere exists at Boalt, students are rarely willing to put their necks on the line. . . . We have debate light. . . . [O]ur behavior is more like that of polite dinner than that of law students. Another student said of another class: "I have witnessed the death of the individual."[31]

Some other pertinent examples of this problem have popped up in recent times, including the shouting down of speakers and some commentary by students about social justice and knowledge. In 2014, a Harvard student writing in the *Harvard Crimson* called for the purging of what in her eyes constitutes nonprogressive thought. "If our university opposes racism, sexism, and heterosexism, why should we put up with research that counters our goals?"[32]

Notice that the writer did not simply pinpoint clearly biased speech; she highlighted any research that in her estimation "counters our goals." This student ignored an important point about social justice: that the meaning of social justice is a very contested matter in the history of political thought. The study of political theory cries out for respect for intellectual diversity. If we assume that only her version should be allowed, the student exhibits a profoundly anti-intellectual attitude. We are left to ask, "From just where did she get this idea?"

The Center for Responsive Politics (CRP) reports donations by organizations for presidential campaigns; the reports consistently show greater donations to Democrats than to Republicans by major higher education institutions and by a wide margin—more than 9 to 1—in the leading institutions. Political diversity is not the same thing as intellectual diversity, but the two forms can be related. The decidedly liberal slant of the donations in the CRP reports is indicative of the political beliefs of those institutions.[33]

Evidence reveals that the leftward tilt of the faculty has accelerated over the course of the past several decades, especially in the humanities and social sciences. In a 2016 study of voter registration for 7,243 faculty members at 40 leading universities in departments of economics, history, journalism or communications, law, and psychology, three leading researchers of faculty politics found 3,623 to be registered Democrats and 314 to be registered Republicans, for a ratio of 11.5:1. "The results indicate that D:R ratios have increased since 2004, and the age profile suggests that in the future they will be even higher. We provide a breakdown by department at each university. The data support the established finding that D:R ratios are highest at the apex of disciplinary pyramids, that is, at the most prestigious departments."[34]

To get a better sense of the effect of ideology in actual practice, we should briefly consider two recent and thorough academic inquiries. In one study, the self-confessed liberal sociologist Neil Gross conducted several empirical inquiries, including (a) a survey of the general public's perceptions of liberal bias in academia; (b) a random survey of the political and social views of 1,400 academics; (c) a review of free-form interviews with 57 professors who teach in five different disciplines; (d) an analysis of the General Social Survey, which has surveyed large numbers of academics and nonacademics since 1970; (e) an examination of a leading longitudinal study of adolescents who went on to graduate school for a PhD; and (f) an email audit survey of directors of graduate programs in five disciplines. Gross then complemented this extensive empirical effort by considering how well the data fit leading social science theories that attempt to explain the politics of academia.

Like previous researchers, Gross found a definite tilt to the left, especially when compared with the general public. Indeed, academia is more liberal than any other occupational group, with the possible exception of authors and journalists. But it is not monolithic. Moving left to right across the different types of academic institutions, one finds 9 percent "radical left," 31 percent "progressive," 14 percent "center-left," 19 percent "moderate," 4 percent "economic conservative," and 23 percent "strong conservative." Not surprisingly, the proportions differ depending on the type of institution and discipline. For example, liberal arts schools are more radical, while community colleges and non–PhD-granting universities are more moderate. Humanities and the social sciences slant decidedly left, with the exception of economics. Engineering and business are more conservative and moderate.

In terms of treatment of colleagues and hiring, Gross found not only less reason for concern than many conservative observers harbor, but also several cases of discrimination and intolerance—a mixed bag of sorts that nonetheless leans in the direction of bias. Rather than attributing the imbalance mainly to intentional discrimination, Gross gives more weight to self-selection by individuals who choose to go into academics and to the longstanding progressive character of higher education since the birth of the modern research university more than a century ago.[35]

Jon A. Shields and Joshua M. Dunn Sr., self-described conservatives, ask similar questions in *Passing on the Right*; they come to conclusions less sanguine than Gross's, but within the same ballpark. They interviewed and surveyed 153 conservative professors in six disciplines in the social sciences and humanities at 84 universities that are a representative sample of public and private institutions. The professors came from the fields of economics, political science, sociology, history, philosophy, and literature. Rather than attempting the thankless task of defining "conservatism," the authors simply let prospective interviewees self-identify. Focusing on those departments makes sense because such departments tend to set the public and political tone of a college or university as a result of their subject matters and the types of students they attract. Engineers, for example, are more conservative, but they are generally less publicly visible in terms of campus opinion and perception.

Shields's and Dunn's ultimate conclusion is nuanced, yet still critical of ideological slant. In summary, whereas they discovered a troubling lack of intellectual and political diversity in many domains and outright hostile treatment of conservatives in too many quarters, they also discovered meaningful exceptions and mitigating factors. In their estimation, the extent of progressive rule in a department appears to be related to at least two factors.

First, the more empirically rigorous a discipline, the less room there generally is for ideology to play a role. In a second and related observation, Shields and Dunn argue that some disciplines and fields are more influenced by what the authors and scholars such as Christian Smith have called the "deeply embedded sacred project" of personal and egalitarian emancipation that derives from the utopian aspirations of the Enlightenment. For example, this project "has shaped the culture of sociology and made it so appealing to generations of social scientists of the left." Because they are less sanguine regarding human nature and its possibilities, conservatives typically do not buy into those more optimistic aspirations. If you disagree with the "project," you run the risk of being considered morally defective—a sense conveyed in myriad ways in campus encounters.[36]

Two points emerge from *Passing on the Right* that are especially relevant to our inquiry. First, because of their generally outsider campus status, conservatives often wrestle with the question of "coming out of the conservative closet." The authors present several interesting examples of this process, applying Erving Goffman's concept of "stigma signals" to illuminate the dynamics of what amounts to a strategic decision. In some cases they even found professors who took special pride in being different and distinctive and in swimming against the tide. I have enjoyed knowing and working with several such people, including conservative or conservative-leaning students who reveled in being different. This posture was always much more refreshing and admirable than was that of those who simmered with resentment or a sense of persecution—a conservative version of identity politics grievance.

More germane to our concerns, Dunn and Shields discuss ways in which the underrepresentation of conservative viewpoints has limited valid perspectives about historical and policy issues, thereby enervating the educational experiences of students and the depth and breadth of knowledge. In language reminiscent of John Stuart Mill's classic defense of intellectual freedom and diversity, the authors write, "The problem is not progressivism. It is the absence of conservatives from many important domains of inquiry."

Examples of the shortcomings of one-sided research that have been rectified by conservatives include the following: the role of religion in the civil rights and other freedom movements; the truths contained in the Moynihan Report's findings about the problems associated with single-parent families, which progressives censured for too long; the illiberal aspects of the link between the historical eugenics movement and the politics of abortion; and the failure of many academic historians to acknowledge the truth of Soviet-inspired infiltrations in the United States, even after the opening of Soviet archives made those facts obvious.[37] In Chapter 7, I present evidence of how liberal and progressive dissent has challenged conventional thinking in ways that have furthered truth and justice.

I would add a recent issue. Important questions remain about how transgender identity is pursued, regardless of how sympathetic one is to the identity. Scholars and doctors have raised empirical questions about related matters such as how sure young people are about their identity when they decide to have a life-changing operation and about the psychological problems that young people struggling with such identity can suffer. Despite the legitimacy of such questions, Brown University recently decided to remove reference on its website to pioneering research by a junior professor on the mental issues at stake. Though the administration claimed that the removal was due to findings about methodological concerns, critics aver that this claim was an expedient pretext, that the decision was essentially political, and that it was made in deference to identity activists.[38] If so, our understanding of the issue is diminished.

In conclusion, whereas one should not exaggerate the problem of a lack of intellectual diversity in higher education, it would be equally wrong to ignore it or to wish it away. It no doubt plays a big role in some institutions but less in others. When it matters, it can harm research, as Dunn and Shields point out. It can also weaken the educational experience of students, who are deprived of exposure to a genuine clash of ideas, inside and outside the classroom. (Gross, Dunn, and Shields do not address this dimension, but it is of obvious importance.) Finally, when a lack of intellectual diversity exists, it can engender a campus climate in which wrongful restrictions on academic free speech are more likely to occur.

CHAPTER 6

CONTEMPORARY SURVEYS: MAKING AMERICA SAFE FOR *PEANUTS*

In Schulz's world, the kids build up confidence and resiliency on their own. They fight their own battles. They stand up for what they think is right . . . and learn how to bounce back after failure. They negotiate, handle taunts and deal with problems—character traits that adults need as well.

—Sally Carpenter, *"The Mystery of the Peanuts' Parents,"*
Ladies of Mystery, *February 6, 2017*[1]

In this chapter, I look at some recent survey research about student and faculty attitudes toward speech. Though hardly conclusive, the surveys perform three major functions. First, they contribute to a fuller understanding of the empirical status of free speech in American higher education, at least in the reported attitudes of the respondents. Second, they offer reasons to be more appropriately nuanced in our assessment of the present and the future, contingent upon what future actions are taken on intellectual freedom's behalf. And third, they help us to refine our assessment of the dangers and threats that academic free speech confronts.

One question in particular looms over the debate: What is the exact nature and extent of the problem? We probably can never definitively answer this empirical question. Thousands of institutions populate the American higher education landscape, and many institutions are little city-states in their own rights, thus making the attempt to know them akin to knowing the streets of Paris. It can be as easy to find outrageous examples of violations of academic free speech as it is to cite incidents of free speech triumphant. When violations happen, they indict themselves and call for conscientious corrective action, while successes may need to be applauded more than they are. Overall, though, the question is about the *extent* of the academic free speech problem, not its *existence*.[2] This chapter attempts to scratch the surface of the question of extent while beckoning further inquiry.

In this chapter, I look at a few findings that I consider representative of the new batch of surveys taken in 2017 and 2018. Recent student surveys show different shades of attitudes, though we have more reasons to be concerned with the status of free speech than did two new surveys about faculty members' and college presidents' opinions. The student surveys are not all in agreement, but a general overall picture emerges: (a) the attitudes of many students reflect the subjective expansion of the concept of hate speech that we examined in Chapter 4; (b) a surprisingly substantial degree, though not a majority, of student opinion supports shouting speakers down, with 10 percent or more even tolerating a resort to violence in a pinch by others, if not themselves; and (c) overall student support for controversial free speech is stronger than surmised by many who blame students for campus political correctness—except for speech deemed offensive to identity-politics groups.

However, speech can cover a broad spectrum of ideas and topics on campuses where issues of identity are predominant, as well as in our culturally pluralistic world. Intellectual freedom does not mean it is okay to allow open discourse about less sensitive topics, but not sensitive ones. Whereas most students personally support wide-open discourse—though less so for hate speech as they define it—most students also maintain that the actual climate for free speech on campus is inhibiting, especially for politically incorrect speech. When asked to rank the importance of wide-open discourse and the norms of sensitivity and diversity, students slightly favor the latter—a finding that is relevant to the discussion of prioritization presented throughout this book.

Political scientist Samuel J. Abrams found widespread faculty support for free speech in his 2018 survey of almost 900 faculty members nationwide. Here are some of the findings, as published in *The American Interest* in April 2018.[3] For reasons of space, I will report Abrams's overall findings for the most part rather than delving more fully into degrees of support.

Generally, college faculty members overwhelmingly supported free speech and open discourse, with both left and right closely agreeing. Thus, 93 percent agreed with this statement: "[U]niversity life requires that people with diverse viewpoints and perspectives encounter each other in an environment where they feel free to speak up and challenge each other."

In terms of the classroom, 80 percent of respondents agreed with this statement: "Faculty members should be free to present in class any idea that they consider relevant." It is perhaps interesting that *liberal* faculty members agreed with this position more than *conservative* ones did, 88 percent to 67 percent. Conservative faculty members were possibly thinking of the public accounts of leftist faculty members making partisan jokes and comments in class.

As we saw in Chapter 3, standards of relevance constitute appropriate limits in principle on classroom pedagogy. Therefore, much depends on what material is construed as relevant. Faculty members in the social sciences and humanities—fields considered the most affected by political correctness—agreed more than 90 percent of the time, compared with 70 percent in business and education.

Classic researches of attitudes about free speech and civil liberties have consistently found greater support for such liberties in the abstract than in more specific, and therefore controversial, applications.[4] The specific situations have included speech for communists, hate groups, moral dissidents, and others. Abrams found a similar reduction when he asked a more specific question comparing a wide-open environment in

Contemporary Surveys: Making America Safe for Peanuts   127

which biased and offensive speech is allowed with a positive climate that restricts such speech. But the results remained substantially in favor of free speech, with 69 percent favoring the open environment compared with 31 percent supporting the positive environment.

Abrams writes, "This strong inclination toward openness mirrors a 2018 Knight poll which found that 29 percent of college students supported a positive environment and 70 percent supported an open environment." This latter comment seems inconsistent with other findings about student support for speech codes, as we will see next. It appears that students have either not thought through the implications of all of their positions, or they believe competing agendas can be balanced without worrying too much about prioritization. Given the politics of a campus, however, 31 percent of faculty members—or a similar percentage of students—who favor sensitivity over free speech could represent backing for censorship.

Abrams found only a slight partisan difference among faculty members in terms of favoring an open versus a positive campus climate: 70 percent of Democrat professors preferred an open climate compared with 66 percent of Republicans. Again, this is a modest finding that nonetheless goes against the grain of common expectations that tend to believe conservatives are more suspicious of free speech limitations because their oxen are more frequently gored by campus policies. Abrams also found that similar percentages of Democrats and Republicans favor the open climate, regardless of field. But here, faculty attitudes differ from student attitudes in the 2018 Knight Foundation survey (see later), which found that when it comes to students, 90 percent of Republicans favored an open environment compared with only 60 percent of Democrats.

Abrams speculates that one reason for the difference in this respect could be because students' time on campus is limited, whereas faculty members become more accepting of academic norms as their careers advance—a hypothesis that holds in my own case. Another explanation is perhaps more plausible: conservative faculty members and students generally feel more set up than do liberal faculty members when it comes to free speech, so they feel the need for an open environment more intensely. Consequently, the free speech issue has engendered more salience for conservatives, thereby placing it more at the center of their radar screen of concerns.

In respect to supporting the new policies that affect discourse on campus, liberal faculty members were overall considerably more supportive of policies such as safe spaces than were conservative faculty members. Abrams reports that 61 percent of faculty members agree or partly agree that safe spaces "help students feel comfortable sharing their perspectives and exploring sensitive subjects." Here we do find a strong partisan split—78 percent versus 39 percent. This difference could be a product of liberals' general greater faith in administrative and regulatory government compared with that of conservatives. Or the percentages could reflect different attitudes regarding character, sensitivity, and the need for toughening up.[5] Furthermore, faculty members at small liberal arts schools were considerably more favorable toward safe spaces (91 percent) than were those at private universities (68 percent) and public universities (65 percent).

Finally, 67 percent of faculty members agree to varying degrees that students who disrupt speakers should be expelled or suspended, with some partisan difference: 84 percent of conservatives were in favor, but just 59 percent of liberals were. Conservatives in general tend to hold more punitive views of punishment than do liberals, which may explain the difference. This is an important finding for two reasons. First, it shows that a clear majority of faculty members believe in academic free speech strongly enough to endorse penalties with real bite for students who violate it, a sign of commitment. Second, as we will see in Chapter 8, one reason for outside legislative intervention into campus disciplinary proceedings is a lack of faith in colleges to properly punish students who indulge in hecklers' vetoes.

Once again, however, we need to zero in on the more precise nature of the problem: a strong majority of faculty members may favor punishment for hecklers who attempt to veto speakers, but the real questions are who makes the decision and whether faculty members will mobilize to ensure that appropriate punishment is meted out. And one-third of faculty members disfavor meaningful punishment: what if this third is the most outspoken and active? Abrams' survey highlights the central practical and strategic issue in this book: the need for faculty members to act on the latent support for academic free speech that they apparently harbor in their breasts.

That, of course, is the $64,000 question, as shown in the discussion of Timur Kuran's theory of public values falsification in Chapter 1.

When a committed minority takes the lead institutionally, it can be easy to create the sense that public opinion lies in one direction, whereas it really lies in the other. (See also the comments of Middlebury's Allison Stanger and Northwestern's Laura Kipnis in Chapter 1.)[6] I would add the actions that students, faculty members, and administrators take in their many encounters and the messages they and others give off in ways both subtle and not so subtle that set the tone for a campus.

A person can claim to favor both X and Y and may sincerely favor both to some degree, but that person's inflections and actions can send a message about where priorities lie when a conflict between them arises. Furthermore, many cases of speech suppression and other violations of rights have taken place beneath the radar screen, as many observers have noted. The lawsuit against the University of Michigan's bias reporting program speaks to this concern, noting that "the most sensitive student on campus effectively dictates the terms under which others may speak." The program threatens to submit offenders to "restorative justice," "individual education," and "unconscious bias training," which "amounts to unconstitutional prior restraint of speech and is too overbroad and vague to give anyone due notice of what is proscribed."[7] And, as underscored in previous chapters of this book, where were the faculty members while this program was germinating?

THE AMERICAN COUNCIL ON EDUCATION PRESIDENTS' SURVEY

In April 2018, the American Council on Education (ACE) conducted a survey of nearly 500 college and university presidents; it was titled *Free Speech and Inclusion: A Survey of College Presidents*. An introduction to a report on its findings states, "Nearly all presidents indicated that promoting an inclusive society (98 percent) *and* protecting freedom of speech (98 percent) are extremely or very important to our democracy, reinforcing the understanding that those two concepts are not mutually exclusive."

The survey began by asking how important the presidents considered two things "to be in our democracy": "[p]romoting an inclusive society that is welcoming to diverse groups" and "[p]rotecting citizens' free speech rights." The finding was that 82 percent considered the former "extremely or very important" and 16 percent "moderately important." No respondent selected "not that important," and 2 percent did not register an opinion. Opinions regarding speech were also strong, but less so than for inclusion. That finding suggested a prioritization given to inclusion over free speech: 74 percent voted for "extremely important" or "very important," with 2 percent not saying.

The next question, however, revealed a much stronger prioritization toward free speech. When asked to choose which is more important, protecting students from speech they consider "offensive or biased," only 4 percent picked this responsibility over "allowing students to be exposed to all types of speech even if they may find it offensive or biased." Apparently, even though campus presidents prioritize inclusiveness over free speech, they also believe that open free speech does not harm inclusiveness, at least in the abstract. Then again, perhaps they are not entertaining the emphasis on speech prioritization that is a key theme of this book.

Most presidents considered the ability of their institutional stakeholders to listen to opposing views to be stronger than those at other institutions. This opinion could be a function of the third-person effect, by which individuals tend to perceive media messages as having greater effect on others than such messages have on themselves. Or it is simply a reflection of the fact that people are inclined to be more generous regarding faults that begin at home. Interestingly, 79 percent believed that their own institutions effectively balanced free speech and inclusion, whereas only 13 percent thought this was so for institutions nationwide—a remarkable difference. The report provides support to those who claim that the support for the suppression of speech is not as sweeping in higher education as critics allege—though, again, the shouting down of speakers is only one of the many ways in which speech can be stifled or inhibited.

Presidents were also largely pessimistic about how the balance between inclusion and free speech would play out in coming years. This particular finding might be a fairly reliable indicator of where the wind is blowing, because college presidents typically are on the scene over several years and have more interaction with the various dimensions of campus life than do other stakeholders. The presidents might feel freer to offer unalloyed views about the situation beyond their own walls.[8]

Overall, the results of this survey point in different directions and provide reasons for guarded optimism as well as ongoing concern. Regardless, those interested in mobilizing for reform should draw on this survey for motivational and strategic purposes.

In Chapter 1, I briefly mentioned that a recent survey on administrators' politics was "much less encouraging" than the surveys on campus leaders. This is another survey by Sam Abrams, which found an overwhelming liberal-progressive tilt among 900 nation's "student-facing administrators. I mentioned this survey in that chapter because of its salience to Laura Kipnis's observations about the bureaucratic elements of the "shadow university" and because it did not ask questions about free and open inquiry. Instead it focused simply on political ideology. Nonetheless, this survey for campus politics that Abrams drew should be borne in mind when thinking about the ACE's president survey. The more deference a college president gives toward such administrators, the more weight their policies and views will have when it comes to actual administrative practice.[9]

STUDENT SURVEYS

As mentioned earlier, student surveys taken in recent times present a less favorable portrait of academic free speech than Abrams's faculty survey does, but they also offer a more nuanced take than many critics of higher education fancy. What stands out is general support for free speech, punctuated by considerably less support of speech deemed to be offensive or biased toward identity groups. In addition, we find undercurrents of support for subjective interpretations of hate speech and for disruption of speakers. Once again, the question is whether there is a silent majority who oppose such trends, what the intensity of their positions is, and what they do about it.

THE KNIGHT SURVEYS

Let us look first at two recent and widely cited surveys undertaken by the Knight Foundation: a survey published in 2018 and conducted with the support of the ACE, the Charles Koch Institute, and the Stanton

Foundation. It is titled *Free Expression on Campus: What College Students Think about First Amendment Issues* and drew on a 2016 survey Knight carried out with Gallup.

KEY FINDINGS OF THE 2016 KNIGHT SURVEY

The 2016 Knight survey found that college students are more likely to feel that free speech in America is secure than is the general public.[10] The 2016 survey also found that 56 percent of adults in the United States considered the right of free speech secure in the country, compared with 73 percent of college students surveyed. For freedom of the press, the figures were 64 percent versus 81 percent; they were 58 percent versus 76 percent for freedom of petition. (The broader General Social Survey has found a similar pattern and has concluded that tolerance for free speech has grown over the years in society at large and among college graduates. The main exception is post-9/11 speech for radical Muslims. Aggregate data from the survey indicate that harder left groups are the most tolerant of the right to engage in hate speech, perhaps because they know that the hard left has often borne the brunt of censorship in history.)

At the same time, many students, especially African Americans and women, were willing in the 2016 Knight survey to accept limitations on hate speech, which the survey defined as intentionally offensive speech to identity groups. However, respondents generally distinguished "political views that are upsetting or offensive to certain groups" from "using slurs or other language that is intentionally offensive to certain groups." Of all students, 27 percent accepted restrictions on general offense, with 72 percent disagreeing. But the numbers shift dramatically when the offense is linked to intentionality and language associated with slurs: 69 percent approve restriction versus 31 percent who do not. This difference is consistent with common sense and even roughly parallels First Amendment doctrine, the latter of which countenances restriction if highly offensive speech is intentionally targeted at someone in the manner of fighting words. Women and African Americans were consistently less protective of speech in those two questions than were whites and males.

An operative question here is whether higher education provides greater opportunities to disrupt and chill discourse than are found outside the academy. Even if the general public is less supportive of controversial speech than is the typical college graduate, this finding does not mean that hecklers' vetoes are more prevalent in public than on campus. It is reasonable to assume that heckler's vetoes are more likely to occur in the more intimate contexts of a college or university than in society at large, where speech acts tend to be swamped by a multitude of other activities and interests. That said, the fact that students ultimately support speech more than does the general public has some salience. It provides one basis for hope so long as this voice is empowered on campus.

KEY FINDINGS FROM THE 2018 KNIGHT SURVEY

The 2018 Knight survey of 3,014 U.S. college students, including 216 at historically black institutions, depicts a slight yet noticeable deterioration in support for free speech among college students compared with 2016, because students no doubt reacted to the many speaker incidents that had taken place between the two surveys and to the demonstrations of the alt right at Charlottesville in 2017 and elsewhere.[11]

First, 56 percent of students say the protection of free speech is extremely important to democracy, with 52 percent affirming the same for promoting a diverse and inclusive society. These are not very high numbers given the importance of the principles. Though a clear majority of students think free speech is very important, when probed further, students tilt in favor of prioritizing diversity and inclusion above free speech. When asked, "If you had to choose, which do you think is more important?" 53 percent voted for a diverse and inclusive society compared with only 46 percent who voted for protecting free speech rights. This finding is important because, as stressed throughout this book, what often matters is *how we prioritize* values when they come into conflict. Therefore, programs and pressures designed to foster diversity and inclusion often stand in tension with academic free speech, especially if what constitutes discriminatory or threatening speech is broadly defined.

The 2016 Knight survey defined hate speech relatively tightly and framed its questioning in terms of intentional offense. Part of the 2018 survey was less definitive when it asked, "Do you think hate speech is a form of expression that should or should not be protected by the First Amendment?" When asked this question, student opinion veered away from the general support elicited by the more abstract questions about speech: 35 percent overall said hate speech should be protected, whereas 64 percent said it should not. (Again, African Americans and women favored such restriction more than did white males.)

On the one hand, when the questioning got more specific about hate, support for restriction increased further: 73 percent favored restricting "slurs/other language that is intentionally offensive to certain groups" (compared with 69 percent in the 2016 survey), and 63 percent favored doing so for costumes that stereotype certain groups (60 percent in 2016). On the other hand, only 27 percent favored banning *politically offensive* speech, compared with 30 percent in 2016.

According to the report, "Black students are more likely than white students to support campus policies that limit these types of expression. Nearly half of blacks, 46 percent, favor limits on political speech, while 28 percent of whites do. Democrats are more likely than are Republicans to favor the restrictions." Note that those findings are generally consistent with the distinction that Jeremy Waldron draws between political or policy positions and that cause offense and intentional vilification, as discussed in Chapters 3 and 4.[12]

Finally, for our purposes, are the questions dealing with specific policies, such as speech codes and safe spaces. We observe that 87 percent overall supported safe spaces where students can find support "if they feel upset or threatened by things they see or hear" (95 percent for Democrats and women). Moreover, 83 percent favored special free speech zones for open discourse, though courts have interpreted most such zones as being overly restrictive of First Amendment rights. When it comes to speech codes "that restrict offensive or biased speech on campus that would be permitted in society more generally," students were close to evenly split between support (49 percent) and disagreement (51 percent).

About 60 percent of African Americans, women, students from historically black colleges and universities, and Democrats favored speech codes, whereas a majority of men, whites, Republicans, and Independents opposed them. The findings indicate substantial student support for the restriction of speech on campus. A partisan student divide prevailed in this most recent survey: 90 percent of student Republicans called for an open environment, whereas only 60 percent of Democrats did. Given the predominance of left-leaning students on most campuses today, this finding appears portentous.

Though students as a whole remained pro–free speech but for the exceptions mentioned, they also increasingly perceived a chilling effect on campus. Alarmingly, 61 percent believed their campus climate prevented people from honestly speaking their thoughts, compared with 54 percent in 2016. Meanwhile, 69 percent think conservatives are free to speak honestly, whereas 92 percent think the same applies to liberals. So, many students do perceive a campus bias in favor of liberal opinion.

Almost 60 percent of students believed that most discussion takes place on social media as opposed to public places on campus, and students who use social media a lot favored restrictions more than did those who use it less. According to the summary, "an increasing percentage of college students agree that social media can stifle free expression because people fear being attacked or blocked by those who disagree with their views." In another finding, 90 percent of students agreed that it is never right to deploy violence against a speaker, with 10 percent saying it can be acceptable. However, 37 percent think that shouting down a speaker is acceptable sometimes. Thus, a sizable percentage of students support hecklers' vetoes.

Finally, 64 percent of college students say freedom of speech is secure in the country as a whole, down from 73 percent in 2016. Three factors could have influenced this significant drop: (a) the media reports about campus speech disruptions nationwide, (b) the media claims that President Trump is hostile to the press and free speech, and (c) the actual climate students perceive on their own campuses.

THE BUCKLEY SURVEY

Other recent surveys broadly paralleled the Knight findings while raising some important further questions and concerns. For example, a September 2017 national survey of undergraduates by Yale's Buckley

Center and the McLaughlin Associates was consistent with other 2017 surveys performed by organizations such as FIRE and the Cato Institute. Its core findings initially sounded alarm bells for academic free speech. But closer examination has lowered the volume to some extent. Like the Knight survey, the Buckley survey showed support for free speech and intellectual diversity in the abstract, but it found considerably less support for speech deemed offensive to identity politics groups. Among its findings were these:

- 83 percent said the First Amendment is important and should continue to be adhered to.
- 52 percent opposed college speech codes versus 38 percent who favored them.
- 84 percent supported administrative programs to promote intellectual diversity of views, including those dealing with politics, race, gender, and religion. Only 10 percent did not endorse such efforts.
- 51 percent believed students should be allowed to express their views anywhere on campus, even if those views were offensive, whereas 40 percent said such views should be limited to certain designated areas (i.e., free speech zones). This finding varied considerably from the survey of just one year earlier, in which 74 percent favored speaking anywhere and only 22 percent supported relegating speech to designated areas. The 2017 survey commented that new wording in the 2017 survey probably accounted for this dramatic difference: It added the words "even if offensive." Thus, a vast majority of students favored limiting offensive speech to quarantined areas of campus, even though the protection of offensive speech is a *sine qua non* of belief in freedom of speech.[13]
- 81 percent felt that "words can be a form of violence." This view is disconcerting, but the word "can" might ameliorate this feeling. After all, some words *are* properly treated as closely linked to violence by courts, as we saw in Chapter 4, including real threats and direct incitement to violence that is likely to occur.

Given the lack of general student knowledge of the specifics of First Amendment law and theory, it is possible that students did not have those constitutionally accepted delimitations in mind, making this finding more disconcerting to free speech advocates.

- 58 percent agreed that their school should prohibit speakers who have engaged in hate speech versus 32 percent who disagreed. In September 2015, 49 percent disagreed, while 46 percent agreed. This decline on the free speech side could be due to the recent spate of alt right speakers. Also, in some schools, the new programs discussed in Chapter 4, which are designed to inhibit certain forms of speech, have had two more years to influence students.[14]

- Most troubling for free speech advocates, 66 percent agreed that "Hate speech is anything that one particular person believes is harmful, racist, or bigoted. Hate speech means something different to everyone, and you just know it when you see or hear it." Only 24 percent disagreed. This finding reflects the problem of subjectivity discussed in Chapter 4. Democrats and African Americans agreed even more strongly.

- 38 percent agreed that "[i]t is sometimes appropriate to shout down or disrupt a speaker on my campus," whereas 56 percent disagreed. That almost 40 percent of college students would support deploying a heckler's veto is not reassuring to defenders of free speech on campus.

THE FIRE AND YOUGOV SURVEY

The FIRE survey of 1,250 U.S. students presented in October 11, 2017, with the assistance of YouGov, had some findings relevant to the issues at hand. First, only 46 percent knew that the First Amendment protects hate speech, and of those, 31 percent thought that the amendment should not do so. Overall, only 35 percent thought such speech *should* be protected speech. In asking about the use of violence against speakers, FIRE's question was more specific than questions in other surveys, asking whether they *personally* might resort to disruption or violence to stop a speaker "with ideas I strongly disagree with." Only 1 percent said "yes." This percentage would naturally be lower than the percentage of those endorsing violence in other surveys because those questions asked only about disruption or violence by anyone, not just the respondent.

FIRE also found that 54 percent of students reported that "they have stopped themselves from sharing an idea or opinion in class at some point since beginning college," a finding that recalls our concern in Chapter 2 about intellectual honesty. But this finding must be balanced with the fact that 87 percent of the respondents reported feeling comfortable about expressing their own views and opinions in the classroom, while 93 percent said speakers of a variety of viewpoints should come to campus.[15] Perhaps opinions about speaking comfort vary in students' minds with the medium at stake, such as social media, face-to-face social settings with peers, and discussions with faculty members. Also, conservative students felt considerably less able to speak freely than did liberal students.

The FIRE survey reflects the different thrusts and tensions of the other surveys: general support for free speech is strong, but students carve out exceptions for hate speech.

THE CATO INSTITUTE SURVEY

This survey asked a broad range of questions relating to different controversial contexts of free speech, including deeply offensive speech toward racial groups, religions, the military, and others; speech that advocates or incites violence; flag burning; sexually offensive speech (obscenity and pornography); not standing for the national anthem; and policies that might chill free speech, such as trigger warnings and microaggressions. In addition, it asks questions about attitudes toward institutions such as colleges and the media and about policies affecting those institutions. Cato surveyed adults 18 years of age and older, with an oversampling of college students and graduate students.[16]

On the positive side for free speech, a clear majority of respondents considered political correctness to be a problem: 70 percent of all respondents "net-agree," including 62 percent of African Americans and

70 percent of Latinos. But a partisan divide prevails here, with 90 percent of Republicans net-agreeing, but only 50 percent of Democrats and 78 percent of Independents. This finding is consistent with conventional wisdom regarding which side experiences the most censorship or chilling on campus. In addition, at least two-thirds of all categories of respondents agreed with this statement reflecting core First Amendment and free speech theory: "Freedom of speech ensures the truth will ultimately win out." This result also means that one-third did not agree.

Once again, more specific and challenging questions engender more divided opinions. In many respects, the Cato survey raises more free speech concerns than do the other surveys we have perused. For example, whereas Republicans are usually more supportive of free speech when it is in tension with identity politics, they head in the opposite direction when it comes to their sacred cows, such as flag burning, which the Supreme Court has upheld as a First Amendment right.[17] A stunning 53 percent of Republicans favor the drastic punishment of *loss of citizenship* for burning the flag, along with 49 percent of Latinos and 28 percent of Democrats. The Supreme Court has ruled that revoking citizenship is a very serious punishment that is justified only in very special circumstances, including—and nearly limited to—committing fraud in the naturalization process, serving in a foreign military, or committing treason. Exercising a constitutional right is certainly not such a special circumstance.[18]

A focus on four questions highlights the most relevant survey findings for our purposes, though one could pick several others as well. The first example explains that when asked if there should be a law that requires people to refer to transgender people by their "preferred gendered pronouns and not according to their biological sex," 51 percent of Democrats were in favor, along with 40 percent of African Americans and 42 percent of Latinos, but only 21 percent of Republicans. One can hardly think of a better display of blurring the difference between the normative encouragement of good manners and actual legal coercion than this example of compelled speech.

The second example deals with the rise of the claim that hate speech and offensive expression constitute actual forms of violence. In response to the question "Is hate speech an act of violence," 53 percent of all respondents said "yes." Understandably, significant differences prevailed according to race and political affiliation: 46 percent of whites, 73 percent of African Americans, 72 percent of Latinos, 66 percent of Democrats, 48 percent of Independents, and 41 percent of Republicans agreed.

The third question I select for this purpose asks if people who don't respect others "deserve" the right to free speech. Despite the obvious practical and normative problems this position raises—it essentially means that disrespectful people are not entitled the right of free speech. Moreover, 44 percent of all respondents agreed: 59 percent of African Americans, 62 percent of Latinos, 36 percent of whites, 47 percent of Democrats, 44 percent of Independents, and 39 percent of Republicans. As far as anyone knows, courts have not allowed First Amendment rights to be limited to those deemed deserving.

The fourth example deals with colleges and offensive speech: "Colleges have an obligation to protect students from offensive speech and ideas that could create a difficult learning environment." Here, 53 percent of all respondents net-agreed, compared with 45 percent net-disagreeing. As with many such questions, whites differed significantly from African Americans and Latinos, whereas political affiliation made a significant difference: 66 percent of Democrats net-agreed, but only 47 percent of Independents and 42 percent of Republicans. Note that the question asked about speech and ideas, which constitute the essence of what a college education is supposed to offer and encourage. Nor did the question limit its scope to the narrow specific contexts in which the Supreme Court has held that sexual and other forms of "harassment" must be prohibited under Title VII.

Another important feature of the Cato survey is that although it focuses mainly on respondents' *attitudes or opinions* about free speech, it also asks about their *knowledge* of the First Amendment's protection of offensive speech and of the new challenges to speech. This distinction matters for at least two reasons, which reflect the three-step process of free speech protection: (a) knowledge is important because *knowing* vital civic facts and principles is the first step in *understanding* them, (b) the second step is then *critical appreciation of and commitment to* the principles of a free society, and (c) the third step is *supportive action.*

Can a constitutional republic be sustained without such knowledge, critical appreciation, and action? Though it touches on knowledge, the Cato survey is weighted toward understanding and appreciation, which are the first two steps in the process of citizenship. Contemporary surveys have consistently shown that the public—and especially younger citizens—have poor basic knowledge of civic facts.[19] E. D. Hirsch has articulated the ways in which a meaningful education requires sufficient cultural literacy in citizens. Cultural literacy entails a basic knowledge of important cultural facts. Similarly, a responsible citizenry needs to possess such civic literacy.[20]

The responses to Cato's first two questions set the stage for what is to come.

Question 1: "Which of the following two statements comes closer to your own view?"

- People should be allowed to express unpopular opinions in public, even those that are deeply offensive to other people.
- Government should *prevent* people from engaging in hate speech against certain groups in public. [Emphasis added.]

This question asks about *opinion*, not *knowledge*. And it asks if respondents are willing to use the coercive force of law to punish speech.

Question 2: "From what you know now, do you believe it is currently legal or illegal for someone to make a racist statement in public?"

Unlike Question 1, Question 2 deals with knowledge. The correct answer is that the First Amendment does protect racist speech except when it amounts to a criminal threat, to a direct incitement to imminent lawless action, or to fighting words narrowly defined in contexts of face-to-face encounters. (See Chapter 4.)

The results were that 75 percent of the overall respondents *knew* that the law protects racist statements in general, though significant differences appear based on race; 83 percent of whites agreed, but only 61 percent of African Americans and 55 percent of Latinos. Whether this difference of knowledge is due to educational attainment or personal experiences of racism is unknown. Political partisanship was not significant, with Republicans, Democrats, and Independents each knowing the law in the 70 percent range.

The big difference arose among *opinions*, which augurs less favorably for the future of the libertarian modern doctrine of speech that permits restriction only in very limited circumstances. When asked if deeply offensive speech *should* be protected, overall support drops to 59 percent, which is made up of 66 percent whites, 42 percent African Americans, and 41 percent Latinos. Among all respondents, 40 percent do not just normatively disapprove of protecting deeply offensive speech, but they contend that government should prevent such speech, which would entail punishment under the criminal law. Racial differences here are significant: 33 percent of white, 56 percent of African American, and 58 percent of Latino respondents took this position.

Political affiliation is also significant in response to this *opinion* question, unlike with the *knowledge* question: 72 percent of Republicans said that deeply offensive speech *should* be allowed, with only 27 percent saying it should be prevented. Though Democrats closely mirrored Republicans in their *knowledge* of the law for this question, 52 percent said the government should prevent deeply offensive speech—a substantial dropoff compared with Democrats' knowledge that the speech is protected by law. The comparable dropoff for Republicans is 6 percent.

TWENGE'S "IGEN" FINDING

In her recent book *iGen*, social and generational psychologist Jean Twenge broadly addresses the mental states and attitudes of young adults today (the generation called iGen), including their positions on free speech. She compares iGen (those born between 1995 and 2012) to the Millennials (1980–1994), Gen Xers (1965–1979), and Boomers (1946–1964) who preceded them. According to those birth years, the 74 million iGens compose 24 percent of the general population.

Twenge acknowledges that those dates are somewhat arbitrary, but she considers them representative of the research. Her work draws on four prominent national databases of older high school students and of college students over several decades, allowing for comparisons based on attitudes at similar ages. Overall, "these surveys show that young people are now quite different from young people in previous decades." She supplemented these data with more qualitative findings as she conducted 23 personal interviews with a cross-section of iGens, posted online interview questions on prominent internet sites, interviewed 250 students in her introductory psychology class at San Diego State, and widely read media accounts of iGens.[21]

Unlike the other surveys considered in this chapter, the data that Twenge probes get at the rising emotional anxieties of college-attending and college-bound students today, including the ways in which they exhibit greater intolerance of conflict and risk taking than have the previous generations of students. Her work has implications for two key aspects of the intellectual *polis*, namely personal character and the openness and courage to engage in genuine intellectual adventure. To the extent that Twenge's findings merit attention, American liberal democracy might have more work on its hands than many assume. A critical divide separates iGens from their predecessors.

Compared with previous generations, iGen young adults are keener on seeking emotional safety, which leads to "the idea that one should be safe not just from car accidents and sexual assault but from people who disagree with you." Often equating speech with physical violence, iGens support things such as safe spaces, trigger warnings, and microaggression policy. "The embrace of safety and protection now extends to course readings, which must be sanitized to remove anything that might offend someone." In her survey of her San Diego State students, Twenge found that 86 percent "agreed with the idea of safe spaces—both during controversial speeches and as a general goal for campuses. These are not fringe ideas but those embraced by the majority in iGen'ers."[22]

In this respect, Twenge's findings provide some empirical support for the social and political analysis of higher education critics such as social theorist Frank Furedi, who has written about two elements: (a) the ways in which college administrative bureaucracies dealing with students' emotional and mental traumas have proliferated in recent years, and (b) the fact that the psychological and cultural line distinguishing college from primary and secondary education has been blurred. And like Furedi, Twenge links the rise in emotional states such as depression and anxiety with the students' desires to limit exposure to upsetting discourse.

Twenge's findings are also consistent with the points in the book *The Coddling of the American Mind* by Greg Lukianoff and Jonathan Haidt.[23] And her work suggests reasons why certain campus bureaucracies have been so busy adopting policies to enforce agendas of safety and emotional well-being: they engage with students in a synergistic fashion.

Of course, we are talking here of statistical differences. Many of us have known iGen students who defy Twenge's generalizations, superb students who motivate instructors to higher levels of pedagogic achievement. iGens are hardly monolithic. But Twenge's statistics show potentially meaningful increases in various measures of risk taking and emotional problems over time that merit attention. And, as seen often in this book, the actions of a few students can set the public tone of an institution if counter-voices and counter-actions remain dormant. A big question that looms in this respect is whether the upgraded adminis-trative mental health apparatus in higher education reflects a necessary response to pre-existing emotional problems, or whether it exacerbates the problem by signaling to students that such feelings are, or should be, a part of their makeup. Or does the truth lie somewhere in the middle?

Deans of students and other campus authorities have told me that students' emotional problems have mushroomed into a major headache for administrators, a claim recently backed by a conversation I had with the chief legal counsel of a major state university. According to her, the problem is genuine and growing.

Twenge found that iGens are highly tolerant of minorities, which is obviously a good thing. But they are also considerably more likely to tolerate censorship in support of sensitivity and tolerance. In her survey of San Diego State students, 28 percent of iGens agreed with the statement, "A faculty member who, on a single occasion, says something racially insen-sitive in class should be fired." Note three key terms in this question: a *single* occasion; "*insensitive*," not "racist" or the like; and "*fired*," the most severe sanction in academia. Meanwhile, a student who does the same should be *expelled* according to 16 percent of Twenge's sample. Twenge remarks, "This is the dark side of tolerance; it begins with the good intentions of including everyone and not offending anyone but ends (at best) with a reluctance to explore deep issues and (at worst) with careers destroyed by a comment someone found offensive and the silencing of all alternative viewpoints."[24]

Finally, Twenge has found that many iGens engage in fewer actual social interactions. She cites the overuse of social media and iPhones as a major culprit of this trend. Teens' lives have "shifted decisively away from in-person interaction. They spend much less time with their friends in person than teens in previous decades did—about an hour a day less. . . . Even when they do see their friends in person, technology, especially texting, allows iGen to avoid social interactions."[25]

Twenge argues that this retreat from personal interaction exacerbates anxiety, depression, and other disorders. It could also harm citizenship by diminishing what Hannah Arendt has depicted as the common sense that underpins the public realm and makes a shared sense of community and reason viable.[26] The more isolated a person is, the more negative subjective fantasies, phobias, and anxieties are allowed to flourish without the check that genuine relations with others can provide in the form of a reality principle. Injudiciously used, social media do not strengthen the social world—they undermine it. The problem of undue subjectivity discussed in Chapter 4 is related to this social media effect, as is the truth decay mentioned in Chapter 5.

To the extent that this finding remains true, it augurs poorly for a key aspect of liberal education that I highlighted in Chapters 2 and 3, namely the interpersonal interactions that take place in the intellectual *polis*. In addition, as seen in the surveys and other data, fear of mobbing and bullying on social media—another anxiety with which Twenge deals—has chilled the exercise of intellectual honesty and reason that are cardinal principles of the university.

CONCLUSION

The survey evidence presented in this chapter provides reasons to be concerned about the status of academic free speech today as well as reasons for guarded optimism, depending on what happens next.

Most students and faculty members believe in the importance of free speech and an open campus environment, along with the qualifications mentioned—especially for identity politics. If academic free speech is to prevail as an integral part of higher education's primary duty, constructive leadership is needed to give presence and power to the freedom side—and to prioritize it.

Twenge's researches in particular are consistent with what many other researchers and ordinary citizens have observed: the decline of everyday freedom for young people today. The phenomenon of helicopter parenting is real—I observed many such cases in the years before I retired in 2015, with parental reach extending into the lives of many of my students.

Everyone has read accounts of parents being targeted by authorities for simply letting their kids walk a few blocks alone to the park—a practice that was commonplace in my youth.[27] Childhood in a free society is a laboratory for preparing the young for the rigors, pleasures, and responsibilities of freedom. Previous generations of children enjoyed a wider-ranging freedom on a daily basis when compared to children today.

Childhood play that is free from parental oversight also prepares the young for freedom's indispensable ally: the rule of law. While playing sports and games without adult supervision, children naturally create consensual rules that they abide by at the same time that they often argue over the interpretation and application—actions that portend what courts and theorists call "ordered liberty." (See also F. A. Hayek and Michael Polanyi on "spontaneous order," which is a linchpin of liberty.)[28] Playing games and sports and having adventures and social interaction free from the oversight of adults help all youths to define themselves and their imagination and to venture into the wider world on their own or with their peers.

The discursive and personal interaction in the intellectual *polis* of higher education that I described in Chapters 2 and 3 is a higher stage of this process, but it begins in one's early years. Higher education champions always say that college should be the beginning of a lifetime of education." This is a half-truth. Education, including education in freedom, begins very early in life. Infants and children are observant and creative "sponges" who take in life with all its intensity. They absorb and respond to the stimuli, emotions, and challenges of playmates, siblings, and parents. Reading to a child at an early age fertilizes imagination, vocabulary, and intellectual acuity. And living in freedom in childhood helps prepare one to expand intellectual horizons in college. We are born to learn, as it were.

Think of the dramatic meaning of the comic strip *Peanuts*, whose stories feature children creating their own identities and interpersonal worlds *free from adults*. I have often wondered if *Peanuts* could have achieved the success it enjoyed had Charles Schulz launched it in this era of managed childhood. Maybe someone should write a book titled *Making America Safe for* Peanuts, subtitled *Upbringing for Freedom*. If such freedom is lost, the seemingly Sisyphean task of higher education will have an even steeper hill to negotiate.

CHAPTER 7

FITTING IT ALL TOGETHER: THE CAMPUS, THE GOOD LIFE, AND THE REPUBLIC

Enlightenment is man's emergence from his self-imposed nonage. Nonage is the inability to use one's own understanding without another's guidance. This nonage is self-imposed if its cause lies not in lack of understanding but in indecision and lack of courage to use one's own mind without another's guidance. Dare to know! (Sapere aude.) *"Have the courage to use your own understanding"* is *therefore the motto of the enlightenment.*

—*Immanuel Kant,* What Is Enlightenment?

The fates of liberal education and liberal democracy are indelibly linked. And freedom of speech and thought is central to each, making it essential to both the university and the republic. In Chapters 2 and 3, we saw the ways in which freedom of speech and academic freedom are defining principles of higher education. In this chapter, I address why this freedom's benefits extend beyond the university's gates to the polity at large. In so doing, I consider some deeper philosophical and functional justifications that are for free speech and that lurk behind the letter of the law.

Rules and laws often have what legal scholar George Fletcher has called "background theories," which can influence legal interpretation and application.[1] My intention in this chapter is to do something similar to what Fletcher does with the criminal law of self-defense: to explore the background justifications for free speech as a constitutional right. Some of the justifications can be found in the case law itself; others, from the thoughts of free speech scholars, theorists, and other sources.

Before moving on, I should say something about two kindred First Amendment rights that are intimately associated with free speech: the rights of religious freedom and personal conscience. James Madison considered the *right of conscience* to be the most fundamental right of all, and it ties the different strands of First Amendment wording and doctrine together. When thinking about freedom of speech, which is our main concern, we must keep this unifying right in mind. It is no accident that religious groups have brought some of the most important First Amendment cases to the Supreme Court and have helped to forge the edifice of First Amendment doctrine and theory.

Free speech has many justifications because speech is a complex phenomenon that is involved in virtually every thought and action. A fundamental distinction between *deontological* and *consequentialist* acts or positions is part of the Western philosophical tradition. First, deontological justifications are based on the inherent significance of a claim or right as an end in itself and are independent of any particular consequences that ensue. Second, consequentialist justifications concern the benefits or harms that flow from an act or claim. In addition, there is a third that we could call *virtue ethical* justifications for free speech: they pertain to the development of individual character. Readers will note that these three categories overlap to some extent, especially because consequences include ethical and character development, and character is certainly an aspect of ethics. But it makes sense to treat each category or realm independently. The coexistence of deontological, consequentialist, and virtue ethical theories parallels the Constitution's overall project of balancing principle and realism.

THE DEONTOLOGICAL VIRTUES OF FREE SPEECH

The deontological justification of free speech has two dimensions: individual and political, or self-governmental. Let us consider the individual aspect first.

INDIVIDUAL ASPECTS

We can think of free speech as an essential unalienable right with which individuals are "endowed by their Creator"—to use the Declaration's language. The key premise in this logic is that although a sufficiently strong state is needed to secure our rights, the rights themselves come to us from God or nature, or by virtue of our being human. Despite the obvious cultural differences that characterize particular conceptions of human rights, human rights theorists recognize that respect for individual freedom and privacy is fundamental to any meaningful understanding of rights.[2]

The Declaration proclaims the divine or natural origin of our rights, and the Constitution is the practical document that creates a government strong enough to "secure the Blessings of Liberty to ourselves and our posterity," as stated in the Preamble—the under-appreciated part of the Constitution that *bestows* power in the first place to the national government before the document later limits that power. In the real world, deontological rights need practical, consequential power in order to prevail. Consider what happened to the civil rights and lives of African Americans in the South when federal power was withdrawn from that region after Reconstruction ended: Their rights were no longer honored, and they were rendered sitting targets of violent mobs and state governments.[3]

Free speech is a cardinal individual right because it is a manifestation of the free mind that constitutes a *self*. To be fully human, we must be able to harbor our own thoughts and to speak our minds without punishment by the state. However much we are educated and influenced by our families, communities, friends, and institutions, in the end we bear responsibility for our own thoughts, speech, and actions. There is a reason that much First Amendment and free speech theory stresses things such as "individual liberty," "personal autonomy," and the like. And, as Justice Robert Jackson wrote in the famous Japanese internment case during World War II, "if any fundamental principle underlies our system, it is that guilt is personal and not inheritable."[4]

Sometimes it takes a person living in crisis under tyranny to fully fathom what Jackson's statement means. Consider the last words of the great Chinese dissident Lin Zhao, words presented in a 137-page letter to the editorial board of the *Chinese People's Daily* three days before the Mao government executed her: "Nobody has the right to tell me: in order to live, you must have chains on your neck and endure the humiliation of slavery."[5]

Improper censorship and intellectual bullying are affronts to respect for the minds of others. In Kant's language, wrongful censorship treats others not as ends in themselves but as means to the censors' ends. It violates the

"Kingdom of Ends."[6] Indeed, the Kantian ethic of treating individuals as ends might be illustrated using several other constitutional provisions in addition to the First Amendment, including the clauses dealing with takings (the state may take private property only for a "public" use, and must provide "just compensation" when it does so), due process, self-incrimination, equal protection, search and seizure, fair trials, and the quartering of soldiers, to mention a few. A similar logic can apply to initiatives such as mandatory and intellectually dogmatic sensitivity and diversity training if conducted in a way that treats attendees in a dismissive rather than an informative way. Studies unsurprisingly confirm that people want to be treated and respected as moral ends unto themselves.[7] Our appreciating the pluralism touted by Isaiah Berlin, which we looked at in Chapter 5, is an important aspect of this Kantian maxim, because the acceptance of pluralism is respectful of differences that constitute individuals.

Many Supreme Court cases trumpet the significance of free speech for individuals as an end in itself, as well as the need for the state to respect this individual freedom. Let us consider two cases. First is Justice Robert H. Jackson's holding in *West Virginia Board of Education v. Barnette*, the case in which the Court upheld the right of a Jehovah's Witness to refuse to salute the flag in class during World War II. *Barnette* exemplifies the ways in which the freedoms of conscience, religion, and speech form a cognate whole. After acknowledging in true Madisonian and Hamiltonian fashion the need for the state to be strong enough to defend itself and to defend public order, Jackson cut to the heart of the matter:

> Those who begin coercive elimination of dissent soon find themselves exterminating dissenters. Compulsory unification of opinion achieves only the unanimity of the graveyard. . . . If there is any fixed star in our constitutional constellation, it is that no official, high or petty, can prescribe what shall be orthodox in politics, nationalism, religion, or other matters of opinion, or force citizens to confess by word or act their faith therein. If there are any circumstances which permit an exception, they do not now occur to us.[8]

The other example is Justice Louis Brandeis's concurrence in the 1927 case of *Whitney v. California*, in which Brandeis presented several justifications that blend deontological or consequential positions, though he points more fully toward the latter. Here, however, I stress the deontological aspects. Brandeis begins a key part of his concurrence by stating, "Those who won our independence believed that the final end of the State was to make men free to develop their faculties, and that, in its government, the deliberative forces should prevail over the arbitrary. They valued liberty both *as an end*, and as a means." [Emphasis added.]

Another Kantian aspect to this part of the decision has direct relevance to the primary mission of the university: the "deliberative" forces—the *mind*—should prevail over the "arbitrary."[9] This posture is brought home later in the opinion when Brandeis presents his model doctrine for speech that poses dangers to social order. The Court did not adopt this formula as its official governing doctrine until 42 years later in *Brandenburg v. Ohio*—yet another example of a Brandeis or Holmes dissent ultimately becoming governing doctrine:

> Fear of serious injury cannot alone justify suppression of free speech and assembly. Men feared witches and burnt women. It is the function of speech to free men from the bondage of irrational fears. . . . There must be reasonable ground to believe ... no danger flowing from speech can be deemed clear and present unless the incidence of the evil apprehended is so imminent that it may befall before there is opportunity for full discussion. If there be time to expose through discussion the falsehood and fallacies, to avert the evil by the processes of education, the remedy to be applied is more speech, not enforced silence.[10]

This doctrine and the thinking behind it envision citizen listeners as moral agents and ends unto themselves; their minds mediate between the speech-stimulus presented and any subsequent action or decision to act. If a speaker advocates unlawful action, as opposed to directly inciting it, then those who act on the speech are the only ones who should be held accountable because they processed the speech through their own independent minds. They are, therefore, responsible for the result.

Instead of the stimulus leading directly to the response (S—R), we have *Mind* mediating between the stimulus and the response (S—M—R). To punish the speaker short of incitement contexts is to assume that listeners are mere tools of the speaker and that they lack their own moral and intellectual agency. On the other side of this coin, note how Brandeis does allow for suppression of the speaker when the deliberative forces of "education" and "discussion" are absent, as when the listeners become a mob that loses its "deliberative force." In those cases, S—M—R becomes S—R.[11]

One aspect of paternalism also at work here is the third-person effect, which we have already encountered: "I can listen to X and act responsibly, but I don't trust other people to do so!"[12] Succumbing to this effect is a form of paternalistic presumption that runs counter to both Kantian norms and political freedom. In higher education, some campus authorities have supported limits on what is said in public and even in private interpersonal conversations because of their distrust of students to do the right thing—and their condescending fear that students can't handle the rigors of robust and critical discourse.[13] But trusting students to make up their own minds in the context of controversial and disturbing discourse is part of education in freedom.

An intriguing aspect of the deontological position is the natural human resistance to being morally or intellectually bullied in a manner that disrespects one's individuality and inner conviction. Coercion of belief can compel outward behavioral change in someone, but it cannot change one's true feelings or beliefs. (Indeed, it can even strengthen one's internal resistance.) Inner conviction can be the product of rational investigation and evidence, or, as in much religious faith, a matter of "seeing the light" in a different kind of sense.

One reason John Locke called for religious toleration is that he considered religious belief and affiliation to be a matter of inner convictions that are resistant to coercion from others. Luther famously justified his rebellion against the Catholic Church, which was so vital to the ultimate rise of religious pluralism and liberal democracy, by stating, *"Hier stehe ich. I kann nicht anders."* (Here I stand. I cannot do otherwise.)[14] Blind conviction can lead to ignorant or dangerous "fighting faiths," as we will see later in this chapter. But the countering of such faiths should heed Locke's insight.

The Kantian "Kingdom of Ends" aspect of free speech theory also points to the universality of free speech and other fundamental rights—however much culture influences particular conceptions and limits.

Such universality exists in dynamic tension with the individual differences that are part of human nature. Free speech belongs to all of us by virtue of our being human. This understanding is especially relevant to our discussion, given higher education's duty to foster a sense of common intellectual citizenship—along with the ability to handle conflict—in the realm of the mind. The idea of inherent rights also embodies the idea of a certain kind of universality.

The commitment to universality should not ignore the conflict and injustices that inescapably exist in a polity, let alone in each soul. The tension between the general and the particular in law, politics, and philosophy coexist in a dialectical relationship. We are all part of humanity, but we also exist as individuals and members of groups in states replete with divisions and struggles. As stressed often in this book, however, conflict can be constructive, as well as destructive, in the absence of sufficient underlying consensus about fundamental principles that also unite us in a basic sense of community.[15]

In addition, the very term "university" begins with three letters that signify the oneness or wholeness of knowledge and truth. And many great universities educate students from around the world. The Latin term "*universitas*" means "the whole." The universality of knowledge must be paralleled by a sufficient sense of the universality of persons. It must be mediated by the differences and conflicts that differentiate us at the same time. Liberal education should sharpen our ability to deal constructively with conflict and difference while making us appreciate what we share as human beings.

Great literature aspires to perform this task while it portrays the tensions and conflicts of the human heart and society and points to universal themes. Similarly, liberal democracy attempts the precarious historical balancing act of creating political regimes of common citizenship and rights out of the particularities of individuals, groups, and what James Madison called "factions."[16] Free speech theory touts tolerance of conflict while promoting support for the speech rights that unite us in common citizenship.

To achieve this balancing act, liberal democratic regimes and higher education must avoid two pitfalls: (a) resorting to coerced conformity in order to solve or ameliorate the conflict problem—the "conformity of the graveyard" problem—and (b) letting our differences and conflicts define us in ways that undermine the universality that makes us a nation or an institution. Forms of identity politics and intersectionality that accentuate difference and attack attempts at forging conscientious connections undermine the common intellectual interest of the university and the polity. Citing E. D. Hirsch, Jonathan Haidt observed in a 2017 speech that "'The American experiment ... is a thoroughly artificial device designed to counterbalance the natural impulses of group suspicions and hatreds. . . . This vast, artificial, trans-tribal construct is what our Founders aimed to achieve.' Intersectionality aims for the exact opposite: an inflaming of tribal suspicions and hatreds in order to stimulate anger and activism in students and in order to recruit them as fighters for the political mission of the professor."[17]

In practical terms that echo its philosophical dimension, universalism means that the project of academic free speech must avoid being partisan at all costs. This obligation is so for both strategic and normative reasons, as I relate in the next chapter. To paraphrase late civil liberty champion Nat Hentoff, free speech must always be for "me *and* thee."[18]

Before moving on, we should consider one other intrinsic element of human nature that steps outside Kant's rationalistic perspective. The Framers of the Constitution aspired to create a governing order that fosters public virtue, and they hoped that virtuous individuals would attain positions of leadership—hard as that might be to believe in 2019. But they were also political and moral realists who knew that liberty itself and the building of an enduring order necessitated accepting unchangeable aspects of human nature while setting up a system that would provide remedies to the deleterious rudiments of its darker side.

As we will see later in this chapter, Mill's fallibility principle is a foundational consequentialist justification for freedom of speech and inquiry. Because no one is infallible, the pursuit of truth must protect dissent and the challenging of conventional conclusions. But a deeper interpretation of the fallibility principle presents a more deontological justification for individual freedom: because we are flawed by nature, a nontyrannical polity must not punish and persecute us for being flawed. It may punish us for our bad or evil deeds only in a legally principled manner. Compelling Utopia is an historically proven recipe for tyranny and totalitarianism.[19]

The due tolerance of human flaws is also woven into America's constitutional fabric. As Alexander Hamilton wrote in *Federalist No. 6*, "Is it not time to awake from the deceitful dream of a golden age and to adopt as a practical maxim for the direction of our political conduct that we as well as other inhabitants of this globe are yet remote from the happy empire of perfect wisdom and perfect virtue?"[20] One reason for the due tolerance of imperfect virtue and the like is the inevitable overkill that would ensue on the slippery slope of application. We would target virtue and liberty in the process. And problems of draftsmanship abound: at what point does an inclination or dreamy sentiment become a coherent "thought" or "belief"? What if an evil thought I have is balanced by a counter-thought? Which thought counts? But a deeper reason calls for our attention beyond the obvious practical concerns.

Beyond this point, as I have often acknowledged in this book, a dark side coexists inextricably with the light of reason in each breast, and this coexistence is good, bad, and mixed. In his famous paean to freedom of speech, *Areopagitica*, John Milton wrote that "Good and evil we know in the field of this world grow up together almost inseparably; and the knowledge of good is . . . involved and interwoven in the knowledge of evil." The good and free society fosters moral virtue and punishes evil conduct that is properly criminalized. However, it cannot punish evil, troubling thoughts, or dispositions that are independent of illegal conduct lest it ends up punishing people for simply being human while incidentally smothering intellectual freedom and creativity, which, as Milton understood, have transgressive aspects. (How to deal with evil thoughts and dispositions outside the criminal sanction is another important moral and practical question, but beyond our present purview.)

Punishing evil or bad thoughts amounts to thought control, which is the quintessential First Amendment sin and a hallmark of an authoritarian or totalitarian state. It is no accident that polities that coerce their vision of a new and perfect form of human nature end up erecting their own versions of gulags.

Such efforts also ineluctably stifle the inner sources of creative tension and rumination that are wellsprings of intellectual and artistic achievement. The pursuit of truth and art are often transgressive, riding forces in which good and evil cannot be cleanly separated. Want to extirpate *all* evil? Then you imperil the good and the creative as well. In commandeering fire for humankind, did not Prometheus commit a crime? Did not the biting of the apple in Eden bestow the gift—and curse—of knowledge? Goethe's Faust, the paradigmatic literary example of the paradoxes embodied in the pursuit of truth and knowledge, understood his controversial quest to have taken on "part of the power which [w]ould ever work evil, but engenders good." Nietzsche had a similar vision: "Be careful, lest in casting out your devil, you cast out the best that is in you."[21]

The *actus reus* ("guilty act") principle in the criminal law of liberal democracies exemplifies this logic: no crime exists in the absence of a voluntary act. In securing a conviction, the state must prove that the requisite mental state, or *mens rea*, was accompanied by a voluntary act that caused, or attempted to cause, the prohibited result. (Similarly, crimes of omission are generally not punishable except when a specific duty of care is necessarily assigned, as for a parent and a child, a captain and the passengers of a ship, and the like.) The *actus reus* principle is a partner of the legal standard that evidence of a defendant's character may not be entered into evidence in a criminal trial unless the defendant chooses to make it part of the case. One is legally culpable for what one does or attempts to do, not for what one is.[22]

As we saw earlier in this chapter and in Chapter 4, free speech cannot flourish unless it, like thoughts, is presumptively considered distinct from action. Necessary exceptions to this presumption exist in First Amendment law when speech is closely connected to action (e.g., criminal solicitation, blackmail, etc.), but they are the exception, not the rule. Accordingly, extending due tolerance toward the evil and dark aspects of human nature—while also working to foster virtue in a manner consistent with freedom—is an important responsibility of a free society. That tolerance is also the interesting underside of the principle of treating citizens as ends unto themselves.

SELF-GOVERNMENT AND THE CONSENT OF THE GOVERNED

The self-government function of free speech is something I have emphasized throughout this book, and it serves as the basis of Robert Post's discussion of core free speech doctrine presented in Chapter 3. Free speech is necessary both for us to govern ourselves *and* for us to behave as responsible citizens. In *Whitney*, Brandeis captures the different dimensions of the political function of free speech: the Framers "believed that freedom to think as you will and to speak as you think are means indispensable to the discovery and spread of political truth . . . that the greatest menace to freedom is an inert people, that public discussion is a political duty, and that this should be a fundamental principle of the American government."

Brandeis endorsed an active concept of democratic citizenship related to classic notions of republican virtue. He modeled his *Whitney* opinion on Thucydides's portrayal of Pericles's Funeral Oration in *The History of Peloponnesian Wars*, in which Pericles praised the unique way that Athens, contra Sparta, combined intellectual achievement with martial excellence, mind with courage.[23]

For Meiklejohn, free speech for We the People is a self-evident logical necessity stemming from the commands of political consent and self-government. In addition to presenting philosophical and practical reasons for this position, Meiklejohn refers to the existence of the Speech and Debate Clause of Article I, which states in part that for members of Congress, "for any Speech or Debate in either House, they shall not be questioned in any other Place." The purpose of the clause is to prevent members of Congress from being held legally liable for speeches they make pursuant to their political duties. According to Meiklejohn, if members of Congress enjoy such privilege, so should the ultimate governors of the republic, We the People, *a fortiori*.[24]

However often We the People get things wrong and are led astray—and recent empirical research raises questions about just how knowledgeable and thoughtful We the People have become—this fact does not justify surrendering our free speech rights to the state or other experts, as that would spell the end of democratic governance.[25]

The most principled response to intellectual irresponsibility is to educate the public to think in truth. The so-called "checking function" of free speech and press is an essential supplement to the checks and balances found elsewhere in the Constitution. This function is an off-shoot of the ultimate "who decides" issue.[26] In a properly democratic government, individuals decide.

A classic Supreme Court endorsement of the self-government theory is the 1964 decision *New York Times v. Sullivan*, in which Justice William Brennan—an heir to Holmes and Brandeis—used Meiklejohn's theory of self-government to justify the establishment of a new standard to be applied in libel cases involving political figures. Unique to the United States, the new doctrine protects citizens' libel of government officials so long as it is not made with actual malice, meaning either intentionally or with reckless disregard for the truth. Though libel even of government officials is not "in principle" protected by the First Amendment, the Court recognized the need to protect such libel short of actual malice for three reasons: (a) in the real world of political commentary, honest mistakes will be made, so "breathing space" must be allowed as a practical matter lest the spirit of political criticism be stifled; (b) criticism of the government is the central meaning of the First Amendment; and (c) the First Amendment is designed not only to tolerate but also to encourage the "profound national commitment to the principle that debate on public issues should be uninhibited, robust, and wide-open and that it may well include vehement, caustic, and sometimes unpleasantly sharp attacks on government and public officials."[27]

In addition to touting the benefits of constructive conflict, Sullivan's core principle is premised on Meiklejohn's theories of consent, self-government, and governmental accountability to We the People as the ultimate governors of the republic. When Meiklejohn heard about the decision shortly before his death, he called it "an occasion for dancing in the streets."[28]

The late legal philosopher Ronald Dworkin presented a justification for free speech that is related to the self-government theory, one that he termed *democratic consent*. In a democracy, being able to present your views about policy and politics is necessary in order for the polity to legitimately obligate you to obey the laws it passes. Why should individuals be obligated to obey the laws when they were not allowed to state their views regarding those laws? Accordingly, even despicable speakers have a right to state their views. "If we expect bigots to accept the verdict of the majority once the majority has spoken, then we must permit them to express their bigotry in the process whose verdict we ask them to respect."[29] Laws and society are always imperfect, so opposition to some laws is a universal condition. Accordingly, we may also envision the First Amendment as a kind of legally sanctioned disobedience, though in speech, not action.[30]

Let us now look at the more practical "consequentialist" justifications for free speech.

THE CONSEQUENTIALIST BENEFITS OF FREE SPEECH

The consequentialist justification for free speech has four dimensions: acknowledging the pursuit of truth; offering an opportunity to challenge the defense mechanisms that all individuals and political society erect and that thwart self-knowledge and the facing of injustices; providing a safety valve for harmful or dangerous groups to let off steam; and enhancing the intellectual project of considering the proper scope and limits of personal freedom, which is an important aspect of citizenship and liberal education. I begin with the pursuit of truth.

THE PURSUIT OF TRUTH AND PRAGMATISM

The pursuit of truth is the most common justification for freedom of speech based on its consequences. Grounding one's argument in the pursuit of truth can also be conceived as an ethical commitment, but it is generally considered a consequential good, in view of the usefulness of true information. History abundantly shows that there is a direct connection between a polity dedicated to protecting the pursuit of truth and respect for freedom and individual rights. To offer just one example, I ask that you consider the importance of truth to the fundamental right to a fair trial. On the practical side, Mill's arguments in *On Liberty* are the most cited support for the necessity of free speech because of the limits and fallibilities of all truth seekers. Mill provided examples of individuals whose truths ultimately prevailed long after they themselves had been persecuted, including the famous examples of Socrates and Christ, who both died for their truths. Mill also stressed that even the truth that we rightfully consider beyond dispute needs to be challenged, lest our commitment and lively understanding of it languish. Mill understood that knowledge exists *in persons*, who have emotions and interests that must be invested in the process of finding and sustaining the truth.[31]

In *Kindly Inquisitors*, Jonathan Rauch presents an extension of Mill's position that underscores the link between free speech and inquiry and the foundations of liberal democracy. He points out that liberal democratic orders consist of three fundamental and interdependent systems of freedom and authority: (a) the free elections for choosing political leaders, (b) the free market for determining economic allocations and arrangements, and (c) the system of freedom of free inquiry—which encompasses what he calls "the liberal model of science"—for determining truth. The three systems reinforce each other.[32]

Exposing the incompleteness or fallacy of existing consensus is a relentless process, with breakthroughs often happening just when consensus seems confirmed. For one example among countless others, in the summer of 2018, the Fermi National Accelerator Lab in Illinois announced that it may have found a new sterile type of neutrino. If so, according to informed sources, this finding could "finally break the Standard Model of particle physics that has reigned since the 1970s. It would also demand 'a new standard model of cosmology.'"[33]

Compared with the underlying data of the natural sciences, the empirics of the social sciences and humanities are even more prone to challenge for a simple reason: human beings do not just behave by responding in a mechanical way to stimuli. Our freedom is obviously constrained by the naturalistic and deterministic forces in us and in the world, including DNA. However, we possess choices and have creative powers that cannot be reduced to reliable deterministic models. We have minds, and we *act*. Human action can be unpredictable, not only because of the vast complexity of human motivation and social relations—a matter of *quantitative* uncertainty—but also because of human freedom. Human action can bring something *qualitatively* new and unexpected into the world.[34]

The ongoing philosophical and scientific debate about the nature of consciousness is most interesting and relevant to such themes in this book, as is the nature of the self, personal and cultural growth, free will and responsibility, interplay between emotion and reason, and tension between lighter and darker forces or aspects of the self.

Debate rages about how to define and locate the origin and place of consciousness in the self and in evolution and about how consciousness is related to classic tensions such as the relationship between mind and body, mind and brain, materialistic and mental reality, and free will and determinism. Michael S. Gazzaniga, a leading neuroscientist who is also schooled in philosophy of mind, wrote in 2018 that "[i]n recent years the topic of consciousness has become red-hot once again. At the same time, despite the modern avalanche of new data, there are few, if any, generally accepted proposals on how the brain builds a mind and, with it, conscious experience." As a neuroscientist, Gazzaniga sides with a naturalistic explanation of consciousness that he embeds in a broadened conception of instinct.[35]

I used to discuss this debate in my classes on free speech and criminal law and justice because of its implications for the assumption of free will and responsibility upon which those enterprises rest. New neuroscience evidence indicates that relevant synapses in the brain fire *before* one becomes conscious of the choice to commit an act, thereby implying a physical cause of human action prior to the mental cause.[36] The criminal law manages to sidestep this dilemma by the way it defines the *mens rea* ("guilty mind") requirement for culpability: the individual must have only the *capacity* to form an intent to act, which is a different question from whether he or she has done so with free will. But the free will question nonetheless still refuses to go away, and the debate over consciousness has yet to be resolved, if it ever can be.

Some philosophers maintain that phenomena such as reason and political freedom have an ontological status that cannot be fully reduced to forces such as emotion, instinct, or natural cause and effect. As physical beings we are affected and determined by naturalistic forces all the time. Beyond this truism, some of the most important emotional and spiritual things in life seem beyond the reach of rational free will, such as the people with whom we fall in love or the subjects that we love or that grab our interest.

And how should we think of freedom and normative obligations? Meiklejohn's theory of free speech stressed the difference between a purely naturalistic scientific model of freedom and a more normative one. The rise and status of natural science and the method of scientific inquiry are integral elements of the history, practice, and theory of liberal democracy.[37] However, in thinking about human and political freedom, we need to use categories that are different in kind from the mechanical and naturalistic forces that compose the data of physical science. We must have recourse to normative and political philosophy. "[W]e need to be not more scientific, but less scientific, not more quantitative, but other than quantitative. We must create and use methods of inquiry, methods of belief which are suitable to the study of men as self-governing persons but not suitable to the study of forces or of machines." Some leading contemporary philosophers have also postulated that mental phenomena such as the ascertainment of truth, the commitment of normative obligation, and the sense of selfhood in relation to others cannot be fully understood by the logic or language of naturalistic science.[38]

In Chapter 5, I mentioned some examples that Jon A. Shields and Joshua Dunn present in *Passing on the Right* about how liberal scholarship has been refined and enriched by conservative challenges, but the arrow naturally also points in the other direction. One such example is how the acknowledgment and understanding of domestic violence was brought to our attention in more telling ways by feminist scholarship. Another is the political power generated by the Second Wave of feminism that burst onto the scene out of the civil rights movement.[39]

Power can be abused, but it can be necessary—not only to secure rights but also to give uncomfortable or previously ignored truths a place at the table. That tension is an aspect of the paradox of power in a constitutional regime. Second Wave feminism was transgressive to conventional thinking in many respects, including that of liberal males in the student and civil rights movements of the 1960s. Those men initially resisted expanding the tent of equal rights to include women in the ways that women began demanding.[40] We have gained a greater understanding of the injustices of domestic violence and racial discrimination through challenges to previous status quo thinking. A similar point applies to the gay rights movement, as Jonathan Rauch has affirmed.

Let me conclude this section with an observation for which Churchill is famously known, though his authorship is disputed: "You can always count on Americans to do the right thing—after they've tried everything else." Whether Churchill said it or not, the statement points to an enduring justification for free speech and its relation to the American spirit: we have earned international leadership in so many areas because we have not been afraid to fail and because we have left the door open to change, challenge, and intellectual rebellion. The willingness to take intellectual risk parallels the willingness to take entrepreneurial and personal risk and to move beyond the sinecures of safe spaces. We forsake this spirit at our peril.

CHALLENGING DEFENSE MECHANISMS OF THE SELF AND SOCIETY

An important and dynamic offshoot of the truth consequence of free speech is the way in which this freedom can be used to challenge us to confront and wrestle with personal and social problems. Starting with the individual, psychiatry teaches us that defense mechanisms make up key aspects of the personality; those defenses can mask disorders or problems and can inhibit the kind of self-understanding that is necessary for mental health and a productive life.

One function of therapy is to help us understand ourselves and our tensions more fully in order to gain more autonomy. If fathoming both tensions and opposing forces is important to the understanding of the external world and to the making of what John Gaddis calls strategy, a similar logic pertains to self-knowledge and maturation. One thing Freud was right about was how we often find security and even pleasure in our disorders (what he called "neuroses"), which makes them hard to shake. Beyond dealing with disorders, introspection is an important vehicle of understanding and discovery. Arendt construed introspection as a conversation with oneself. The self is a mystery, so probing the self can be viewed as a kind of adventure into the unknown within—unless the project slides into counterproductive self-indulgence or obsession. One way to prevent that slide may lie in the self's ability to draw on and assimilate many different external sources of information. In that way, the freedom of expression may even lead to better mental health.

Free speech may play a role in exposing social dysfunction. Perfect social or political justice exists only in the imagination of utopians and totalitarians. In the real world that we know, every social order has built-in tensions and aspects of injustice because of the omnipresence of self-interest and the drive for power. In addition, the consequences of even virtuous, selfless acts can be detrimental in unanticipated ways in a tragic world.[41]

In *Moral Man and Immoral Society*, theologian and moral realist Reinhold Niebuhr analyzed the ways in which social orders embed different forms of injustice regardless of the virtues of the individuals who compose those social orders.[42] Accordingly, one function of free speech is to challenge injustices. And, as mentioned before, speakers have a right to take their challenges directly to where the problem lies rather than being relegated to free speech zones or Hyde Parks. This ability to locate one's speech may sometimes face legally sanctioned limits regarding time, place, and manner, but the symbolic importance of locating one's speech means that those limits ought to be few. An exemplar of this use of free speech is Martin Luther King Jr. and other civil rights demonstrators who took their messages to the source of social and political injustice: state houses, jails, discriminatory businesses, and racist neighborhoods.

SAFETY VALVE

The safety valve theory of free speech is relevant here. This consequentialist theory is an empirical offshoot of both the self-government and the consent justifications for free speech. The idea is that letting potentially subversive groups state their views makes them less likely to resort to actual subversion or violence, either for the reasons to which Dworkin alluded earlier or because they will be sufficiently satisfied to simply let off steam—hence the term "safety valve."

Brandeis pointed to this justification in *Whitney* when he said, "[T]he path of safety lies in the opportunity to discuss freely supposed grievances and proposed remedies, and that the fitting remedy for evil counsels is good ones."[43] No one to my knowledge has conducted a serious empirical inquiry into the validity of the safety valve claim, but it has at least initial plausibility. In a related vein, I often think of the irony of the Nazi Party in the Skokie case as it proclaimed its constitutional entitlement to equal First Amendment rights in the same breath with which its members declared their intent to deprive Jews, blacks, homosexuals, Catholics, and others of their rights. The Nazi Party's mere affirmation of its own rights exposed the hypocrisy lying in its members' hearts.

The safety valve theory is relevant to campus life. First, it is possible that students have resorted to hateful clandestine messages because they feel that their voices have been suppressed or disrespectfully discouraged. Second, there is strong circumstantial evidence that student groups have resorted to inviting inappropriately provocative speakers simply to stick it to what they consider an intellectually intolerant campus.

Finally, by going public, dangerous groups expose themselves in ways that can facilitate the polity to keep a more watchful and knowledgeable eye on them—the "know thy enemy" point discussed in Chapter 3. This benefit coexists with the potential harm of such groups gaining influence through speech, which then necessitates concerted and conscientious counter-speech and other measures. As Brandeis wrote, the practice of free speech obligates the citizenry to be active, not inert.

DISCUSSION OF LIMITS AND LIBERAL EDUCATION

Given the constant sifting and winnowing that is endemic to the pursuit of truth and knowledge, no university worth its salt would allow the process to be limited by political or other non-intellectual criteria. Where it is more responsible to talk about limits is in the *application* of certain findings. (Enforcing limits in practice raises further questions, of course.) Atomic research goes on, but we don't let individuals own their own bombs. Similarly, knowledge about cloning should be allowed to proceed, but it is appropriate to consider ethical limits to its applications because of the moral implications of its use, especially on humans.

More than a decade ago, ethicist Leon Kass and other thinkers wrote influential works about the ethical dangers of taking cloning into the human realm. More recently, Jennifer Doudna, an award-winning University of California–Berkeley pioneer in the discovery of the revolutionary CRISPR-Cas9 gene-editing tool, has written a book in which she celebrates this discovery. The tool holds unprecedented promise for curing diseases through DNA engineering. However, after the pages that portray the excitement of the tortuous path that led to the scientific breakthrough, she devotes many other pages to warning us about the potential moral dangers of using the tool to create a new super race that genetically outclasses the rest of us.

Doudna recently admitted to having a nightmare about her work in which she encounters Hitler, the master eugenicist.[44] Her analysis exemplifies another dimension of the tension between a purely natural science model of thinking and an ethical versus philosophical model. Given a genuinely new question with obvious ethical dimensions and widespread disagreement about how that question should be answered, the value of free inquiry and free expression becomes obvious.

Human nature and community are complex phenomena consisting of many tensions and contradictions; being cognizant of the downsides of intellectual freedom should accompany our dedication to it.[45] Social theorists such as Philip Rieff and Roger Shattuck have written about how certain taboos regarding what we should study or do are part of the human story, beginning with the Book of Genesis. Thus, it is natural to have qualms about pushing the pursuit of truth without any concern for ethical limits. Great literature such as Goethe's *Faust* and Mary Shelley's *Frankenstein* warn us of treading into certain forbidden domains without ethical and philosophical qualms or guidance.

Rieff portrays absolute and unreflective freedom of the mind as leading to what he calls the "deathworks" because of the darkness in the human soul that can be encouraged or unleashed by a lack of appropriate restraints. Human nature is not all benign. (Rieff was a scholar of Freud, whose work indicated that total freedom empowers not just good angels, but also demons. Freud also taught that repression of the instincts was necessary at the same it made us unhappy—hence his valid claim to being a tragedian.)

In *Why Liberalism Failed*, political theorist Patrick Deneen claims that liberalism has betrayed a proper sense of community by the way it has allegedly eviscerated the collective sense of limits. Those positions challenge the strong defense of intellectual freedom that animates this book, but the honest pursuit of truth should take heed of the downside of such freedom, which is itself an aspect of truth. A free speech advocate might respond as follows. It is one thing to *think the unthinkable* but another thing to *do the unthinkable*. (The subtitle to Doudna and Sternberg's recent book on CRISPR-Cas9 captures this tension: *Gene Editing and the Unthinkable Power of Controlling Evolution*.) Being able to think the unthinkable may well save us from many instances in which, without thinking, we would do the unthinkable.

Struggling with the tension between freedom and limits is an important aspect of liberal education and constitutional citizenship. Learning the First Amendment, for example, requires knowing not only why strong protections for free speech are part of the DNA of constitutional freedom, but also why well-ordered society requires proper limits to free expression, as well as self-discipline in the exercise of freedom. (Recall the discussion of the reciprocal rights and duties attendant upon the system of free speech in Chapter 3.)

Deliberating about the tension between free speech and its limits contributes to several intellectual and ethical benefits. They include learning how to make arguments on both sides of the ledger; thinking more deeply about the relationships among freedom, self-control, social order, and its limits; deciding who should make the critical decisions about how to draw the balance; and determining how best to enact good policy in this domain. This process is part of intellectual responsibility.

Students learn that both speech and censorship can be harmful. Thus in many respects, free speech adjudication is a matter of judicial and societal risk assessment: when do harm and risk rise to the level of justifying censorship? The modern doctrine of speech is grounded on the operating principle that we are willing to take significant risks in order to protect the good of intellectual freedom. Hence the court requires strict scrutiny in most free speech cases. It has placed limits on the exceptions to free speech, such as illegal incitement, true threats, and extreme fighting words, but legitimate lines do properly exist.

And even though the court has expanded First Amendment protection of commercial speech (advertising) in recent decades, it still rightly upholds stricter regulation, especially for false advertising. False advertising is similar to libel in that both can cause very direct harm and can seriously compromise or distort the honest pursuit of truth. What the court does protect strongly in the realm of commercial speech is that truthful information be provided to consumers, which can assist them in making informed choices.[46] Thinking about how to draw lines enhances the critical judgment that is a mark of thoughtful citizenship.[47]

I used to present two statements by George Kennan early in my First Amendment course. First is the quotation I will present later in this chapter that addresses McCarthyism's harmful effect on the American state of mind. The second is from a controversial book that features Kennan's engaging conversation with student activists back in the late 1960s. In the conversation, he chided the students' commitment to unconditional freedom. Kennan was one of America's leading diplomats and foreign policy thinkers of the 20th century. Some of my students who were most committed to free speech as a principle and practice told me that this comment was one of the most memorable statements they encountered in the course. Kennan's advocacy of self-discipline here echoes Alexander Meiklejohn's teaching that "Political freedom does not mean freedom from control. It means self-control." Here is an excerpt of the statement I read to them:

> There is not, and cannot be, such a thing as total freedom. Freedom, for this reason, is definable only in terms of the obligations and restraints and sacrifices it accepts . . . and that means commitment, duty, self-restraint.

> Every great artist has known this. Every great philosopher has recognized it. . . . Tell me what framework of discipline you are prepared to accept, and I will attempt to tell you what freedom might mean for you. . . . I will tell you, as Dostoevsky told his readers, that you are destined to become the most unfree of men . . . for freedom . . . grows only with struggle, and self-discipline, and faith.[48]

As we have seen throughout this book, one aspect of this struggle and faith is the duty to protect freedom of speech itself.

I treat the character justification separately as an *ethical* aspect of free speech because it speaks to personal virtue, which is distinct from inherent rights and communal consequences, though it affects both. I consider it under two related rubrics: democratic character and courage.

COURAGE, FEAR, AND OVERCOMING

The *courage* to face challenging and upsetting ideas plays a central role in free speech jurisprudence. In *Whitney*, Brandeis touted courage as fundamental to the constitutional republic:

> Those who won our independence by revolution were not cowards. They did not fear political change. They did not exalt order at the cost of liberty. To courageous, self-reliant men, with confidence in the power of free and fearless reasoning applied through the processes of popular government, no danger flowing from speech can be deemed clear and present unless the incidence of the evil apprehended is so imminent that it may befall before there is opportunity for full discussion.

Courage has both a personal and a civic dimension: it is an anchor for our other virtues, and it is necessary to protect our freedoms from our enemies by standing up for freedom when it is verbally or physically attacked. In her praise of the ancient Greek concept of politics, Hannah Arendt wrote that courage "became the political virtue, *par excellence*."[49] To the extent that courage is now a neglected or marginalized virtue in higher education and its administrative apparatuses, we are letting our young people down, as well as our republic.

As discussed in Chapter 5, First Amendment theory is also designed to teach us how to deal with *fear*. It distinguishes rationally based fear from irrationally based fear. One of the cardinal norms of First Amendment jurisprudence is requiring the state to prove that an actual harm exists in a meaningful fashion before restriction of speech may be countenanced. Undifferentiated fear of disorder is an insufficient basis.[50] Emotion must yield to reason. Undifferentiated fear commits two wrongs: (a) it freezes and diminishes the self, thereby undermining its other virtues; and (b) it has engendered significant injustices, some of which we have witnessed on campuses across the United States today in programs designed to encourage anonymous reporting and espying the discrimination and threats that allegedly hide behind too many bushes.

In *Dennis v. United States* (1951), the leading Communist Party case decided during the McCarthy era, Justice Hugo Black wrote similar words in the conclusion of his dissent, in which he disagreed with the court's affirming the convictions of leading members of the Communist Party U.S.A.: "Public opinion being what it now is, few will protest the conviction of these Communist petitioners. There is hope, however, that, in calmer times, when present pressures, passions, and fears subside, this or some later Court will restore the First Amendment liberties to the high preferred place where they belong in a free society."[51]

In teaching free speech jurisprudence, however, I have learned that it is wise not to simply denounce decisions such as *Dennis*. Communism *did* pose dangers, as the release of evidence from Soviet archives in the 1990s proves beyond all reasonable doubt. It is always easier to look back and see that one has overreacted, but much more difficult to listen to reason under the pressures of real time. In class, I always asked students to place themselves in the shoes of the decisionmakers and to contemplate how they might react in the face of the unknown future. They should also think about how learning First Amendment jurisprudence might help prepare them to think more clearly during future crises.

The conception of courage has evolved over historical time, though its core qualities seem universal.[52] In his *Nicomachean Ethics*, Aristotle treated courage and fear in a manner consistent with his more general philosophy of the golden mean. Learning to fear the right things—rational fear—is part of ethical and practical maturation. One should fear real dangers and things such as the loss of one's reputation. But irrational fear, or fearing the wrong things, undermines ethical integrity.

In a similar vein, Aristotle taught that courage lies at the mean between the extremes of rash boldness (*tharsos*), incognizant of real dangers—and of being a coward (*deilos*). Courage is not being afraid to act in the face of fear *for the right reasons*. For example, a soldier facing death, a fearful thing, is courageous because defense of the *polis* is among the highest duties. Courage is perhaps the highest virtue because it entails acting rightly for worthy ends in the face of pressure and fear.[53]

Core First Amendment doctrine regarding fear and reason parallels the criminal law doctrine of self-defense in illuminating ways. The 1969 *Brandenburg* test dealing with the central question of how the law should treat advocacy of unlawful action contains three prongs: (a) the speech must be a direct incitement (b) to imminent unlawful action (c) that is likely to occur. Only speech closely connected to actual illegal conduct is subject to punishment.[54] The state must prove all three *Brandenburg* prongs in order to punish the speaker.

The criminal law of self-defense is remarkably similar: first, one may use deadly force against another person(s) only if one "*reasonably believes* that the person(s) confronts one with *imminent* death or serious bodily harm." [Emphasis added.]

Second, the law of self-defense, like law in general, requires assuming the perspective of the reasonable person: it demands the exercise of reason in the face of danger, which is the paradigmatic situation in which fear takes over. The doctrine is demanding and requires the exercise of reason even when situations of danger ignite the primitive impulse of fear. Physiologically, fear is housed in the primitive limbic system of the brain, not the frontal cortex, which is the home of reason and foresight.[55] So self-defense doctrine is a demanding standard: how many of us are able to be governed by reason when our limbic system is ignited? But the law has no choice here; the alternative is to authorize the use of deadly force when it is not necessary, which would endanger innocent people and society at large. Sometimes the law is properly demanding of citizens to preserve order and to protect others, and the law of self-defense is an outstanding example of this obligation. Meiklejohn and Kennan are right: self-control is essential to political freedom and the rights of others. As the house of reason, the university should contribute to the education of citizens in this respect as well.

Third, the doctrine of self-defense is premised on the larger legal doctrine of *necessity*: resort to deadly force can be justified only when it is truly necessary to do so, and imminent harm is the most reliable indicator of such necessity. The imminence standard of self-defense serves to keep the self-defense claim *honest*. If the apprehension of danger is reasonably perceived as necessary and imminent, the defender's options are very limited, making the claim of self-defense intrinsically or presumptively credible. Indeed, almost all states require the prosecution to prove the absence of imminence beyond a reasonable doubt once sufficient evidence is produced to make the self-defense claim part of the case. (Retreat is another option that some laws of self-defense require, but only if retreat does not further endanger the retreater.)

If, however, deadly force is deployed when the harm is *not* imminent, then other motives for its deployment enter the picture as possibilities, such as revenge or opportunity.[56] The same logic applies to free speech doctrine: if the state censors speech when the harm is not imminent, as *Brandenburg* requires, the specter of improper motives enters the scene, such as the state's disfavoring the message in violation of the cardinal anti-viewpoint discrimination doctrine or such as improper paternalism in the form of an undifferentiated fear that the evil counsels will be acted upon.

But how can we productively strive to mitigate the natural force of fear in us—if not overcome it? One method that is consistent with free speech theory is to face the problem and to learn how to give reason its due. Let me briefly explore some ideas relating to this position. One model to consider is Bruno Bettelheim's in his book, *The Uses of Enchantment*, which is winner of two prestigious book awards. Bettelheim has something to teach us about overcoming adversity and trauma.[57] His significant experiences and intellectual work—surviving a concentration camp under Hitler, working extensively with children, and understanding different intellectual traditions—made him a credible source on many human problems.

The basic theme of *Uses of Enchantment* is that children have throughout history used their reading and hearing of scary fairy tales to three constructive ends: recognizing in the stories the fears and dark feelings that naturally lie in their own breasts, wrestling with those inner fears and desires in order to constructively overcome them, and using the stories to develop the imagination, which is a gift in this life.

I have spent much space in this chapter discussing the rationalistic benefits that come from the sifting and winnowing of ideas. But we must not undervalue the singular importance of imagination, either. Imagination is related to artistic and literary inquiries into life, and even rational and scientific advances are often fueled by imagination's stretching the bounds of accepted thinking and paradigms. In his recent book about Leonardo, for example, Walter Isaacson celebrates the ways in which Leonardo's work ingeniously synthesized imagination and science.[58] And many works have portrayed the role of imagination in furthering breakthroughs in the most serious of scientific endeavors.

If the young are sheltered from being thus exposed in this or other ways, as many are today, they can end up lacking critical tools for dealing with their inner fears and dark impulses; their imaginations will have had less nourishment. In Jung's terms, they will lack the self-knowledge and nourishment that can come from dealing with the shadow within.[59]

In a section titled "Fairy Tales and the Existential Predicament," Bettelheim observes that by reading dark fairy tales "a child fits unconscious content into conscious fantasies, which then enable him to deal with that content, . . . The dominant culture wishes to pretend, particularly, where children are concerned, that the dark side of man does not exist, and that professes a belief in optimistic meliorism. . . . Psychoanalysis was created to accept the problematic nature of life without being defeated by it, or giving in to escapism. . . . 'Safe' stories mention neither death nor aging, the limits to our existence, nor the wish for eternal life. The fairy tale, by contrast, confronts the child squarely with the basic human predicaments."[60]

Cognitive-behavioral therapy (CBT) has largely replaced psychoanalysis as an accepted model of therapy, but its teachings related to dealing with fears and anxiety are similar in interesting ways. Models of CBT teach that a sufferer should face the problem while also developing constructive cognitive and behavioral strategies that point the way out. Clinging to the problem as part of one's very identity or refusing to confront it—for example, always expecting bad things by negative fortune telling, "castastrophizing," and similar psychological acts—only perpetuates the negative mental traits and the sense of victimization. Yet in their *Atlantic* article on trigger warnings, microaggression policies, and related matters, Jonathan Haidt and Greg Lukianoff present examples of college policies that do precisely what CBT counsels against.[61] In addition, a recent controlled study by Harvard researchers about the effect of trigger warnings on two groups of readers—one whose readings were accompanied by triggers, the other whose readings were not—show that those who read after being given triggers registered increases in anxiety when reading. Though not large, the differences are meaningful. The empirical findings regarding trigger warnings are still a work in progress, but this and other findings support a heightened level of concern.[62]

CBT and other tested theories support an inspiring claim: that productive human striving and a sense of accomplishment can be found in *overcoming* problems and setbacks. As in Kennan's observation, we may say not only that internal and external struggles are facts attending the exercise of freedom, but also that they are often part of what makes overcoming so meaningful and distinctive. Indeed, becoming a mature and successful adult requires (a) struggling with the conflicts and tensions that exist in the world and in oneself and (b) integrating them as much as is feasible in the self. This process means making conscious much of what has been unconscious or repressed.[63]

Such struggles can deepen one's understanding of the human condition and the plights of others, as Joshua Wolf Shenk illustrates convincingly in his book titled *Lincoln's Melancholy: How Depression Challenged a President and Fueled His Greatness.*[64] I have had students who succeeded despite limitations such as dyslexia, chaotic backgrounds, and emotional struggles and who took special pride in their perseverance. Taking this point seriously does not justify victimization or indifference to human suffering, but it does counsel us that challenging students and expecting them to strive in the face of obstacles can be beneficial.

CHUTZPAH, DUE DOUBT, AND DEMOCRATIC CHARACTER

The other virtue ethical aspect of free speech theory involves chutzpah, which in turn involves the paradox of *assertion and due doubt*. As we have seen, developing new truths and challenging established truths and convictions can take courage and willfulness. (Recall Madison on checks and balances: "[A]mbition must be made to counteract ambition.") Self-assertion, self-confidence, and intellectual ambition are part of mental health and the pursuit of truth, as is self-reliance, which is a classic American character trait that is under unfair attack today.

In *On Liberty*, Mill praised those who possess the courage, wherewithal, stubbornness, and even obsession to push their truths to their ultimate depths and into the world. I once read that in challenging the Catholic Church's heliocentric view of the universe, Copernicus was filled with a powerful yet dreadful sense of challenging God—chutzpah or transgression of the highest order. We want courageous, self-reliant citizens who stand up for themselves and their beliefs rather than doubtful souls who wallow in fear and destructive guilt. The undue spread of castrating guilt is detrimental to the health and prospect of liberal democracy.[65]

But Mill is also the most famous advocate of the fallibility principle, which calls for due modesty and doubt about truth. So what gives here? One solution to this puzzle of assertion and doubt is to distinguish the process of truth determination—the marketplace of ideas or whatever we want to call it—from the individuals and groups who present their truths in it. Let participants be assertive as much as they desire, so long as the rest of us evaluators more objectively sift and winnow what is presented. This process is similar to two attorneys fighting it out in court: let the two sides assert their evidence and arguments while the neutral jury considers the evidence under the guidance of the judge. The real problem arises when we jurors ourselves are taken over by dogmatism or ignorance. Absent that, as Jonathan Rauch has declared, "An enlightened, and efficient, intellectual regime lets a million prejudices bloom, including hateful ones."[66]

Another solution is individuals learning how to negotiate this tension within themselves. This solution means balancing the self-confidence and assertion that are the marks of a healthy, self-reliant character with the due doubt that signifies self-control, respect for others, and the ability of citizens with different beliefs to live together in freedom. It is the capacity to harbor this tension that I call "democratic character." This tension courses its way through First Amendment jurisprudence, but its most illustrative expression in First Amendment law is Justice Oliver

Wendell Holmes Jr.'s famous 1919 dissent in *Abrams v. United States*, in which he presented the first official legal and philosophical doctrine underlying the modern doctrine of speech.

In addition to providing the first Supreme Court version of the incitement test that ultimately found its way into majority status in *Brandenburg* 50 years later, Holmes introduced the famous marketplace of ideas metaphor, which combines elements of epistemic skepticism, psychological insight, due doubt, appropriate distrust of government, and an image of character conducive to constitutional democracy. It is noteworthy that in writing this lonely dissent, Holmes had changed his own mind regarding the scope of free speech that he had staked out just a few months previously when he had authored the famous decisions upholding the convictions of leading critics of World War I on grounds highly deferential to the government. His dissent thus encapsulates aspects of free speech theory, as well as autobiography and the existential aspects of justice.

Holmes's switch highlights some key themes of this book: how strongly held beliefs and truths can be wrong and properly reconsidered, how dissenting positions can come to be widely accepted truths, and how the courage to dissent is an important part of constitutional citizenship. Holmes's statement merits lengthy quotation:

> Persecution for the expression of opinions seems to me perfectly logical. If you have no doubt of your premises or your power, and want a certain result with all your heart, you naturally express your wishes in law, and sweep away all opposition. . . . But when men have realized that time has upset many fighting faiths, they may come to believe even more than they believe the very foundations of their own conduct that the ultimate good desired is better reached by free trade in ideas—that the best test of truth is the power of the thought to get itself accepted in the competition of the market, and that truth is the only ground upon which their wishes safely can be carried out. That, at any rate, is the theory of our Constitution. It is an experiment, as all life is an experiment. . . . [W]e should be eternally vigilant against attempts to check the expression of opinions that we loathe and believe to be fraught with death, unless they so imminently threaten immediate interference with the lawful and pressing purposes of the law that an immediate check is required to save the country.[67]

Meiklejohn disapproved of Holmes's concept of the marketplace and argued that it improperly reduced the political significance of free speech to economic transactions. But some aspects of the dissent are highly relevant to the First Amendment's effects on citizenship and character. Let me simply list them:

- How we acknowledge the fallibility or incompleteness of human knowledge. The pursuit of truth is never ending.

- How implying that the question of "who decides" is central to First Amendment theory. The best interpretation of the "marketplace" model is that it boils down to a practical question: if not people in the market, then just who else should we trust to decide public truth? Perhaps Meiklejohn would have been happier had Holmes used the term "public forum" rather than "marketplace."

- How we should establish an appreciation of the fact that our professed truths and beliefs are often tied to our emotions and passions, our "fighting faiths"—an understanding that echoes the positions of Hume, Haidt, and others discussed in Chapter 2 earlier. And of how a sense of justice unmoored from due doubt and respect for rights can lead us to fall into uncontrolled or unreflective moral anger that undermines justice and rule of law. (See Chapter 5.)

- How democratic freedom entails accepting the risk of letting people speak their minds and of not letting illegitimate fears take over. The "theory of our Constitution" is "an experiment," as Holmes wrote.

- How democratic character requires the ability to balance doubt and conviction. In Chapter 2, I discussed how a key mission of higher education is to sublimate passion and emotion into more reasoned thinking. This point is related to the virtue of due doubt because due doubt is based on self-restraint and on sublimating the passion that animates self-interest and self-righteousness. Holmes's statement in *Abrams* is explicitly premised upon this process, which hopes to turn fighting faiths into reasoned faiths.[68]

In *The Tolerant Society*, First Amendment scholar (and now president of Columbia University) Lee C. Bollinger based his defense of the constitutional protection of hate speech and what Holmes called the "freedom for the thought we hate" on the way in which tolerance of the free speech rights of such speakers—not of the speeches' content—requires us to control our emotions. Coexistence in a liberal democracy requires due tolerance of things we do not like. Bollinger refers to the kind of intellectual virtue and emotional control we demand of *jurors*, who are duty bound to think objectively and fairly about the facts and the culpability of defendants regardless of the jurors' strong feelings about the crime or the defendant. Reason must control the jerking knee.[69]

Tocqueville and others have conceived of the jury as a laboratory for democratic citizenship. First, the jury's primary duty is to think objectively and fairly.[70] The duty of the jury is also directly analogous to the mission of the university, which is likewise to seek the truth through standards of reason. Like the university, the jury is guided by standards of evidence that are designed to limit prejudice and passion. The jury duly considers the cases presented by both sides. In addition, the jury must strive to exercise *good judgment*.

Determining legal culpability is not a mechanical process, especially in the small percentage of cases that end up going to trial. One must first ascertain often incomplete and conflicting facts and then must apply legal standards of culpability and proof to those facts. This exercise often requires making difficult assessments and discerning judgments in the face of some level of uncertainty—even the highest standard of "beyond a reasonable doubt" is less than "certainty." Except in clear-cut cases, such judgment often requires being able to live with the possibility that one might be wrong, which can be an existential burden to bear. Developing the mental and emotional skills to pull this responsibility off makes for more virtuous citizens. Such skills are related to our discussion in Chapter 5 of John Gaddis's take on the importance of considering pluralism and tensions in the making of sound policy.[71]

In his *Memoirs*, George F. Kennan presented a perspective on McCarthyism in the late 1940s and the 1950s that pointed to both strategic and ethical aspects in a manner that directly speaks to the importance of intellectual freedom. Kennan acknowledged that Soviet communism did indeed infiltrate and pose a danger to the United States at the same time that he warned us of losing our objectivity and presence of mind over this danger. A free society must face such external danger with commitment, but in a manner that does not forsake reason and the quality of mind that make us what we are. His words have clear relevance to higher education today. We must avoid

> . . . a danger that something may occur in our own minds and souls which will make us no longer be like the persons by whose efforts this republic was founded and held together, but rather like the representatives of that very power we are trying to combat: intolerant, secretive, suspicious, cruel, and terrified of internal dissent. . . .

> America, after all, was not just territory and people; it was something in our minds that caused us to believe in certain things and to behave in certain ways. It is what distinguished us from others. If that went, there would be no America left to defend. . . .[72]

CONCLUSION

This chapter has presented different justifications for freedom of thought and speech that reveal the many ways in which this freedom is indeed what Justice Benjamin Cardozo called "the matrix, the indispensable condition, of nearly every other form of freedom."[73] The justifications I presented signify the many ways in which the first freedom has worked and woven itself into so many domains of our constitutional republic, thereby making it a fundamental element of American character.

The question then arises: Okay, it matters. But what has been done or can be done to back this acknowledgment and commitment up with action? I will address this practical question in the next chapter.

CHAPTER 8
CAMPUS MOBILIZATION AND ADMINISTRATIVE REFORM

The freedom of mind which befits the members of a self-governing society is not a given and fixed part of human nature. It can be increased and established by learning, by teaching, by the unhindered flow of accurate information, by giving men health and vigor and security, by bringing them together in activities of communication and mutual understanding.
—*Alexander Meiklejohn,* Free Speech and Its Relation to Self-Government

In this chapter, I address the practical and normative question of remedies for the challenges to academic free speech. It reflects a theme that has run throughout the book: the significance of combining knowledge of what is at stake with the commitment and power to actualize this knowledge in the real world—a pact between education and strategy. The picture I offer is meant to be only illustrative and instructive rather than exhaustive. A full treatment of the political, policy, and legal aspects of remedies would require writing a separate book.

LOCAL VERSUS EXTERNAL ACTION

My first focus is on how activist groups inside and outside campus can generate support either to prevent or rescind speech-inhibiting policies and actions or to construct speech-friendly policy and actions. I then look at administrative leadership and institutionally supported efforts that are more emblematic of top-down efforts. In actual practice, top-down and bottom-up actions often go hand in hand, but it makes sense for purposes of analysis to treat them separately.

LOCAL PREFERENCE

My preference is for remedial action within the institution itself, though seeking outside help can be a constructive option if necessary and if conscientiously deployed. Speech-friendly policies are much more effective and morally justified when they are the product of a process that includes persuasion, consent, and an opportunity to be heard—as the discussion of Kant and Ronald Dworkin noted in Chapter 7. Persuasion treats others as moral ends, not just means to an end. But internal remedial action also has a practical aspect that reflects Alexander Hamilton's observation in *Federalist No. 84* that rights are more enduring if supported by "the general spirit of the people and of the government." It is in this spirit that "we must seek for the only solid basis of all our rights."[1] Research has shown that court rulings about major social and political issues can suffer resistance if the culture at hand is not supportive. This fact is often quite pertinent to higher education institutions, which can be insular worlds with their own incentive systems.

Across the land, individuals and groups have taken countless actions on their respective campuses, most of which have not received public notice. Simply speaking up at a faculty senate, department, or committee meeting would qualify as constructive action, as would questioning an effort by an administration or student group to stifle honest discourse. And letting people know about such actions can inspire others to come out of the woodwork.

That said, confrontation in the form of a lawsuit or hardball internal politics can be necessary when persuasion is simply not possible. And more confrontational approaches can spill over into persuasion in a political process if the circumstances are ripe, thereby giving rise to a kind of middle way that blends some features of both approaches. A classic example of the need to sue is the lawsuit that Marquette University political scientist John McAdams won against his institution in the Wisconsin Supreme Court in July 2018. The university had fired the recalcitrant associate professor for writing a piece in his blog, *Marquette Warrior*, in which he critiqued and exposed a graduate student lecturer who had denied a conservative student the opportunity to raise critical questions about gay marriage in a class discussing equality and rights— questions that were directly relevant to the class. The instructor claimed that simply raising the questions could constitute harassment, a claim that committed two intellectual errors: it violated the cardinal principle of viewpoint neutrality in academic discussion while exemplifying unprincipled expansion of the concept of harassment to cover politically incorrect presentation of ideas. (Echoes of Laura Kipnis!)

The case was complicated by the fact that the student secretly recorded his private conversation with the instructor, and McAdams's exposure included publicizing the instructor's contact information, which Marquette claimed implicated McAdams in the extreme online bullying of the instructor by people who were hostile to her stifling the student's speech, both actions constituting affronts to *the instructor's* academic freedom in their own right, to say nothing about the simple inhumanness of the bullying. But the court ruled that McAdams's speech constituted protected extramural discourse about an important public matter and that Marquette's procedures violated its own contractual commitment to academic freedom and free speech as protected by the First Amendment. Isolated on campus, McAdams had no choice but to seek redress in the courts.[2]

Working with outside allies can also be effective and justified, but due caution is advised. Expanding the scope of the conflict is a classic but double-edged tactic for gaining power in a local situation in which one is at a disadvantage. On the negative edge, the Wisconsin legislature's passage of the 2017 pro–free speech bill that I discuss later in this chapter actually gave second thoughts to some potential free speech allies who were poised to jump off the fence. They demurred because the politics and background of the bill came across to many as a partisan, pro-conservative bill and because some of them worried that the bill violated the academic freedom principle of institutional autonomy.

This reaction was strategically important independent of the substantive merits or demerits of the bill. And I was personally involved in a case in which CAFAR's reaching out to the local press early in our tenure created unexpected stress on a client we were defending, even though he had originally told us the outreach was fine. We learned this lesson the hard way. But expanding the scope has played a significant and positive role in the historical expansion of civil liberties and civil rights in the United States.[3]

The key question is where the major initiative lies. For example, campus movements to adopt institutional versions of the University of Chicago Principles of Free Expression have been weighted toward local forms of mobilization that draw on the national model provided by Chicago. As of June 15, 2018, 42 colleges or universities had passed their own versions of the Chicago Statement, thus taking different routes to get there in terms of who took the most initiative among faculty, administration, and trustees or regents.[4] Organizations such as the Foundation for Individual Rights in Education and the Institute for Humane Studies, with which I have been affiliated, have provided advice and resources to local individuals and groups who want their respective schools to adopt a version of the Chicago Statement.

I should briefly mention another form of local action that has a connection to outside sources: centers established on campus with outside funding. Such centers have been around a long time and receive support from both private and governmental sources. The centers can broaden the research and intellectual horizons of a campus while often striving to expand intellectual diversity and academic free speech. Many centers are dedicated to teaching and researching the core principles of liberal and constitutional democracy. Some even include freedom of speech as a major part of their programs, including the James Madison Program at Princeton, the Center for the Study of Liberal Democracy at UW–Madison, the Center for the Study of Institutions and Innovation (at UW-Stout), the Thomas Jefferson Center for the Protection of Free Expression at the University of Virginia, and the Center for Political Thought and Leadership at Arizona State University.

The best centers wrestle with important intellectual and policy questions; they also provide different perspectives and viewpoints regarding such questions. Controversy has arisen, however, over the way in which outside funding can compromise institutional autonomy, which is one component of academic freedom. As a matter of principle and institutional academic freedom, all centers must resist funder interference with intellectual judgment and must abide by the same operational rules that apply to other centers—assuming such rules exist in the first place. Those rules should include appropriate deference to faculty oversight and openness regarding funding. Special treatment should be *verboten*. If such adherence prevails, the key questions should be intellectual regardless of funding: do the ideas and questions presented by the center contribute to the intellectual life of the institution? These stipulations should apply regardless of the politics of the center and its funders, be the politics conservative-libertarian (e.g., the Koch Foundation), liberal-progressive (e.g., the Soros Foundation), or any other orientation.

As Jason Brennan points out in an essay about outside funding in *The Value and Limits of Academic Speech*, three interrelated questions are germane: (a) Can good intellectual arguments be made for the center's contributions? (b) Does the center enhance the intellectual climate by providing a presence for ideas that are unduly underrepresented on campus? (c) Is the campus improperly ideologically biased in the first place, thereby calling out for a center to balance the scales?[5]

The need to maintain valid institutional autonomy is one reason that I am reluctant to enlist legislative or government backing in the fight for academic free speech: politicians wield the ultimate power, and they are often interested in furthering their own agendas. Recall the problems that the new Title IX regulations caused for campus freedom at the same time that they addressed the pressing need to punish those responsible for sexual misconduct.

Internal campus mobilization can be difficult to pull off for several reasons, including these: an unfavorable campus climate, culturally, politically, or both; a fear of being criticized or appearing to be insensitive or even hostile to identity politics claims, as Middlebury's Allison Stanger observed in Chapter 1; a reluctance to offend colleagues who oppose your stance (jeopardizing "professional courtesy," as it were); and an element of being too busy performing other tasks of one's job, such as research, teaching, service, and outreach. Alan Kors, a cofounder of

FIRE and the leader of the academic free speech movement at Penn for several years, has underscored in private conversations with others and me the burdens one must be willing to assume if one decides to engage in academic free speech activism.

Despite the valid precautions, nationally based groups have been invaluable to the campus free speech movement, especially those who work conscientiously and with local campus groups so as to maintain sufficient local initiative. Each engages the campaign in its own distinctive fashion. Each uses methods that include garnering media attention, assisting in lawsuits, providing forums and information about the cause, facilitating communications and cooperation among activists at different locations, presenting research, grading the status of academic free speech and rights at different institutions, and conducting surveys of campus attitudes and beliefs and related matters.

The major organizations, which span the ideological spectrum, include FIRE (the preeminent organization), the AAUP, the ACLU, the Open Inquiry Project of the Institute for Humane Studies' Free Speech and Open Inquiry Initiative, the National Association of Scholars, the American Council of Trustees and Alumni, the Heterodox Academy, the Cato Institute, Speech First, *Spiked*, and PEN America and PEN International.[6]

STRATEGIES FOR LOCAL MOBILIZATION AND OUTREACH: PROTECTING ACADEMIC FREE SPEECH THROUGH POWER AND PERSUASION

As I have made clear throughout this book, the first task in the preservation of freedom is for citizens to acquire the requisite knowledge of what freedom entails and why it matters. The second task is to care about the principles embedded in this knowledge. The third is to do something about it, which means backing freedom with power. As you read the following portrayals of strategic and tactical keys, keep in mind the distinctions just discussed between internal and external solutions and between confrontation and persuasion.

An example of a predominantly *internal and cooperative model* of action for reform with a touch of outside help is Georgetown University. Business and law professor John Hasnas and his allies have worked there as internal entrepreneurs to build broad consensus to effectuate positive change in the institution. As Hasnas has told audiences at events sponsored by the Institute for Humane Studies (IHS) such as the one in Charlotte, North Carolina, and at Chapman University in California (both of which I attended), he worked quietly behind the scenes with relevant faculty members and administrators while educating and persuading them to adopt policies friendly to free speech and due process. His strategy involved letting others take credit for results, assuming the goodwill of administrators and colleagues who just might not be fully informed of the law and academic standards, and being patient while internal authorities worked things out.

The method succeeded in persuading the university to adopt a version of the Chicago Free Speech Statement. According to FIRE's report, "By adopting a strong statement committing the university to upholding freedom of expression, Georgetown takes an important first step in righting past wrongs." And it went a long way in persuading the university to reform its overly broad harassment policy to make it consistent with the Supreme Court's definition of harassment. But then the reaction to Donald Trump's election compelled the university to back off reform—an example of how internal dynamics and incentives can change as a result of political circumstances.[7]

This strategy worked as well as it did because Hasnas enjoyed receptive colleagues, at least until Trump's surprising win. An example of a confrontational entrepreneur is found in the way Alan Charles Kors battled the administration of the University of Pennsylvania in the notorious case in 1993. In that case, a student was improperly charged with violating Penn's speech code for calling some African American students "water buffaloes" for being loud and raucous outside his dorm room early in the morning. Along with a small list of allies, Kors successfully fought the administration tooth and nail, and he expanded the scope of the politics by masterfully deploying the press and other outside supporters.[8]

In a presentation at a 2017 national conference on campus freedom in Dallas sponsored by FIRE, I presented a list of several factors that can contribute to success in internal campus mobilization. Let me relate the points here, along with some commentary about how actions by campus groups and figures around the country reflect their use. Of course, local movements often embody several of the points.

Civic commitment to the institution as an intellectual *polis* comes first because no one is willing to act without this a priori incentive. As Madison put it in *Federalist No. 51*, one must wed one's own ambition to the mission of the institution. And as accentuated throughout this book, such an undertaking requires getting one's priorities right and acting on behalf of this understanding.

Second, it is vital to give the ideas and principles of academic free speech *public presence on campus*. Public presence can be built upon to enlist support from those who otherwise might remain silent. Speaking out can also stop a bad thing in its tracks. It is often easier to prevent a rule in the first place than to rescind it. A classic example of the importance of speaking out in this way is the action that professors Bradley Thompson, Alan Grubb, and Bradley Meyer took at Clemson University in 2015 to head off vociferous student calls for anti–free speech policy. Among other things, students demanded a public commitment from Clemson's administration to prosecute "criminally predatory behaviors and *defamatory speech* committed by members of the Clemson University community (including, but not limited to, those facilitated by usage of social media)." [Emphasis added.] The term "defamatory" was not meant to be limited to what established legal doctrine considers libelous but rather to views that the group considered contrary to their cause.

When the threesome received word that a large faculty group was going to take out a full-page ad in the student paper in support of the demand to punish constitutionally protected speech, they submitted a counter-ad that forcefully opposed the call and declared support for student free speech. "In the name of genuine tolerance and diversity, let there be no thought crimes or thought police at Clemson University," it declared. As a result, Thompson told FIRE, "[L]arge swaths of the campus rallied in support of our open letter to Clemson students," and several faculty members who had signed onto the original full-page ad began to feel embarrassed about doing so. The call for censorship failed.[9]

One good way to generate public presence is to *enlist the support of the student press*, or at least its indulgence. Though the student press has succumbed to the pressures of political correctness in different degrees in recent years, it can still be an invaluable ally for free speech advocates, especially if those advocates remind the press of its historical role in our polity.

A recent AAUP report is appropriately critical of how administrations have been illegitimately cracking down on the student press for publishing pieces deemed detrimental to administrative and campus interests. The report generated significant critical commentary around the country.[10] The significance of the student press points to a related point: *the importance of enlisting student groups as allies in general.* Student claims have credibility on campus, especially when the policy at stake is intended to help students. And participation in the cause is educational for students as well as for faculty members.

Working with conscientious and energetic student press leaders and other students is always a joy. UW–Madison would probably still have its old offending faculty speech code had key students not joined the movement against it in the late 1990s. Teaching courses about free speech principles and law can also provide public presence. The large First Amendment lecture course that I taught at UW–Madison for 30 years was designed to teach First Amendment law, theory, history, and politics, but it also gave public presence to the subject. I discuss my course further later in this chapter.

In a related vein, it can be important for *individuals or a critical core to take the initiative,* because we hope that action engenders what Timur Kuran has called a "bandwagon movement." One example is political scientist Mitch Pickerill, a former graduate student of mine who now teaches at Northern Illinois University. In the early 2000s, when he taught at Washington State, Pickerill attended a public hearing that included a proposal for a new speech code that raised serious free speech concerns regarding scope and vagueness. The measure was drawn from an anti-harassment code that had been created by an outside private company's human resources manual. (Yet another example of the detrimental "corporatization" of higher education.)

The university's general counsel attended this meeting, but according to Pickerill, she knew little about First Amendment law—not an exceptionally unusual situation on many campuses. Pickerill stood up and spoke against the measure, and because of his comments, the counsel then asked him to meet with her to discuss the matter. "I walked her through things, and essentially I proposed the changes that would limit the code to covering actions only (stalking and actual harassment) and protecting speech/expression."

Meantime, FIRE had gotten involved in other speech-related incidents on campus, so Pickerill proceeded to set up a campus conference at the university's Foley Institute about "Speech Codes and Speech on Campus" with four panelists: Fire's then-president David French; John Wilson of Illinois State University, a leading national voice for academic freedom; the head of the campus's diversity office; and me.[11] Pickerill succeeded because of his own efforts and by widening the scope of his efforts to include campus officials, some faculty members, and supportive outsiders. The university counsel's openness to Pickerill's input is an example of the point stressed earlier about the potential goodwill of administrators.

The more allies you enlist, the more seriously you will be taken, and the more universal and nonpartisan your efforts will both be and appear. The expansion of rights in America over time has consisted of outsider groups appealing to the universal constitutional principles that they rightfully claim should be extended to them. They *strive for expanding inclusion in the constitutional regime as equal citizens.*[12]

The effort to mobilize allies should include a vital tactic: separating traditional liberals who believe in fundamental principles such as free speech and due process from less intellectually tolerant contingents of the left who put their commitment to their own social justice visions ahead of their commitment to free speech and civil liberty. Virtually every mobilization effort I know of that has enjoyed any measure of success has accomplished this task in some form. Liberals are more likely to be uncomfortable about creating opposition to censorship motivated by social justice claims than are conservatives, though conservatives have their own distinctive reasons for remaining "in the closet," as we saw in Chapter 5.[13]

At UW–Madison, CAFAR took up several cases involving threats to the left's speech rights for reasons of both principle and strategy, and we were successful in our efforts. In one case in 2006, we publicly defended the right of a student group at UW–Whitewater to bring in Ward Churchill to speak despite strong legislative calls for his disinvitation that included a threat to cut state funding unless Whitewater complied with the conservatives' wishes. Churchill was reviled for his hard-left politics and his comments after the 9/11 attacks in New York in which he had called people working in the Twin Towers "crypto Nazis." CAFAR leaders wrote a memo for the provost about Whitewater's defending the right to invite Churchill, the university used it as a press release, and two of us met with the leading legislative critic to dissuade him from his threat. The Churchill case is but one example of such support.

Actions undertaken by faculty members at the University of Montana epitomize the process of gaining allies. Several years ago, a diverse group of almost 50 individuals from several departments—an unusually large critical mass that augurs well for success—formed a group they named University of Montana Scholars for Academic Freedom (UMSAF), with seven serving as the entrepreneurial core. UMSAF opposed a series of measures that the administration had designed to promote diversity while circumventing the normal processes of shared governance. The concern was that the entrenchment of such policies would engender a stifling, conformist campus climate for free thought. The administrative policies included the following: (a) restrictions on speech that contained a student conduct code that proposed a broad definition of hate speech; (b) diversity measures containing language restricting ostensibly offensive speech; (c) "abbreviated" faculty position searches that did not reach out to a national pool; (d) allegedly unfounded accusations of harassment that featured expansive definitions of harassment and the inclusion of opinions above and beyond legal standards; and (e) recommendations of the Rape and Sexual Assault Task Force that involved censoring a syllabus and class readings.

According to a group leader, Linda S. Frey, the UMSAF raised its own money and strategically accentuated diversity of ideas "as essential to the university's mission," while also enlisting student support and speaking out publicly about the threat of speech codes. Members of the group wrote letters to the local newspapers and organized to win seats in the faculty senate. And they "appealed to the Human Rights Commission of Montana and sent a long report to and met with the Commissioner of Higher Education. . . . We pride ourselves on stopping some of the egregious actions and perhaps even in preventing others." Linda Frey's sister, Marsha, was a leader in a similar movement at the University of Kansas to fight back against overzealous diversity policies and the bypassing of "all faculty governance procedures."[14]

Another good example of alliance building and cooperative interaction is the way that academic freedom advocates at Johns Hopkins University forged a broad movement that led to the university's formally adopting an official policy, *Academic Freedom at Johns Hopkins* in 2015. It is one of the best statements on academic freedom principles and philosophy in the land. Led by the late political scientist and legal scholar Joel Grossman—a revered former colleague and mentor of mine at Madison and a model of institutional commitment—a 14-member Task Force on Academic Freedom worked for several months to build broad consensus for the strongly worded measure.

According to a press release, the Task Force "reviewed background materials on the topic of academic freedom; gathered feedback from faculty, staff, students, and alumni from every corner of the university; and met to deliberate the appropriate bounds of the principles." The statement recalls the powerful arguments of Justice Louis Brandeis. It reads in part, "But academic freedom necessarily permits the expression of views that even the vast majority of the community may find misguided, ignorant, or offensive. The appropriate response to such statements in an academic setting is not to censor or punish, but to challenge, criticize, and persuade."[15]

As we have seen, whereas many higher education institutions today are riven with conflict over mission prioritization, most have charters and contract or policy statements that promise rights consistent with the principles that shaped the advent of the modern nonproprietary college or university. Though embattled in many places, the founding principles of intellectual freedom generally remain in place, but, as John Stuart Mill would advise if he were brought back to life, they need to be revivified in order to speak to us.

When the UW–Madison faculty senate began its several debates over the ill-fated faculty speech code in the late 1990s, the university was about to celebrate its sesquicentennial. So the historical moment was propitious for academic free speech advocates because we were able to invoke the founding principles of the university that had played a significant part in the rise of academic freedom and the pursuit of truth as the paramount principles of higher education. For example, two UW–Madison professors were among the 15 original signees of the classic AAUP 1915 *Declaration of Principles on Academic Freedom and Academic Tenure*, more than any other institution. And the university's official motto to this day is an excerpt from a 1894 Board of Regents statement about academic freedom written in the aftermath of a famous academic freedom dispute back then: "Whatever may be the limitations which trammel inquiry elsewhere, we believe that the great state University of Wisconsin shall ever encourage continuous and fearless sifting and winnowing of ideas by which alone truth may be found."[16] And we reminded colleagues that their own oxen could be gored in the future if censorship changed ideological direction.

The next tactic is to *take advantage of crises both to raise the issue of intellectual freedom and to show the campus why it matters.* It is one thing to preach the virtues of intellectual freedom when things appear okay, another to actually have a problem or violation at hand that captures salience and attention. This point reflects the reality of the significance of emotion in relation to reason: being confronted with an actual case of injustice galvanizes support. As discussed in other places in this book, free speech can receive support from two different groups: from those dedicated to the principle in a universal respect and from those who accept it for reasons of self-interest. Members of the latter group support the rights of their intellectual foes in order to protect their own rights in a mutual interest pact, a kind of implicit social contract or insurance policy.[17] Being able to point to the actual casualties of censorship and wrongful investigations serves both methods. Strategically, this effort can awaken those who support intellectual freedom but who have taken its presence for granted.

At UW–Madison, CAFAR took advantage of several such examples to gain allies and support in the drive to abolish the faculty speech code in 1999 and on other occasions. Indeed, CAFAR was founded in reaction to an explosive case of an invalid investigation on campus, and my own conversion to a strong free speech position was accelerated by witnessing the harms inflicted on persons and principle by improper censorship and investigation. In the Montana case mentioned earlier, the activists pointed to the wrongful censorship of course and syllabus material to galvanize support for their side.

Recall also the discussion in Chapter 4 about the 2011 political mobilization at UW–Stout sparked by the university's reaction to a faculty member's placement of a *Firefly* poster on his office door. The administration backed down in the face of FIRE's intervention, media attention, and internal pressure exerted by campus forces led by noted free speech philosopher Timothy Shiell and his allies. Shiell and his partners then used this tailwind to assemble a First Amendment Study Group to inform the campus of the contours of academic free speech. Later they established the Center for the Study of Institutions and Innovation, which includes a significant and innovative First Amendment Project that connects the University of Wisconsin System campuses in a pro–free speech network.[18]

In late 2013, Louisiana State University (LSU) professor Teresa Buchanan provoked complaints by using obscenities and sexual innuendo in class. The AAUP described her as "a highly productive scholar and teacher," and many sources believed her speech was germane and pedagogically acceptable. A faculty committee that looked into the matter did recommend censure, but it strongly stood against any further sanctions. Under pressure, however, the school fired Buchanan in 2015, a decision a deferential federal court upheld in early 2018. In response, the AAUP censured LSU on substantive and procedural grounds. Spurred by this incident, LSU's faculty senate condemned the dismissal, and then a diverse movement of faculty members organized, held events, and ultimately passed a resolution espousing principles based on the University of Chicago Principles.[19]

Cooperation and compromise can both be acceptable. This tactical or strategic principle applies to groups that operate over a period of time and that need to maintain support. Though persuasion is best, sometimes willingness to engage in conflict is called for. Thus, one needs to appreciate how one can still be devoted to one's institution while also engaging in conflict with its leaders or one's colleagues.

In a related vein, as Aristotle observed, the *polis* is its constitution, which is not the same thing as the people in power at any particular time: it is also an embodiment of a historical mission. One needs to learn how to navigate between the institution as a historical and living idea and as a community consisting of colleagues. Too much collegiality can be detrimental to the institution, as can unjustified noncollegiality. The AAUP has correctly held that, standing alone, collegiality should not be grounds for discipline or denial of tenure; similarly, civility should be pursued if properly defined, but never made grounds for sanction or censorship. (See Chapter 2 on civility.)[20]

CAFAR strove to be accurate about problems as it distinguished among black, white, and gray. If a group overreacts by improperly shouting "academic freedom," that group can be seen as Chicken Little and not taken seriously when it matters. Similarly, one needs to know when to push for total victory and when to compromise. Sometimes compromise is simply required by the circumstances or the interest of a client if an individual case is at hand. It can also be a strategic decision to maintain relations among those you have to deal with in the future. Such compromise and cooperation are fraught with the risk that one is selling out or sacrificing too much. Therefore, strategic judgment—something no one possesses with perfection—is the goal.

One example of compromise is CAFAR's reluctant support a few years ago of UW–Madison's new "bullying" policy. With CAFAR's input, the university adopted a bullying policy that FIRE considered a model for a green light. However, our preference was not to have such a policy at all because of the potential for abuse. We decided to work with the sponsors because we believed that senate passage was inevitable and that it was tactically more productive to enter negotiations in order to tighten the policy. One must look at the larger picture: the stronger stances that we had taken in the past gave sufficient credibility to our opposition, so the policy sponsors felt compelled to welcome our input, almost all of which they adopted.[21] But to this day former CAFAR members remain uncomfortable and unsure about our decision. Indeed, in 2019, some faculty members related to me examples of how the policy has been improperly manipulated by several campus personnel. Today, I consider this erstwhile compromise effort to be a failure.

I could write a paper—even a book!—about the strategic and intellectual mistakes CAFAR and its members made over the years at Wisconsin. The core fallibility principle that underlies free speech theory certainly applied to us as well. The list of our mistakes along the way includes overreacting, underreacting, misjudging a situation or a client, and even occasionally being lazy—among other human foibles. We achieved good results for all our clients, yet the paths of our successes were not always smooth. I cannot speak for other movements discussed in this chapter, but I assume that they experienced their own mistakes as well. *The point is to learn from mistakes, to expect them, and not to let them deter you from acting when you should.*

Finally, faculty members and students who are thinking about engaging in campus free speech politics should realize that such *engagement can be both engaging and fun*. I know several individuals whose careers were energized and given more meaning when they threw their hats into this ring. Such engagement can be uniquely rewarding, especially when you make unexpected progress toward your goal. Like liberal education, it is an adventure. Seek and ye shall find.

LEGISLATIVE ACTIONS: MORE OVERT OUTSIDE INTERVENTION

Outside governmental intervention is a final issue to consider in today's campus speech battles. I leave out government administrative orders and rules, such as the Obama administration's policies enforcing Title IX, because those have tended to be infringements on academic free speech rather than aids, which is the subject of this chapter. One exception is the DOE's Office for Civil Rights letter to colleges and universities in 2003; it stated that an institution's rules against harassment must not be interpreted or applied in ways that infringe on First Amendment rights. This DOE action was spearheaded by input from FIRE's cofounder Alan Charles Kors.[22] Of course, the DOE was quite different under the next administration.

As mentioned already, I am ambivalent about outside legislative measures, especially if they entail deeper intervention into institutional autonomy. But we should recognize the ways those measures and proposals signify how forces in the general public are becoming increasingly aware of the need for colleges and universities to do what is necessary to protect academic free speech and to make it and the pursuit of truth the primary priorities of higher education. The problem is that outside intervention can open its own Pandora's box, so due respect for institutional autonomy is called for—depending on the situation.

In recent times, several states have passed legislation or pressured their state institutions to adopt two related forms of policy: (a) a policy that expressly protects campus speakers against disruption, that mandates penalties for violators, and that requires equal, nondiscriminatory treatment of the viewpoints of all lawful speakers and student groups; and (b) a policy that outlaws free speech zones that limit free speech on campus to certain Hyde Park areas that essentially serve to quarantine free speech as if it is some kind of infectious disease. As of mid-2018, at least 11 states had passed legislation regarding free speech zones.[23]

The original blueprint for more intrusive measures came from the Goldwater Institute in Arizona, which presented the model at a press conference in Washington, DC, in early 2017. Among other things, the proposal calls for these: laws protecting the rights of speakers and audiences, meaningful sanctions for disrupters, prohibitions against disinviting speakers, legal remedies for speakers and their invitees who are disrupted, and campus commissions to monitor the status of free speech on campus.[24]

The American Executive Legislative Council (ALEC) has proposed similar bills based on its model proposal, "Forming Open and Robust University Minds (FORUM)." FIRE's Joe Cohn has worked closely with many state legislatures in constructive ways that have made actual or pending legislation much more principled—including a proposed bill in Wisconsin that led to the Board of Regents passing policy on its own for the UW System.

Former CAFAR members worked behind the scenes with Tim Higgins and other regents to improve the pending bill, thus leading to the final Regent Policy. But most of us did not formally endorse the final product because of our concerns about political intervention of this nature. The new Regent Policy is a clear improvement over the original legislative proposal, and Higgins is a model of what a regent should be: actively and conscientiously concerned with the intellectual mission of the university and higher education, as well as willing to walk the walk. He spearheaded the effort that led to the board's adoption of the University of Wisconsin version of the Chicago Statement in December 2015.

But our concerns about letting the legislature's nose into the tent have been buttressed by legislators' more recent attempts to go after professors on the basis of wording in their course descriptions or syllabi—sometimes in reaction to a single disgruntled student's complaining to the legislature. In one case in early 2019, a colleague of mine was subjected to threatening email bullying by right-wing internet bullies, thereby calling for police attention and security forces being placed in his class. (I withhold his name for reasons of his security.) Such consequences do not exactly make one more sanguine about bringing state politicians on board in the fight for free speech.

As of mid-2018, two states had passed versions of FORUM, with five not doing so after a bill was introduced; four states had adopted their version of the Goldwater model by May 15, 2018.[25] In 2018, the U.S. Congress held hearings about a similar bill at the national level, but nothing has come of this matter as of this writing. According to a report by the National Association of Student Personnel Administrators, a large international organization founded at the University of Wisconsin in 1918, "Notably, most of the witnesses seemed to agree that the best remedy to the concerns was not to legislate additional requirements for college campuses, but rather to continue conspicuous oversight so that campuses remain vigilant in protecting the rights of all their students."[26]

John Hardin, director of university relations at the Charles Koch Foundation, agreed in a 2018 *New York Times* op-ed that "[s]uch broad measures are vulnerable to abuse. Our criminal justice system has already seen the destructive effects of similar mandatory minimums in sentencing, and there is little reason to think they would fare better in the environment of a college campus."[27] Those bills involve more outside oversight of internal campus operations than of the free speech zone cases, thereby raising more questions of institutional autonomy.

Another problem is that state bills are often viewed—not without reason in some cases—as partisan. Such was the case in Wisconsin, where the proposed legislative bill followed in the wake of other very controversial legislative measures that had potentially deleterious effects on tenure, shared governance, curricular decisions, and financial considerations of UW institutions. (See Chapter 5.) Fairly or unfairly, many critics viewed the bill as yet another partisan attack on the university.

On the other side of the coin, at the February 2018 conference at ASU that I discussed in Chapter 3, James Manley of the Goldwater Institute reported an interesting experience he had at UW–Madison. When Fox News's Katie Pavlich came to UW to give a talk on "Women and Guns" in November 2017, a student group held a protest outside Bascom Hall, where the event took place. Manley was on hand and asked the group's leader why her group remained outside rather than choosing to disrupt the talk inside. According to Manley, she replied that they had planned to disrupt the talk, but that they decided simply to hold a legitimate protest outside. Why? "Because we didn't want to get expelled due to the new Regent Policy," she replied. Deterrence worked.

The acceptability of such intervention varies inversely with the extent of the internal campus problem; the use of courts when individuals' rights have been violated is certainly legitimate. Individuals and groups should also consider the use of tort action against those who violate their free speech rights—an approach that merits more attention in the discussion of legal remedies and leaves the initiative to take constructive action in the hands of those affected.

ADMINISTRATIVE AND INSTITUTIONAL REFORM

The emphasis in the previous section was on bottom-up actions that can bubble up to influence institutional policy and culture. In this section, I deal with institutional policy that is ultimately the product of administrative leadership working with faculty members and students. The idea is to create a campus-wide culture for the *polis*, which is buttressed by policy that honors the preeminence of academic free speech as primary to institutional mission.

CAMPUS LEADERSHIP

The first matter for renewal is campus leadership that understands that academic free speech is indispensable to the primary mission of the university, namely the shared pursuit of truth. Other missions such as diversity, student well-being, and financial concerns merit attention, but never in a manner that harms this *raison d'être*.

If one is to achieve success, it is imperative for administrative leaders to reach out to relevant campus stakeholders to enlist them in the project. Efforts must be made to combine genuine commitment with persuasion. In other words, political acumen is required. In Chapter 3, we looked at the painstaking efforts that University of Florida leaders undertook to prepare for Richard Spencer's coming to campus in October 2017. The task included a firm commitment to upholding the viewpoint neutrality principle in the university's limited public forum, as well as a concerted effort to reach out to various campus constituencies, including those who were most upset about the event. The administration assured the community that its commitment to free speech in no way compromised the commitment to the equal respect for all campus citizens, and it provided alternative venues for protest and discussion. (See the following about the principle of inclusive speech.)

As discussed in Chapter 3, free speech involves a system of reciprocal rights and duties that make up the framework for ordered liberty. Outreach should bring in students, faculty members, administrators, campus police officers, and regents or trustees. Even key alumni and members of the local public are viable partners. The only proviso is not letting the widening outreach detract from the mission by bogging it down or leading to undue compromise. Recall the essentiality of focused prioritization.

A fine example of administrative leadership at the top of an institution is Howard Gillman, chancellor at the University of California–Irvine. In addition to coauthoring the recent book, *Free Speech on Campus*, that we dealt with in Chapter 3, Gillman has put his money where his mouth is on a variety of levels, including the following: (a) teaching a course about free speech; (b) cochairing the University of California's National Center for Free Speech and Civic Engagement; (c) cochairing a variety of panels and actions with the presidents of the Association of American Universities and Association of Public and Land-Grant Universities; (d) giving presentations to the National Association of College and University Attorneys; (e) networking with other UC campus groups; and (f) participating in events around the country. If more Howard Gillmans headed universities and colleges around the country, books like this would not have to be written. Gillman's coauthor, Erwin Chemerinsky, has also been an administrative leader in such efforts at Irvine, Berkeley, and other institutions.

INCLUSIVE SPEECH AND OTHER NONCENSORIAL MEASURES

Such outreach must make one thing clear: students and the groups with whom they are associated have free speech rights to present and advocate their own views, as well as to protest speakers and events in a manner that does not entail a heckler's veto. Academic free speech applies to all. At the same time, such outreach must not shy away from holding students to the same obligations regarding respect for academic free speech that are expected of all campus citizens.

In her 2016 book, Sigal R. Ben-Porath maintains that we can appropriately balance free speech with identity politics and with personal and group dignity if we work hard enough. She cites the drive for equal respect as the primary motivator of campus identity politics. (See also Chapter 2.) The resolution to the contradiction between identity politics and free speech is not to censor any ideas, however contentious, but to take affirmative steps to ensure that the classroom, public forum, and marketplace of ideas voluntarily include the voices of all marginalized groups—what she calls "inclusive speech" policy. Ben-Porath also supports what she considers to be reasonable uses of new policies or practices such as trigger warnings, safe spaces, microaggression theory, and bias reporting programs. Concerns about the anti-intellectual implications of these and related policies are unwarranted in her eyes. Students need to learn more about free speech and its history, but "generally the change of focus that they, as a generation, introduce into the debate is not one that should be of concern to the self-appointed guardians of democracy. Universities and colleges are institutions with aims that go well beyond the general goals of a democratic society, and it makes sense for them to be organized and managed based on additional principles."[28]

The concept of inclusive speech is important, and Ben-Porath helps to show us why. But she is too insouciant about the abuse of the policies that she endorses and about the ways in which radical or separatist forms of identity politics and what Frank Furedi calls "emotional correctness" can be detrimental if their tenets become part of actual policies or campus culture. The right of identity politics advocates to speak their truths is one thing, but basing actual speech policies on the censorial aspects of identity politics is another.

As stressed in Chapter 2, the struggle for identity is universal, but there are varying forms of it that have different implications for free speech and the universality of rights. Also, Ben-Porath's claim that higher education institutions should "be organized and managed based on additional principles" opens the door to losing the central intellectual mission of higher education in the thickening forest of other missions, some of which are not friendly to academic free speech. Speech policy should be a matter of prioritizing speech, not of making it equal to other missions. So *how* the necessary policy of inclusive speech is carried out matters.

In Chapter 8 of her book *Hate*, Nadine Strossen offers other non-censorial measures along with some evidence of their potential effectiveness. Her remedies compose a balance among enhanced teaching of adhering to free speech principles, showing toughness of character, following principles needed to be effective, and taking reasonable student concerns and causes seriously. She emphasizes the classic remedy of counter-speech championed by Justice Louis Brandeis as explained in Chapter 7 of this book, as well as the need for campus leaders to speak out against genuine hate when it appears. In so doing, they demonstrate respect for all campus citizens.

In researching *Nazis in Skokie*, I asked Holocaust survivor leader Erna Gans if there was one main lesson she learned from the Holocaust. "Be your brother's keeper," she replied.[29] In terms of campus speech conflict, we must be our brothers' and sisters' keepers in a way that demonstrates due and inclusive respect for all students, just as we expect them to have the wherewithal to handle the obligations of constitutional citizenship. If you don't like a speaker, protest constitutionally. Don't veto.

ORIENTATION AND THE IMPORTANCE OF PRIMING

Psychologists have shown how individuals' expectations and interpretations of encounters are affected by the thoughts and feelings that they bring to new experiences. So it makes sense to prime students ahead of time to expect new challenges that will arise, as well as to instruct them on how to deal constructively with conflict.[30]

Today most institutions incentivize priming orientation sessions that address matters such as diversity and discrimination. Now, responding to the rising national concern, some schools have developed orientation programs that are for students and that teach the principles of academic free speech and open inquiry. Examples include the Civil Discourse 101 programs mentioned in Chapter 1. Befitting its hallowed intellectual freedom tradition, the University of Chicago is a key proponent of such programs. The effort began with the school's 2015 *Report of the Committee on Freedom of Expression*, which was headed by noted free speech scholar and advocate law professor Geoffrey Stone. That report became the now famous *Chicago Statement on the Principles of Free Expression*. The presentation of the statement incentivized the administration to hold campus-wide discussions about the issue.

In the fall of 2016, the dean of students sent a letter to new first-year students calling for the fostering of a campus state of mind that was conducive to robust academic free speech and was accompanied by a commitment to civility that can nourish a culture of open inquiry and respect for intellectual diversity. Along with the letter, the dean included a copy of a monograph that informed the students of the rich intellectual freedom history of the storied institution: *Academic Freedom and the Modern University: The Experience of the University of Chicago*, written by Dean John W. Boyer.

In 2017, the university followed up by publishing the *Revised Final Report of the Committee on University Discipline for Disruptive Conduct*, which recommended policies for protecting academic free speech. The committee later called for "Co-Curricular Educational Programming" that is dedicated to fostering the "free-speech commons at the university." The memo declared, "Sustaining a free speech environment requires concerted effort to educate and inform students (and the University staff who support them) about the University's values, goals, policies, and procedures around freedom of expression, protest, and dissent."[31]

In 2017, the University of Wisconsin's Board of Regents promulgated Regent Policy 4-21, which dealt with campus free speech in response to the state legislature's moves to enact a version of the Goldwater model. Policy 4-21 includes protections against heckler's vetoes and calls for sanctions against students who disrupt legitimate speakers. It also necessarily protects the right to protest, which includes protest of speakers. The policy touted the university's "courageous sifting and winnowing" mission and declared that "[e]ach UW institution shall include an orientation for freshmen and transfer students [that provides] information regarding freedom of expression consistent with this policy."[32]

Even before the advent of Policy 4-21, UW–Madison began providing its own orientation primer or toolkit in response to the 2015 Regent Statement on Academic Freedom and Freedom of Expression. The document instructed students about the primacy of academic free speech and about cultivating a campus climate of civil discourse. Kevin Helmkamp (now retired assistant vice provost and associate dean of students) and a CAFAR member put the primer together in early 2016, shortly after the Regent vote on their statement in December 2015. A passage reads:

> When you enter the university, you will encounter fellow students, professors, and staff that represent a wide diversity of backgrounds and ideas. Sometimes these differences will stimulate interesting and engaging discussion and learning. At other times they will generate strong disagreements and emotions. In order for a university and educational experience to succeed, we must find a way to live with our intellectual differences in a constructive way that contributes to the common goals of the educational process.[33]

This UW–Madison primer also said something about the importance of civility, which was understood in the manner that I related in

Chapter 2 earlier. It defined civility as a quality of self-control and reason that nourishes the ability to engage in intellectual discussion and conflict in a forceful yet constructive manner.

COURSES

Another means of priming is to teach courses related to constitutional and intellectual freedom. An institution can hold such a course for new students, can offer it later in students' academic careers depending on need, or both. In recent years, I have heard extensive discussion at my old school and elsewhere about the importance of teaching such courses. Recall the report that I mentioned in Chapter 5 by the American Council of Trustees and Alumni about the decline of American history courses in higher education: what is taught matters.[34]

My intent in teaching my First Amendment course at Wisconsin was threefold: to teach the basic principles and law of First Amendment jurisprudence in historical, political, philosophical, and doctrinal contexts; to strive for a Socratic way of thinking about constitutional adjudication; and to give public presence to this subject. Each time it was taught, two things appeared to take place as the course proceeded.

First, students exhibited greater knowledge of the legal issues at stake. Second, in terms of state of mind, students became more thoughtful when we dealt with controversial and even painful cases rather than resorting to their immediate feelings. In one case a few years ago, students reacted emotionally to a pro-life minister who displayed a large and very offensive picture of a fetus in a public forum in front of Memorial Union, the campus nerve center. I was impressed by how my students— most of whom were pro-choice and very upset at this display—dealt with the First Amendment questions at stake; they used reason and argument. Becoming knowledgeable about the law made all the difference *in terms of attitude and posture,* thus serving as a kind of filter that protected the reasoning process from undue emotion and anger. Moral anger was sublimated into more reasoned reflection.

The students' reasoning process itself improved, the way the students thought through the different aspects of the case from more than one position. I found the same virtues on display when students dealt with other offensive forms of speech that regularly erupted on campus, including the many crises that arose regarding the *Badger Herald* student paper. In terms of public presence, I sought out leaders in student government and the student press who, in turn, networked with other students, faculty members, and staff members about the course and its relevance to liberal education and campus affairs. I conceived of the course as a pedagogical and civic duty and as a supplement to the work we did on CAFAR.

DIVERSITY TRAINING AND RELATED POLICIES

Diversity is a valued part of American history and culture; it merits respect. The problem is when it becomes an obsession or even a secular form of religion that de-prioritizes the intellectual freedom that is indispensable to the truth mission of higher education. I have lost track of how many faculty members I have encountered who have felt simple and fair resentment over being exposed to mandatory diversity programs that indulge in presumptions of discriminatory intent and intellectual simplicities. I recommend three ways to make diversity training or advocacy more consistent with the university's core mission.

First, as Yale law professor Peter Schuck has maintained, diversity is something that policymakers should simply let happen from the bottom up, as it naturally will, so long as wrongful discrimination is prevented. It should not be force-fed by a top-heavy and dogmatic approach.[35] A key idea here is related to a constant theme in this book: moral or intellectual bullying is no way to generate genuine respect for something. Diversity's proponents must strive to persuade by treating others as moral ends. Of course, more forceful means are called for in situations of discriminatory conduct, laws, and policy.

Schuck's position finds support in a 2016 article in the *Harvard Business Review*; the article reviewed studies of a host of diversity programs in practice. The authors underscore the importance of generating genuine consent to diversity, which involves a presumption in favor of more voluntary compliance that is consistent with free minds.

Not only are dogmatism and brow-beating inconsistent with genuine respect for differences and intellectual freedom and standards, but also they are ineffectual because of the natural human impulse to rebel against being treated dogmatically, which means being treated as someone else's end.

> [L]aboratory studies show that this kind of force-feeding can activate bias rather than stamp it out. As social scientists have found, people often rebel against rules to assert their autonomy. Try to coerce me to do X, Y, or Z, and I'll do the opposite just to prove that I'm my own person. It's more effective to engage managers in solving the problem, increase their on-the-job contact with female and minority workers, and promote social accountability—the desire to look fair-minded. . . . You won't get managers on board by blaming and shaming them with rules and reeducation.[36]

Second, programs dealing with diversity and sensitivity should take *intellectual diversity* seriously, especially in universities and colleges. This statement is true for two reasons: (a) intellectual diversity is intimately related to the primary mission of higher education, and (b) the concept of diversity itself is naturally open to contestation in terms of its substantive meaning and its application. As political theorist Dana Villa has written about the need for Socratic inquiry, "The implication of Socratic examination is that virtually every moral belief becomes false and an invitation to injustice the moment it becomes unquestioned or unquestionable."[37] Villa's maxim is especially pertinent to a concept as substantive and open to interpretation as diversity. And even if we agree on what it means, debate over how to implement it is unavoidable. In the legal history of antidiscrimination law, the most pressing normative and constitutional question is often about means, not just ends. This point certainly applies to social justice as a concept, which is about both means and ends.

Third, university policy should strive to be as universal as possible and should move away from an emphasis on the categories of identity politics. One way to achieve this result is to concentrate on the equal respect that each of us deserves because of our basic humanity, which I discussed in Chapter 7's section on the deontological dimension of free speech as a right. Think of diversity in terms of human rights rather than the divisions that sharpen under the gaze of identity politics as it is practiced today.[38] Important issues of racism, sexism, and history can be addressed in this approach, but in a context that appeals to human rights as a widely shared principle that is capable of appealing to students of any background, including those who have traditionally enjoyed social power or privilege.

LIMITS ON SPEECH

As argued in Chapter 7, understanding and thinking about the limits of free speech are important aspects of learning and citizenship whether, generally speaking, in the classroom or in the campus public forum.

GENERAL LIMITS

We must respect proper general limits on speech. We have seen that one threat to academic free speech is spurious claims to its protection when they are not merited, as in the case of the heckler attempting a veto. Moreover, we saw in Chapter 7 how thinking about limits can contribute to liberal education. The University of Chicago Statement delineates classic limits that apply to the campus as a whole; in addition, there are limits germane to the classroom, as we discussed in Chapter 3. The Chicago principles are consistent with basic First Amendment law and the Supreme Court's definitions of such speech as harassment, threats, libel, privacy, obscenity, and incitement to illegal action:

> The University may restrict expression that violates the law, that falsely defames a specific individual, that constitutes a genuine threat or harassment, that unjustifiably invades substantial privacy or confidentiality interests, or that is otherwise directly incompatible with the functioning of the University. In addition, the University may reasonably regulate the time, place, and manner of expression to ensure that it does not disrupt the ordinary activities of the University. But these are narrow exceptions to the general principle of freedom of

expression, and it is vitally important that these exceptions never be used in a manner that is inconsistent with the University's commitment to a completely free and open discussion of ideas.[39]

Harassment is also an important general limit. However, as stressed in Chapter 4 and elsewhere, in order to protect free speech, legal standards limit the definition of harassment to objective and specific circumstances. According to the Supreme Court, harassment takes place only when it is discriminatory, targeted, and "so severe, pervasive, and objectively offensive, and that so undermines and detracts from the victims' educational experience, that the victim-students are effectively denied equal access to an institution's resources and opportunities."[40] Bias reporting programs that encourage the reporting of speech that falls outside this limit are especially hazardous to the health of the campus conceived as an intellectual *polis*. FIRE urges campuses to limit such programs to covering speech similar to that which the Supreme Court considers "harassment."

CLASSROOM

In addition, as Chapter 3 lays out, further limits are legitimate in professional settings such as the classroom. Taking into consideration appropriate wiggle room or breathing space made for intellectual exploration (heuristics) and human error, speech must be relevant or germane to the matter at hand. Of course, intellectual fraud and plagiarism are necessarily prohibited. And intellectual standards must be upheld, again with due consideration of reasonable differences of interpretation and conclusions.

A trickier issue pertains to offensive statements and civility in the classroom. No teacher worth his or her salt would allow intentional racial vilification directed at students or the like in class.[41] As mentioned in Chapter 3, personal gratuitous offense unrelated to valid pedagogical purposes crosses a line in principle, though we need to be careful about protecting all *ideas*, however offensive, that are related to the subject matter at hand. UW–Madison's official statement about harassment in instructional settings, which was adopted by the faculty senate in 1999 after we abolished the faculty speech code, talks about the importance of respect, civility, and tolerance in class, but it emphasizes the paramount (prioritized) importance of academic freedom. "All expression" that is "germane" is protected.[42]

HATE SPEECH AND OUTSIDE SPEAKERS

The problem of hate speech by campus speakers in invited venues or campus public forums is perhaps the most pressing free speech problem on campus today, though it appears to be waning in importance as I conclude this book. (To wit, a national "White Civil Rights" rally in Washington, DC, in August 2018 ended up attracting fewer than 20 followers.)[43] Historically, severe challenges to established free speech doctrine have tended to raise similar concerns about doctrinal sustainability, only to wane with time. The Skokie case generated fears of Nazis and other hate groups taking to the public forum in increasing waves, thereby provoking large and potentially violent counter-demonstrations that threatened to unleash financial havoc and massive planning problems.[44] Similarly, many commentators feared that the doctrine of prior restraint would take a hit if newspapers began publishing pieces clearly detrimental to national security in the wake of the Pentagon Papers case (*New York Times Co. v. United States*) in 1971. But this trend did not materialize, either, and the doctrine of prior restraint remains secure. Stakeholders have a way of adjusting to deal with new problems, especially in a free society.[45]

In August 2017, white nationalist demonstrators spewing hate provoked violent reactions from protesters in Charlottesville, home of the University of Virginia. Police stood down as the two sides went at it. A white nationalist thug even killed a protester in the process. The scene evoked deep emotions and fears about similar events erupting on other campuses. Many sources claim that wealthy right-wing funders are backing provocative right-wing speakers to appear on campuses in order to highlight campus intolerance of speech or simply to cause trouble and financial strain.

UC–Berkeley had to deal with a series of trying situations in 2016 and 2017 involving provocateur Milos Yiannopoulos and hecklers' reactions to mainstream conservative speakers such as Ben Shapiro.

The Milos event led to large-scale violence, most of which was perpetrated by outside agitators on the far left. Some speakers had been invited by registered student organizations (RSOs), whereas others appeared in the public forum on their own. Cash-strapped UC–Berkeley estimates that the costs it incurred preparing for controversial speakers amounted to $4 million during that span. In late 2017, the chancellor appointed the Berkeley Free Speech Commission to recommend policy reform.

The commission presented its report in April 2018. Its recommendations included some measures I discussed earlier: (a) offering a course for all freshmen about free speech and constitutional principles; (b) having enhanced data collection about speaker events; (c) working with police to be more effective in promoting security while also being less intimidating to students; (d) training students about how to deal constructively with disagreement and debate, including building "logic and empirical inquiry skills"; (e) educating students about the "harms of hateful speech and the reasons hateful speech is unrestricted"; and (f) encouraging the campus to hold "alternative events that feature multiple viewpoints on sensitive subjects"—a form of inclusive speech.

The commission also called on students to "[h]onor not just the campus's Principles of Community but its mission of education, research, and public service by voluntarily balancing their right to hold events with their responsibility to the community." Responsibility to the community essentially entails being aware of the financial, security, and emotional strains some speakers can engender, and giving due regard to whether the quality of the speaker befits the pedagogical and intellectual standards of the university.[46]

More controversially, the commission proposed two other actions. First, that RSOs "[s]ubmit a public statement in support of events that require additional security, addressing (a) the rationale for the event, (b) what new perspectives the event will bring to discussion on campus, and (c) how the event is consistent with Berkeley's Principles of Community." Critics worried that this proposal could lead to a Permission Committee that improperly influences the historically vibrant student speech network. (In the fall semester alone, Berkeley hosted more than 11,000 student events!)

Drawing on the work of Nobel Prize laureate Elinor Ostrom and Vincent Ostrom, IHS CEO Emily Chamlee-Wright has pointed out in correspondence and a forthcoming paper about the matter that this policy could be subject to the classic pitfalls that can arise with empowering such a top-down body. Those pitfalls include ideological conformity or bias and "epistemological problems" associated with the lack of adequate understanding or appreciation of an RSO's reasons for bringing a speaker to campus. Chamlee-Wright argues for a "bottom-up," "local knowledge" process that clearly delegates the discretion of whom to invite to the groups themselves. She leaves it to the institution to provide background thoughts and information about the institutional and pedagogical values that student groups may rightly consider.

> [The Ostroms'] research suggests that as long as we have good general (constitutional) rules, (e.g., no one can violate the individual rights of another person), local communities tend to be fairly good at generating the more specific rules they need to achieve positive outcomes. The key insight is that such rules tend to work best when they are defined, monitored, and enforced from the bottom up."[47]

In the end, this proposal was dropped from the final version of Berkeley's plan. This version is also clear about the need for viewpoint neutrality. "All criteria for assessing Major Events must be applied in a viewpoint-neutral manner and without regard to the content of any performance or speaking aspect of the event." According to Gillman, Berkeley's commitment to free speech events is clear and substantial.[48]

The highly active network of student RSOs is an important pedagogical feature of many schools, as I highlighted in Chapter 3. In principle, it is appropriate for university leadership to ensure that students are aware of the different dimensions at stake in inviting speakers to campus, including the effect on the intellectual quality of life. The problem with such educational effort is similar to the problem that can arise with diversity training and the like: if top-heavy and bullying, it stifles the intellectual diversity, vitality, and honesty of the institutional climate. Applied to RSOs, it can be paternalistic and therefore disrespectful of the moral agency of students as young adults.

The second further action that the commission called for implicates an issue that we dealt with in Chapter 3 when we distinguished academic speech, free speech, and their respective campus realms: to what extent should the institution limit or discourage speakers with low intellectual quality or whose primary objective is to disrupt rather than to instruct?

The Commission held that it is appropriate for faculty members—in particular those who are advisers to a student group—to recommend that students at least think twice about inviting a speaker for intellectual reasons. Inviting a speaker is different from letting a person or group speak in a classic or limited public forum. The commission mentioned how a conservative UCLA sociologist convinced UCLA College Republicans to disinvite Milo Yiannopoulos in early 2018. In an open letter to the community, the sociologist wrote, "Your conscience should tell you that you never want anything to do with someone whose entire career is not reasoned argument, but shock jock performance art. In the 1980s conservatives made fun of 'artists' who defecated on stage for the purpose of upsetting conservatives. Now apparently, conservatives are willing to embrace a man who says despicable things for the purpose of 'triggering snowflakes.'"

Such action by a faculty member connected to a group can be consistent with academic free speech principles so long as it is done with due respect for the students and an open mind about the different ways in which pedagogical value can be gained by a speaker. Indeed, many institutions require student groups to obtain sponsorship from a faculty member or department in order to secure a room for a speaker or to obtain security protection. Again, such requirements can be consistent with free speech standards so long as they do not provide cover for viewpoint discrimination and as long as other safeguards are in place.

The fact that the UCLA case involved a disinvitation is unsettling, as is the fact that the professor chose a public statement rather than speaking privately with the student inviters in a noncoercive manner. Principled faculty members who advise can facilitate free speech while upholding intellectual standards that are so important to the academic side of free speech, as long as they do so in a way respectful of student rights and autonomy.

We have covered much ground in this book as we have addressed the academic free speech question from a variety of empirical, analytical, and normative perspectives. I began the project almost two years before we entered the final publication process at Cato, and one thing that strikes my mind as I write this concluding comment is how much the fields of scholarship and action surrounding the issue evolved as I wrote. Articles, books, speeches, and interviews have piled up, and many individuals and organizations have joined the politics of campus free speech and academic freedom locally, nationally, and internationally. Consequently, I had to account for new literature and assessments of the status of campus freedom as I updated new drafts. I hope this book contributes something to those ongoing efforts. The fact that the discussion and debate continue is itself befitting of a free society.

But despite the positive movements, the good, the bad, the ugly, and, yes, the beautiful still compete for ascendance. As I write this final thought, I just read that Harvard University has fired Ronald Sullivan, a prominent Harvard law professor, from his deanship of a residence hall for the sin of being one of Harvey Weinstein's attorneys in his famous criminal case. The veritable Valhalla of higher education caved before the pressure of students who claimed that the dean's acting in honor of the foundational principles of due process and a fair trial in a case taking place far away from the campus traumatized them and made them feel unsafe.

Harvard's action has direct relevance for the status of intellectual freedom and constitutional rights on campus. In language echoing this book's emphasis on prioritization, journalist Conor Friedersdorf wrote in *The Atlantic* that "protecting the norms around the right to counsel is *orders of magnitude more important* than the 'unenlightened or misplaced' discomfort of some Harvard undergraduates."[49] [Emphasis in the original.]

On the other side of the ledger, the president of Philadelphia University of the Arts has recently stood firm in upholding the free speech and academic freedom rights of the redoubtable Camille Paglia against student claims that she be fired for ostensible insensitivity to transgender students. (Itself a highly implausible claim given Paglia's philosophy of life and works.) In April, students also stopped her speech at the school in its tracks by pulling a fire alarm, thereby emptying the tall building in which she was speaking.[50]

In this book's Introduction, I wrote that we are currently debating what version of higher education we want to pursue and are focusing on three ideal-type models: traditional proprietary, liberal freedom, and social justice. A free society properly makes room for all three because of the right to charter one's own destiny, the fallibility of human endeavor, and the reality of value and cultural pluralism in democratic regimes.

But when the dust of inevitable conflict settles, it is the ascendency of the liberal freedom model that enables this balance to prevail and to endure in a principled and just manner. Let us hope that the guarded optimism of this book is merited. Only our knowledge, commitment, prioritization, and action to support "the First Freedom" can make it so.

ACKNOWLEDGMENTS

I am indebted to many individuals who helped to pave the way for *Free Speech and Liberal Education* to appear. First, I thank my wife, Susan Downs, and our children, Jackie Dorris and Alex Downs, who have shared the allegiance to intellectual freedom with me for many decades. They have thus made this commitment part of our family identity. The spirit now extends to our son-in-law and daughter-in-law, Matthew Dorris and Megan Downs, and to our grandchildren, Maddie, Jolie, and Jackson Dorris.

Free Speech and Liberal Education is both hopeful and less than sanguine about the prospects of liberal democracy in the world today. Gladly, knowing the young people in our family nourishes the hopeful side of the ledger. Susan merits further praise for having the patience to put up with my writing this book during the early years of my retirement from the University of Wisconsin–Madison.

Second, I am indebted to my colleagues and friends of the late Committee for Academic Freedom and Rights (CAFAR), a nonpartisan group of a dozen or so faculty members established as an independent force in 1996 to fight for academic freedom, free speech, and due process at UW–Madison. Working with this distinctive set of individuals over the course of 20 years was a highlight of my career, as well as a genuine honor and privilege. In addition to being distinguished scholars in their respective fields, those colleagues possessed the knowledge, commitment, and willingness to act that are necessary for the sustenance of free polities and institutions. My CAFAR colleagues taught me invaluable lessons by virtue of their minds and deeds. I refer to their efforts often in this book.

Third, my students showed me why universities still matter. Their dedication to learning and to intellectual engagement and challenge constantly renewed my spirit, making each class a new dawn. Special recognition is due to those many students who participated in our free speech movement at Wisconsin in various capacities and who taught us that a university needs citizenship along with respect for learning.

Fourth, I want to thank the people who worked with me on the Open Inquiry Project of the Institute for Humane Studies' Free Speech and Open Inquiry Initiative in Arlington, Virginia. IHS allowed me to continue work in the academic free speech arena after my retirement from Wisconsin in 2015, and I benefited from the excellent intellectual and collegial input and experiential opportunities it gave me for several years. Hopefully the national project we launched made some meaningful contributions to the cause during our tenure together.

I am also grateful to the Cato Institute for the support it provided in seeing *Free Speech and Liberal Education* into print. Cato's dedication and intellectual excellence in the service of liberty are well known and widely valued, and I am pleased to have the book placed there.

Special thanks go to John Samples and Jason Kuznicki, two mainstays of the Institute. John, a vice president of Cato and director of its Center for Representative Government, gave me invaluable editorial advice and insights as he shepherded the book through its first rounds of review. He helped turn a rambling, meandering endeavor into something more cogent. His patience is superhuman. Jason, editor of Cato Books and *Cato Unbound*, picked up where John left off in the final stage. He offered probing advice and stipulations that strengthened the work while preserving my intent—editorial assistance at its best. John and Jason are deeply knowledgeable, and few writers have been as fortunate as I in receiving such editorial expertise. I also received excellent editorial advice that I took to heart from two anonymous reviewers of the first draft. And Eleanor O'Connor, managing editor at Cato, provided excellent assistance to me in the copyediting process, as did the copy editor, Barbara B. Hart, Publications Professionals LLC. Their professionalism and dedication to the task are much appreciated.

Finally, I want to thank the University of Wisconsin–Madison, my institutional home. True to its venerable tradition, it challenged me, educated me, and provided me with the resources to expand intellectually and experientially, even when my CAFAR allies challenged it and opposed certain policies and actions. Our positions embodied what Michael Walzer called "connected criticism"—critique from an insider friend rather than an outsider bearing hostility. But we also understood that "the University" is not the same thing as the people who run it. Through friendship, collegiality, and, yes, *Sturm und Drang*, my love for Wisconsin as an institution with its own history, character, and distinct intellectual mission grew each year.

NOTES

EPIGRAPH

José Ortega y Gasset, *The Revolt of the Masses* (New York: W. W. Norton & Company, 1932), p. 48.

INTRODUCTION

1. Albert Lepawsky, "Intellectual Responsibility and Political Conduct," in *The Berkeley Student Revolt: Facts and Interpretations*, ed. Seymour Martin Lipset and Sheldon S. Wolin (New York: Doubleday Anchor, 1965), p. 22.

2. I will often use the term "academic free speech" because free speech and academic freedom are intimately related yet are distinct concepts and practices, as I will articulate in Chapters 2 and 3.

3. John Etchemendy, "The Threat From Within: Intellectual Intolerance Poses an Existential Danger to the University," *Chronicle of Higher Education*, March 3, 2017. Critical scholars who have recently addressed such policies and practices include, among others, Jonathan Zimmerman, *Campus Politics: What Everyone Needs to Know* (New York: Oxford University Press, 2016); Frank Furedi, *What's Happened to the University?* (Abingdon, UK, and New York: Routledge, 2016); Erwin Chemerinsky and Howard Gillman, *Free Speech on Campus* (New Haven, CT: Yale University Press, 2017); Keith Whittington, *Speak Freely: Why Universities Must Defend Free Speech* (Princeton, NJ: Princeton University Press, 2018); and Nadine Strossen, *Hate: Why We Should Resist It with Free Speech, Not Censorship* (New York: Oxford University Press, 2018).

4. Arianne Shahvisi, "From Academic Freedom to Academic Responsibility," in *The Value and Limits of Academic Speech*, ed. Donald A. Downs and Chris W. Surprenant (Abingdon, UK, and New York: Routledge, 2018), p. 266.

5. Even if individuals were to be perfectly moral—a matter of hypothesis only—organized society by its very nature always includes aspects of struggle and conflict, thereby requiring free speech to address. See, e.g., Reinhold Niebuhr, *Moral Man and Immoral Society* (New York: Scribner, 1932).

6. See, e.g., Justice Oliver Wendell Holmes Jr. dissenting in *Abrams v. United States*, 250 U.S. 616 (1919), p. 630. The "theory of our Constitution" is "an experiment, as all life is an experiment." Alexander Meiklejohn, "Free Speech and Its Relation to Self-Government," in *Political Freedom: The Constitutional Powers of the People* (New York: Oxford University Press, 1965), pp. 27–28.

7. On the history of CAFAR, see Donald A. Downs and Stanley G. Payne, "The Wisconsin Fight for Academic Freedom," *Academic Questions* 29, no. 2 (2016). See also Donald A. Downs, *Restoring Free Speech and Liberty on Campus* (Cambridge: Cambridge University Press, 2005).

8. See, e.g., Michael Kent Curtis, *Free Speech, "The People's Darling Privilege": Struggles for Freedom of Expression in American History* (Durham, NC: Duke University Press, 2000). See also Alexis de Tocqueville, *Democracy in America*, trans. Richard Reeves (New York: Schocken Books, 1961). On bureaucracy as a necessary institution within bounds, see James Q. Wilson, *Bureaucracy: What Government Agencies Do and Why They Do It* (New York: Basic Books, 1989).

9. Ralph Ellison, "What These Children Are Like," *Teaching American History*, September 1963.

10. See Dana Villa, *Socratic Citizenship* (Princeton: NJ: Princeton University Press, 2001). On how responsible policymaking requires attention to conflict, tension, and contradiction, see John Gaddis, *On Grand Strategy* (New York: Penguin Random House, 2018). Gaddis's political theory model of this way of thinking is Isaiah Berlin.

11. See, e.g., Richard K. Vedder, *Restoring the Promise: Higher Education in America* (Oakland, CA: Independent Institute, 2019).

12. See *Palm Beach Post*, "Charles Krauthammer, Conservative Columnist and Pundit, Dies," June 22, 2018.

CHAPTER 1

1. Evan Charney, "The End of Being a Duke Professor and What It Means for the Future of Higher Education," James G. Martin Center, April 22, 2019.

2. Frank Furedi documents the alliance between student emotional regression and campus bureaucracies at length in *What's Happened to the University?* (Abingdon, UK, and New York: Routledge, 2016). See also Greg Lukianoff and Jonathan Haidt, *The Coddling of the American Mind: How Good Intentions and Bad Ideas Are Setting Up a Generation for Failure* (New York: Penguin Press, 2018).

3. Alan C. Kors and Harvey Silverglate, *The Shadow University: The Betrayal of Liberty on America's Campuses* (New York: Free Press, 1998).

4. *Tinker v. Des Moines Sch. Dist.*, 393 U.S. 503 (1969), pp. 512–13.

5. See, e.g., FIRE's website that chronicles campus speaker disruptions over the years: https://www.thefire.org/?s=speech+disruptions; see also Adam Steinbaugh, "Hecklers Shout Down California Attorney General, Assembly Majority Leader at Whittier College," FIRE Newsdesk, October 13, 2017.

6. Allison Stanger, "Understanding the Angry Mob at Middlebury That Gave Me a Concussion," *New York Times*, March 13, 2017.

7. Allison Stanger, "Middlebury, My Divided Campus," *New York Times*, April 3, 2017. I held long phone conversations with a leader of the pro–free speech group beforehand. The group's preparation was extensive. So was the negative reaction to their position.

8. See, e.g., *Board of Education of Island Trees Free School District No. 26 v. Pico*, 457 U.S. 853 (1982). Removal of a public school library book as a result of pressure creates more of a presumption of discriminatory motive than does the initial book selection process.

9. Josh Logue, "Uninvited to Williams," *Inside Higher Ed*, October 21, 2015.

10. FIRE, "Disinvitation Database," https://www.thefire.org/resources /disinvitation-database/. My Cornell experience was in reaction to the publication of my book titled *Cornell '69: Liberalism and the Crisis of the American University* (Cornell University Press, 1999).

11. Jeffrey A. Sachs, "The 'Campus Free Speech Crisis' Ended Last Year," Niskanen Center, January 25, 2019.

12. Jeremy Bauer-Wolf, "Free Speech 'Meltdown': Williams Plans to Revise Its Policies after a Faculty Petition to Adopt Free Speech Guidelines Enraged Student Activists," *Inside Higher Education*, April 23, 2019.

13. C-SPAN, "Q & A with John Gaddis," May 8, 2018.

14. Laura Kipnis, "Sexual Paranoia Strikes Academe," *Chronicle of Higher Education*, February 27, 2015.

15. See, e.g., Evan Gerstmann, *Campus Sexual Assault: Constitutional Rights and Fundamental Fairness* (Cambridge: Cambridge University Press, 2019).

16. Laura Kipnis, *Unwanted Advances: Sexual Paranoia Comes to Campus* (New York: Harper Collins, 2017), pp. 2–3.

17. Kipnis, *Unwanted Advances*, p. 6. [Emphasis added.] See also Alan Charles Kors and Harvey A. Silverglate, *The Shadow University: The Betrayal of Liberty on America's Campuses* (New York: Free Press, 1998).

18. David Jesse, "University of Michigan to Invest $85 Million in Diversity Programs," *Detroit Free Press*, October 6, 2016.

19. Heather Mac Donald, "At Yale, 'Diversity' Means More of the Same," *Wall Street Journal,* April 23, 2019; Heather Mac Donald, *The Diversity Delusion* (New York: St. Martin's Press, 2018); and Frederick R. Lynch, *The Diversity Machine* (New York: Free Press, 1997).

20. Alexis de Tocqueville, *Democracy in America*, trans. Richard Reeves (New York: Schocken Books, 1961).

21. The information here is based on email correspondence with members of Georgetown's Department of Political Science over the course of 2018.

22. See, e.g., Samuel J. Abrams, "Professors Support Free Speech," *American Interest*, April 14, 2018; Samuel J. Abrams, "Think Professors Are Liberal? Try College Administrators," *New York Times*, October 16, 2018.

23. I have encountered them at two national academic free speech events. For a report on the 2017 incident and its aftermath, see Scott Jaschik, "Evergreen Calls Off Day of Absence," *Inside Higher Ed*, February 22, 2018.

24. See, e.g., Bari Weiss, "When the Left Turns on Its Own," *New York Times*, June 1, 2017; Jillian Kay Melchior, "Rough Justice at Evergreen State," *Wall Street Journal*, May 22, 2018.

25. See, e.g., Chris Bodenner, "The Surprising Revolt at the Most Liberal College in America," *Atlantic Monthly*, November 2, 2017.

26. Bari Weiss, "Meet the Renegades of the Intellectual Dark Web," *New York Times*, May 8, 2018.

27. "Cowardice and Courage at Middlebury," *Wall Street Journal*, April 19, 2019; Dominic Aiello, "What I Saw at Middlebury College," *Quillette*, April 27, 2019.

28. Melissa Korn, "New Topic on Campus: Civil Discourse 101," *Wall Street Journal*, August 15, 2018.

29. Allan Bloom, *The Closing of the American Mind* (New York: Simon and Schuster, 1987), p. 249.

30. Timur Kuran, *Private Truths, Public Lies: The Social Consequences of Preference Falsification* (Cambridge, MA: Harvard University Press, 1995). As Hannah Arendt has discerned, totalitarianism's "success" depends on keeping citizens as isolated as possible, as well as unorganized and immobilized. See her book *The Origins of Totalitarianism* (New York: Harcourt Brace, 1951).

31. See Donald A. Downs, *Restoring Free Speech and Liberty on Campus* (Cambridge: Cambridge University Press for the Independent Institute, 2005).

CHAPTER 2

1. See, e.g., Paul Horwitz, *First Amendment Institutions* (Cambridge, MA: Harvard University Press, 2013), esp. chap. 5.

2. Clark Kerr, *The Uses of the University* (Cambridge, MA: Harvard University Press, 1963).

3. Jack Stripling, "Inside Auburn's Secret Effort to Advance an Athlete-Friendly Curriculum," *Chronicle of Higher Education*, February 16, 2018.

4. University of California San Diego, "Contributions to Diversity Statements." See, e.g., Mark J. Perry, "All Applicants for Faculty Positions at UCSD Now Required to Submit a 'Contribution to Diversity Statement,'" *American Enterprise Institute, Carpe Diem* (blog), April 28, 2018. See also Sarah Brown, "More Colleges Are Asking Faculty for Diversity Statements," *Chronicle of Higher Education*, January 29, 2019.

5. Keith E. Whittington, *Speak Freely: Why Universities Must Defend Free Speech* (Princeton, NJ: Princeton University Press, 2018).

6. On the key distinction between ontology and epistemology, see John Searle, *The Rediscovery of the Mind* (Cambridge, MA: MIT Press, 1988), esp. chap. 1. See also Chapter 8 of this book.

7. In physics, this is known as the "observer effect." See also Kant on the unattainability of the "thing in itself."

8. See, e.g., "Vince Lombardi Jr. Quotes," https://www.goodreads.com/quotes /32550-gentlemen-we-will-chase-perfection-and-we-will-chase-it. See also Jonathan Rauch, "The Constitution of Knowledge," *National Affairs*, Fall 2018.

9. Stanley Fish, *Versions of Academic Freedom* (Chicago: University of Chicago Press, 2014). See also Judith Jarvis Thompson, "Ideology and Faculty Selection," in *Freedom and Tenure in the Academy*, ed. William van Alstyne (Durham, NC: Duke University Press, 1993).

10. See, e.g., Society for Applied Anthropology, "Human Rights and Social Justice Committee."

11. I am indebted to Jaroslav Pelikan, *The Idea of the University: A Reexamination* (New Haven, CT: Yale University Press, 1992), for emphasizing the first three virtues that compose the heart of the university. I added the fourth.

12. Crane Brinton, *The Shaping of the Modern Mind* (New York: New American Library, 1953). See also Thomas Kuhn, *The Structure of Scientific Revolutions* (Chicago: University of Chicago Press, 1962).

13. William Shakespeare, *Hamlet*, Act I, Scene 5; Kenneth Clark, in Walter Isaacson, *Leonardo Da Vinci* (New York: Simon and Schuster, 2017), p. 463; Friedrich Nietzsche, *The Birth of Tragedy*, in *The Birth of Tragedy and the Case of Wagner*, trans. Walter Kaufmann (New York: Vintage, 1967); On how liberal education should provide an intellectual tool for students to examine themselves and the deeper aspects and conflicts of life, including the meaning of life, death, and struggles of the soul, see Anthony Kronman, *Education's End: How Our Colleges and Universities Have Given Up on the Meaning of Life* (New Haven, CT: Yale University Press, 2007).

14. Friedrich Nietzsche, *Beyond Good and Evil: Prelude to a Philosophy of the Future*, trans. Walter Kaufmann (New York: Vintage, 1966).

15. Meiklejohn, "Free Speech and Its Relation to Self-Government," in *Political Freedom: The Constitutional Powers of the People* (New York: Oxford University Press, 1965), p. 75.

16. Daniel Kahneman, *Thinking Fast and Slow* (New York: Macmillan, 2012). John Searle's notion of the "background to the mind" is helpful in terms of linking the two systems of thought. What we learn from "slow" thinking can be stored in memory, affecting conscious life when triggered by experience and recollection. Searle, *The Rediscovery of the Mind*.

17. Jonathan Haidt, *The Righteous Mind: Why Good People Are Divided by Politics and Religion* (New York: Pantheon Books, 2012).

18. See Michael S. Gazzaniga, *The Consciousness Instinct: Unraveling the Mystery of How the Brain Makes the Mind* (New York: Farrar, Straus, and Giroux, 2018), chap. 6.

19. On the humanities and the vicissitudes of human nature, see Anthony T. Kronman, *Education's End: Why Our Colleges and Universities Have Given Up on the Meaning of Life* (New Haven, CT: Yale University Press, 2007).

20. On the ways in which the striving for affirmation of one's identity conflicts with the institutional commitment to critical thought, see Frank Furedi, *What's Happened to the University?* (Abingdon, UK, and New York: Routledge, 2016); John Stuart Mill, *On Liberty*.

21. Mark Lilla, *The Once and Future Liberal: After Identity Politics* (New York: HarperCollins, 2017), p. 10. Lilla's critique echoes that of Richard Sennett's 1974 critique of turning politics into psychological needs in *The Fall of Public Man* (New York: Knopf, 1976). "Identity politics" was a less known term 40 years ago.

22. Jonathan Haidt, "The Age of Outrage," speech, Manhattan Institute's Wriston Lecture, New York, NY, November 15, 2017. The quotation is from E. D. Hirsch.

23. See, e.g., Charles Taylor, "The Politics of Recognition," in *Multiculturalism: Examining the Politics of Recognition*, ed. Amy Gutmann (Princeton, NJ: Princeton University Press, 1992), p. 26.

24. See, e.g., David Moshman, "Martin Luther King on the First Amendment," *Huffington Post*, January 4, 2017.

25. See, e.g., Donald A. Downs, *Restoring Free Speech and Liberty on Campus* (Cambridge: Cambridge University Press for the Independent Institute, 2005), chaps. 6 and 7.

26. Anthony Giddens, *Modernity and Self-Identity: Self and Society in the Late Modern Age* (Palo Alto, CA: Stanford University Press, 1991).

27. In the following discussion of civility, I am indebted to what I learned from reading Richard Sennett's insightful book titled *The Fall of Public Man* (New York: Knopf, 1976), which discusses civility and other qualities related to the character and psychological attributes that support a healthy public realm.

28. See, e.g., *Cohen v. California*, 403 U.S. 15 (1971), p. 26: ". . . much linguistic expression serves a dual communicative function: it conveys not only ideas capable of relatively precise, detached explication, but otherwise inexpressible emotions as well."

29. American Association of University Professors (AAUP), "On Collegiality as a Criterion for Faculty Evaluation," 2016.

30. Definitions from Lexico, https://en.oxforddictionaries.com/definition/civility.

31. See, e.g., Philip Rieff's classic book, *The Triumph of the Therapeutic: Uses of Faith after Freud* (New York: Harper and Row, 1966). See also Elizabeth Lasch-Quinn, *Race Experts: How Racial Etiquette, Sensitivity Training, and New Age Therapy Hijacked the Civil Rights Movement* (New York: W. W. Norton, 2001); Richard Sennett, *The Fall of Public Man*.

32. Hannah Arendt, *The Human Condition* (Chicago: University of Chicago Press, 1958), p. 36.

33. Simone de Beauvoir, *The Second Sex*, ed. and trans. H. M. Parshley (New York: Vintage Books, 1952); Meiklejohn, "Free Speech and Its Relation to Self-Government," p. 9.

34. See, e.g., Laurence Tribe, *American Constitutional Law*, 3rd ed. (Foundation Press, 2000), chap. 12.

35. See, e.g., *Schenck v. United States*, 249 U.S. 47 (1919) (distributing anti-war letters to draftees); *Debs v. United States,* 249 U.S. 211 (1919) (making an anti-war speech in a park); *Frohwerk v. United States,* 249 U.S. 204 (1919) (publishing anti-war sentiment); *Masses Publishing Company v. Patten*, 244 Fed.535 (S.D.N.Y. 1917) (sending an anti-war magazine in the mail). In general, see David Rabban, *Free Speech in Its Forgotten Years: 1870–1920* (Cambridge: Cambridge University Press, 1997).

36. *R.A.V. v. St. Paul*, 505 U.S. 377 (1992). See also Edward J. Cleary, *Beyond the Burning Cross: A Landmark Case of Race, Law, and the First Amendment* (New York: Vintage, 1994), p. 44.

37. An illustrative book on how socio-political evolution and revolution have affected the development of Western law, see Harold J. Berman's *Law and Revolution: The Formation of the Western Legal Tradition* (Cambridge, MA: Harvard University Press, 1983).

38. *McCulloch v. Maryland*, 17 U.S. 316 (1819), p. 407. [Emphasis in original.]

39. See, e.g., Donald A. Downs, *Arms and the University: Military Presence and the Civic Education of Non-Military Students* (Cambridge: Cambridge University Press, 2012).

40. AAUP, "Appendix I: 1915 Declaration of Principles on Academic Freedom and Tenure," https://www.aaup.org/NR/rdonlyres/A6520A9D-0A9A-47B3-B550-C006B5B224E7/0/1915Declaration.pdf.

41. Furedi, *What's Happened to the University?*

42. Tocqueville, *Democracy in America*, trans. Richard Reeves, (New York: Schocken Books, 1961).

43. On the "monarchical" qualities of the unchecked administrative state, see Philip Hamburger, *Is Administrative Law Unlawful?* (Chicago: University of Chicago Press, 2014). See also Michael Kent Curtis, *Free Speech, "The People's Darling Privilege": Struggles for Freedom of Expression in American History* (Durham, NC: Duke University Press, 2000).

44. See, e.g., David Moshman, "Martin Luther King on the First Amendment," *HuffPost*, January 4, 2017. On the crucial role of free speech and the civil rights movement, see Timothy Shiell, *African Americans and the First Amendment* (Albany, NY: SUNY Press, 2019).

45. AAUP, *1915 Declaration of Principles on Academic Freedom and Tenure*. See also *Whitney v. California*, 274 U.S. 357 (1927), p. 377.

46. See, e.g., George M. Marsden, *The Soul of the American University: From Protestant Establishment to Established Nonbelief* (New York: Oxford University Press, 1994). See also Albert Hirschman, *Exit, Voice, and Loyalty* (Cambridge, MA: Harvard University Press, 1970).

47. On competing *nomos*, see Robert Cover, "Foreword: *Nomos* and Narrative," *Harvard Law Review* 97, no. 1 (1983): 4–68. In a related vein, see Samuel Huntington, *American Politics: The Promise of Disharmony* (Cambridge, MA: Harvard University Press, 1981), and Jacob Levy's *Rationalism, Pluralism, and Freedom* (New York: Oxford University Press, 2015). On checks and balances and uniformity of opinion, see Paul Eidelberg, *The Philosophy of the American Constitution: A Reinterpretation of the Intentions of the Founding Fathers* (New York: Free Press, 1968), esp. p. 153.

48. See Adam Laats, *Fundamentalist U: Keeping the Faith in American Higher Education* (New York: Oxford University Press, 2018).

49. Patrick Deneen, *Why Liberalism Failed* (New Haven, CT: Yale University Press, 2018).

50. See, e.g., Berns, *Making Patriots* (Chicago: University of Chicago Press, 2001). Berns resigned from Cornell in 1969 when the university turned its back on academic freedom in favor of the demands of social justice advocates bearing guns on campus. See Donald A. Downs, *Cornell '69: Liberalism and the Crisis of the American University* (Ithica, NY: Cornell University Press, 1999).

51. See, e.g., Robert Booth Fowler, *Unconventional Partners: Religion and Liberal Culture in the United States* (Grand Rapids, MI: W. B. Eerdmans, 1989); Bernard Yack, ed., *Liberalism without Illusions: Essays on Liberal Theory and the Political Vision of Judith N. Shklar* (Chicago: University of Chicago Press, 1996).

52. *New State Ice Co. v. Liebmann*, 285 U.S. 262 (1932), Brandeis dissenting, p. 285.

53. *John McAdams v. Marquette University*, Wisconsin Supreme Court, Case No. 2014AP1240 (July 6, 2018). In Chapter 8 I discuss the ambiguities and tensions in this case.

54. John Hasnas, "Freedom of Expression at the Private University," in *The Value and Limits of Academic Free Speech*, ed. Donald A. Downs and Chris W. Surprenant (Abingdon, UK, and New York: Routledge, 2018), chap. 5. See also Greg Lukianoff, "Liberty University, Free Speech, and the Private University," June 3, 2009, FIRE Newsdesk (web page), https://www.thefire.org/liberty -university-free-speech-and-the-private-university/.

CHAPTER 3

1. See also Robert Post, *Democracy, Expertise, and Academic Freedom: A First Amendment Jurisprudence for the Modern State* (New Haven, CT: Yale University Press, 2013). See also Robert Post, "The Classic First Amendment Tradition Under Stress: Freedom of Speech and the University," keynote address for conference on *Free Speech and Intellectual Diversity in Higher Education: Implications for American Society*, School of Civic and Economic Thought and Leadership, Arizona State University, February 23–25, 2018. Cosponsored by ASU Walter Cronkite School of Journalism and Mass Communication and by Sandra Day O'Connor School of Law, https://scetl.asu.edu/content/2018-spring-conference-%E2%80%94-free-speech-and-intellectual-diversity-higher-education.

2. See, e.g., James R. Stoner, "Are Academic Freedom and Freedom of Speech Congruent or Opposed?" in *The Value and Limits of Academic Speech*, ed. Donald A. Downs and Chris W. Surprenant (Abingdon, UK, and New York: Routledge, 2018), chap. 4.

3. John H. Newman, "Discourse VII: Knowledge Viewed in Relation to Professional Skill" (1852), in *The Idea of a University: Defined and Illustrated*, ed. T. Ker (Oxford: Clarendon Press, 1976), p. 154.

4. Other justifications of free speech include things such as the elusive pursuit of truth, self-realization and happiness, social change, speech as a safety valve for dissent, inherent individual rights, consent theory, and distrust of government, among others. In this book, see Chapter 7, "Fitting It All Together."

5. Though Post did not mention his name, Alexander Meiklejohn is the most prominent advocate of this theory of free speech. See Meiklejohn, "Free Speech and Its Relation to Self-Government," in *Political Freedom: The Constitutional Powers of the People* (New York: Oxford University Press, 1965).

6. Frank Furedi, "Growing Up Disturbed," in *The Value and Limits of Academic Free Speech*, ed. Donald A. Downs and Chris W. Surprenant (Abingdon, UK, and New York: Routledge, 2018), chap. 12. See also Furedi, *What's Happened to the University?* Other empirical critiques of the self-government theory abound today, largely maintaining that economic, social, and political power are now too concentrated and top-heavy for liberal democracy to flourish. See, e.g., Patrick Deneen, *Why Liberalism Failed* (New Haven, CT: Yale University Press, 2018).

7. *Gertz v. Robert Welch, Inc.*, 418 U.S. 323 (1974), p. 340.

8. John Rawls, *Political Liberalism* (New York: Columbia University Press, 2005), p. 427. In *Kindly Inquisitors*, Jonathan Rauch defends what he calls the "empirical rule," which means that truth claims must be demonstrated by relevant facts rather than simply deferring to the conclusions of people with authority or prestige. But note that Rauch also correctly stresses that it is profoundly wrong to hold that all ideas are entitled to equal respect. He critiques the "Egalitarian Principle" in this regard in *Kindly Inquisitors: The New Attacks on Free Thought* (Chicago: University of Chicago Press, 1993), chaps. 1 and 2.

9. *West Virginia State Bd. of Educ. v. Barnette,* 319 U.S. 624 (1943).

10. See, e.g., Frederick Schauer, *Free Speech: A Philosophical Enquiry* (Cambridge, MA: Harvard University Press, 1982).

11. See, e.g., Matthew Finkin and Robert Post, *For the Common Good: Principles of American Academic Freedom* (New Haven: Yale University Press, 2009), esp. p. 94.

12. Jeremy Waldron, *The Harm in Hate Speech* (Cambridge, MA: Harvard University Press, 2012), p. 27.

13. On the practical and administrative slippery slope regarding Waldron's definition of hate speech even in the higher education context, see C. K. Miles, "Skepticism About Title IX Culture," in Downs and Suprenant, *The Value and Limits of Academic Free Speech,* chap. 15.

14. *Axson-Flynn v. Johnson,* 356 F.3d 1277 (10th Cir. 2004).

15. *Sweezy v. New Hampshire,* 354 U.S. 234 (1957), p. 263.

16. AAUP, *A Statement of the Association's Council: Freedom and Responsibility,* October 1970. On this aspect of duty—to protect rights—see, e.g., Wesley Newcomb Hohfeld, *Fundamental Legal Conceptions as Applied in Judicial Reasoning* (New Haven, CT: Yale University Press, 1946).

17. Robert Post, "There Is No 1st Amendment Right to Speak on a College Campus," *Vox,* October 25, 2017.

18. Amy M. Hass, general counsel for the University of Florida, related this background to the panel and audience at the University of Tampa on April 6, 2018, at a symposium on "Free Speech and Academic Freedom." See also Jeremy Bauer-Wolf, "Lessons from Spencer's Florida Speech," *Inside Higher Education,* October 23, 2017.

19. Donald A. Downs, *The New Politics of Pornography* (Chicago: University of Chicago Press, 1989), p. 130.

20. See Aryeh Neier, *Defending My Enemy: American Nazis, the Skokie Case, and the Risks of Freedom* (New York: Dutton, 1979); Donald A. Downs, *Nazis in Skokie: Freedom, Community, and the First Amendment* (Notre Dame, IN: University of Notre Dame Press, 1985), chap. 6.

21. See, e.g., Calum Miller, "The Plausibility of Abhorrent Views, and Why It Matters," in Downs and Surprenant, *The Value and Limits of Academic Free Speech,* chap. 19.

22. On how academic institutions have an obligation to uphold the distinction between truth and intellectual propaganda in teaching and research, see, e.g., Mary Lefkowitz, *History Lesson: A Race Odyssey* (New Haven, CT: Yale University Press, 2008).

23. Erwin Chemerinsky and Howard Gillman, *Free Speech on Campus* (New Haven, CT: Yale University Press, 2017), pp. 75, 77.

24. Keith E. Whittington, *Speak Freely: Why Universities Must Defend Free Speech* (Princeton, NJ: Princeton University Press, 2018), pp. 150–60.

25. *Garcetti v. Ceballos*, 547 U.S. 410 (2006).

26. Yale College, *Report of the Committee on Free Expression at Yale* (1974), Section 1, "Of Values and Priorities." [Emphasis added.]

27. *Tinker v. Des Moines Sch. Dist.*, 393 U.S. 503 (1969), pp. 512–13. [Emphasis added.] When it comes to precollege institutions, *Tinker* has been limited by subsequent decisions that are more deferential to school authorities, but its central holding hangs on, perhaps precariously, and its message remains normatively strong, especially for higher education.

28. In the wake of California Proposition 209 in the late 1990s that limited the use of race as a criterion for admission to public higher education, a climate of severe intolerance of different viewpoints about race arose at Berkeley's Boalt Law School. Many students chose to express their disagreements with this silencing on the bathroom stalls rather than in more public domains. Even students opposed to 209 were more upset at the effect of the broad silencing on their educations. See David Wienir and Marc Berley, eds., *The Diversity Hoax: Law Students Report from Berkeley* (Foundation for Academic Standards and Tradition, 1999), pp. 52–53, 155. See also Donald A. Downs, *Restoring Free Speech and Liberty on Campus* (Cambridge: Cambridge University Press, 2006), chap. 4. Listen to the words of Simon and Garfunkel, "The Sounds of Silence," https://www.youtube.com/watch?v=--DbgPXwLlM.

29. Laura Kipnis, *Unwanted Advances: Sexual Paranoia Comes to Campus* (New York: HarperCollins, 2017), p. 49.

30. Boris Pasternak, *Doctor Zhivago*, trans. Richard Pevear and Larissa Volokhonsky (New York: Pantheon, 2010). Soviet political theory also invented the idea of "socialist realism," which assimilated individual intellectual, scientific, and artistic exploration and imagination to the imperatives of the Communist Party.

31. Burkay Ozturk and Bob Fischer, "Speech and War: Rethinking the Ethics of Speech Restrictions," in Downs and Surprenant, *The Value and Limits of Academic Speech*, chap. 11.

32. Robert Cover, "Foreward: *Nomos* and Narrative: *Harvard Law Review* 97, no. 1 (1983–1984): 4–68. See also, Samuel Huntington, *American Politics: The Promise of Disharmony* (Cambridge, MA: Harvard University Press, 1981).

33. Hans-Georg Gadamer, *Truth and Method*, trans. Garrett Barden and John Cumming (New York: Seabury Press, 1975), pp. 92–210. William Shakespeare, *Hamlet*, Act 2, Scene 2.

34. See Harry Kalven Jr., *The Negro and the First Amendment* (Chicago: University of Chicago Press, 1965).

35. In legal parlance, this rule is an example of "legitimated disobedience," which means it is okay to disobey the law. Examples include the disobeying of

an unconstitutional statute or administrative order, the nullification of a jury's decision, and the necessity defense in criminal law, which includes self-defense. See Mortimer R. Kadish and Sanford H. Kadish, *Discretion to Disobey: A Study of Lawful Departures from Legal Rules* (Palo Alto, CA: Stanford University Press, 1973).

36. See, e.g., *Bible Believers v. Wayne County*, 805 F. 3d. 228 (2015), which summarizes these rules nicely. The modern jurisprudence of the heckler's veto is built on another famous dissent, this time Justice Hugo Black's in *Feiner v. New York*, in which the Supreme Court upheld Feiner's conviction because he failed to obey a police order in which police did not abide by those rules. Black's dissent became governing doctrine when the Court began fashioning the Modern Doctrine of Speech.

37. See Thomas Emerson, *The System of Freedom of Expression* (New Haven, CT: Yale University Press, 1970). The Supreme Court has used the concept of "ordered liberty" often in its jurisprudence. See, e.g., its use of the concept in its cases involving the incorporation of the Bill of Rights to apply to the states. *Palko v. Connecticut*, 302 U.S. 319 (1937). Political theorists ranging from Burke, Tocqueville, the Framers, and Meiklejohn have used the concept as a limit on freedom. See also Michael G. Kammen, *Spheres of Liberty: Changing Perceptions of Liberty in American Culture* (Ithica, NY: Cornell University Press, 1985).

38. *Report of the Chancellor's Commission on Free Speech*, UC–Berkeley, April 9, 2018.

39. UW–Madison's definition of "academic freedom" similarly connects academic freedom and free speech norms. See "Statement on Principles of Free Expression," University of Chicago, July 2012, https://provost.uchicago.edu/sites /default/files/documents/reports/FOECommitteeReport.pdf. See also Donald A. Downs, "The University of Wisconsin Counters *Garcetti v. Ceballos*," AAUP.

40. See, e.g., *Roberts v. Haragan*, 346 F. Supp. 2d 853 (N.D. Tex. 2004), which struck down Texas Tech University's "free speech zone" policy restricting free speech to a very small space and requiring a permit be acquired prior to the speech. On funding of student groups, see *Board of Regents of the University of Wisconsin System v. Southworth*, 529 U.S. 217 (2000). On speech codes, see *UWM Post v. Board of Regents*, 773 F. Supp. 1163 (E.D. Wis., 1991).

41. See Brian Leiter, "Why Academic Freedom?" in Downs and Surprenant, *The Value and Limits of Academic Free Speech*.

42. José Ortega y Gasset, *Mission of the University* (New York: W. W. Norton, 1966).

43. Hans J. Morgenthau, "The Purpose of Political Science," in *A Design for Political Science: Scope, Objectives, and Methods*, ed. James C. Charlesworth (Philadelphia, PA: American Academy of Political and Social Science, 1966); Karl Marx, *Eleven Theses on Feuerbach*.

44. See also Roger Scruton, *The Soul of the World* (Princeton, NJ: Princeton University Press, 2014). Human character and community are forged through the encounter of the self with the "other" as a free person with distinctively human characteristics that cannot be reduced to instinct and other purely naturalistic forces.

45. Whittington, *Speak Freely*. Whittington accentuated the same point in an address at UW–Madison on April 20, 2018.

47. Paul Eidelberg, *The Philosophy of the American Constitution: A Reinterpretation of the Intentions of the Founding Fathers* (New York: Free Press, 1968), p. 153.

48. See, e.g., David M. Rabban, "Academic Freedom, Individual or Institutional? Most Federal Courts Agree that Academic Freedom Is a First Amendment Right, But Whose Right Is It?" *Academe*, November–December 2001.

49. For a learned treatise on the role of distrust in constitutional adjudication, see John Hart Ely, *Democracy and Distrust: A Theory of Judicial Review* (Cambridge, MA: Harvard University Press, 1980).

CHAPTER 4

1. University of California Microaggression List, https://sites.google.com/site /cacmnow/university-of-california-microaggression-lisy. Eugene Volokh, "UC Teaching Faculty Members Not to Criticize Race-Based Affirmative Action, Call America 'Melting pot,' and More," *Washington Post*, June 16, 2015.

2. Office for Civil Rights Resolution Agreement with University of Montana. OCR Case No. 10126001, DOJ DJ No. 169-44-9 (2013), https://www2.ed.gov /about/offices/list/ocr/docs/investigations/more/10126001-b.pdf.

3. "Department of Education Issues Proposed Title IX Regulations of Sexual Harassment," Association of Governing Boards of Colleges and Universities, February 22, 2019.

4. Laura Kipnis, *Unwanted Advances: Sexual Paranoia Comes to Campus* (New York: Harper Collins, 2017), pp. 1–2.

5. See, e.g., Alison Flood, "U.S. Students Request 'Trigger Warnings' on Literature," *The Guardian*, May 19, 2014; Katy Waldman, "Reading Ovid in the Age of #MeToo," *New Yorker*, February 12, 2018.

6. Greg Lukianoff and Jonathan Haidt, "The Coddling of the American Mind," *Atlantic Monthly*, September 2015.

7. Jonathan Zimmerman, *Campus Politics: What Everyone Needs to Know* (New York: Oxford University Press, 2016), pp. 99–103.

8. AAUP, "On Trigger Warnings" (2014); National Coalition Against Censorship, "NCAC Report: What's All This About Trigger Warnings?" (2014).

9. Diane Ravitch, *The Language Police: How Pressure Groups Restrict What Students Can Learn* (New York: Knopf, 2003).

10. See, e.g., Conor Friedersdorf, "Why Critics of the 'Microaggressions' Framework Are Skeptical," *Atlantic Monthly*, September 14, 2015.

11. Evan Gerstmann, "Sex, Liberty, and Freedom of Sexual Expression at the American University," in *The Value and Limits of Academic Free Speech*, ed. Donald A. Downs and Chris W. Surprenant (Abingdon, UK, and New York: Routledge, 2018); Evan Gerstmann, *Campus Sexual Assault: Constitutional Rights and Fundamental Fairness* (Cambridge: Cambridge University Press), chap. 6.

12. I draw this language from an informative essay about BRTs by Jeffrey Aaron Snyder and Amna Khalid, "The Rise of 'Bias Response' Teams," *The New Republic*, March 30, 2016.

13. FIRE, *Bias Response Team Report 2017*.

14. Sometimes such incidents are not genuine examples of hate, though we also have ample examples of legitimate claims. Samantha Schmidt, "A Black Student Wrote Those Messages That Shook the Air Force Academy, School Says," *Washington Post*, November 8, 2017.

15. "Bias Review Team," Portland State University, https://www.pdx.edu/diversity/bias-response-team; Michael McGrady, "University Tells Students to Report 'Incidents of Discomfort' to Campus Police," The College Fix, February 15, 2016.

16. *Keyishian v. Board of Regents*, 385 U.S. 589 (1967), p. 603. See also *Healy v. James* in which college campuses are "peculiarly the 'marketplace of ideas.'" *Healy v. James*, 408 U.S. 169, 180 (1972). [Internal citation omitted.]

17. Snyder and Khalid, "The Rise of 'Bias Response' Teams."

18. Snyder and Khalid, "The Rise of 'Bias Response' Teams."

19. On pedagogic heuristics, see Matthew W. Finkin and Robert C. Post, *For the Common Good: Principles of Academic Freedom* (New Haven, CT: Yale University Press, 2009), p. 92. See also Conrad Russell, *Academic Freedom* (Abingdon, UK, and New York: Routledge, 1993).

20. Knight Foundation and Gallup, *Free Expression on Campus: What College Students Think About First Amendment Issues* (2018); Jean M. Twenge, *iGen: Why Today's Super-Connected Kids Are Growing Up Less Rebellious, More Tolerant, Less Happy—and Completely Unprepared for Adulthood* (New York: Atria Books, 2017), pp. 145, 152–54, 156, and, generally, chap. 9.

21. For a defense of safe spaces rightly understood, which strives to reconcile diversity and free speech, see John Palfrey, *Safe Spaces, Brave Spaces: Diversity and Free Expression in Education* (Cambridge, MA: MIT Press, 2017).

22. John McWhorter, "The Know-Nothing Campus 'Protest' Movement," *Daily Beast*, May 1, 2017.

23. See, e.g., Sean Stevens, "Campus Speaker Disinvitations: Recent Trends (Part 1 of 2)," Heterodox Academy, January 24, 2017.

24. Donald Alexander Downs, *Cornell '69: Liberalism and the Crisis of the American University* (Ithaca, NY: Cornell University Press, 1999).

25. Dana Rose Falcone, "Jerry Seinfeld: 'College Students Don't Know What the Hell They're Talking About,'" *Entertainment Weekly*, June 8, 2015.

26. Edward Johnson, "Don't Make Me Laugh: Speech Codes and the Humorless Campus," in Downs and Surprenant, *The Value and Limits of Academic Free Speech*.

27. Eric Owens, "University of Michigan Tries—and Fails—to Scrub Trump Trauma Play-Doh Event from Website," *Daily Caller*, November 12, 2016.

28. See Jeannie Suk Gersen, "The Trouble with Teaching Rape Law," *New Yorker*, December 15, 2014.

29. See, e.g., Eugene Volokh, "At the University of Oregon, No More Free Speech for Professors on Such Subjects As Race, Religion, and Sexual Orientation," *Washington Post*, December 26, 2016.

30. See FIRE, "Victory at UW–Stout: Chancellor Folds after Censorship of 'Firefly' and Anti-Fascism Posters," October 11, 2011.

31. Katherine Timpf, "Student Protesters: Defending the First Amendment Is 'Violent,'" *National Review*, December 5, 2017.

32. See, e.g., Mark Lilla, *The Once and Future Liberal: After Identity Politics* (New York: Harper Collins, 2017), p. 10. See also Richard Sennett, The Fall of Public Man (New York: Knopf, 1976).

33. Frank Furedi, "Growing Up Disturbed," in Downs and Surprenant, *The Value and Limits of Academic Speech*, p. 218. See also Furedi, *What's Happened to the University?* (Abingdon, UK, and New York: Routledge, 2016). For a broader perspective about the rise of therapeutic consciousness in the West, see Philip Rieff's classic book, *The Triumph of the Therapeutic: Uses of Faith after Freud* (New York: Harper and Row, 1966). See also Jonathan Haidt, "Forget the Money: Follow the Sacredness," *New York Times*, March 17, 2012. This is a theme also in Haidt, *The Righteous Mind: Why Good People Are Divided by Politics and Religion* (New York: Pantheon Books, 2012).

34. Nina Petraro, "Harmful Speech and True Threats: *Virginia v. Black* and the First Amendment in an Age of Terrorism," *Journal of Civil Rights and Economic Development* 20, no. 2 (2006): 546; *Virginia v. Black*, 538 U.S. 343 (2003).

35. On incitement, see *Brandenburg v. Ohio*, 395 U.S. 444 (1969); on fighting words and hostile speech, see *Cohen v. California*, 403 U.S. 15 (1971), and *Snyder v. Phelps*, 562 U.S. 443 (2010).

36. See Nadine Strossen, *Hate: Why We Should Resist It with Free Speech, Not Censorship* (New York: Oxford University Press, 2018), p. 79. Strossen also provides several other examples of this expansion.

37. *Beauharnais v. Illinois*, 343 U.S. 250 (1952). [Emphasis added.]

38. Jeremy Waldron, *The Harm in Hate Speech* (Cambridge, MA: Harvard University Press, 2012). On Waldron's definition of opening a door to abuse in actual application, see J. K. Miles, "Skepticism About Title IX Culture," in *The Value and Limits of Academic Free Speech,* ed. Donald A. Downs and Chris W. Surprenant, (Abingdon, UK, and New York, NY: Routledge, 2018).

39. See David M. Rabban, *Free Speech in Its Forgotten Years: 1870–1920* (Cambridge: Cambridge University Press, 1997), esp. chap. 8.

40. Václav Havel, "Words on Words," *New York Review of Books,* January 18, 1990. On the complexity of the "causation" question, see Anuj C. Desai, "Attacking Brandenburg with History: Does the Long Term Harm of Biased Speech Justify a Criminal Statute Suppressing It?" *Federal Communications Law Journal* 55, no. 2 (2003). For a thorough analysis of the various political, cultural, and economic forces that led to the fall of the Weimar Republic, see Benjamin Carter Hett, *The Death of Democracy: Hitler's Rise to Power and the Downfall of the Weimar Republic* (New York: Henry Holt & Co., 2018).

41. See Lynn Payer, *Medicine and Culture: Varieties of Treatment in the United States, England, West Germany, and France* (New York: Penguin, 1988). See also Joseph A. Amato, *Victims and Values: A History and a Theory of Suffering* (Westport, CT: Praeger, 1990). *The Value and Limits of Academic Free Speech,* cited earlier, contains several essays dealing with the "harm principle" and its application to campus speech. See, e.g., Andrew J. Cohen, "Harm: An Event-Based Feinbergian Account," which is Chapter 7 in the previously mentioned book.

42. See, e.g., Bernard E. Harcourt, "The Collapse of the Harm Principle," *Journal of Criminal Law and Criminology* 90, no. 1 (1999).

43. On "responsive law" as activist law distinguished from "autonomous law," see Philippe Nonet and Philip Selznick, *Law and Society in Transition: Toward Responsive Law* (Piscataway, NJ: Transaction Books, 2001), esp. chap. IV, "Responsive Law."

44. Herbert Marcuse, "Repressive Tolerance," in *A Critique of Pure Tolerance* (Boston, MA: Beacon Press, 1969). The minority report of the 1974 Woodward Report at Yale took a largely Marcusean line in justifying progressive grounds for restrictions of free speech on campus.

45. A key case in this development is *Edwards v. South Carolina,* 372 U.S. 229 (1963), which involved the grounds outside of the statehouse.

46. *National Socialist Party of America v. Village of Skokie,* 432 U.S. 43 (1977); *Collin v. Smith,* 575 F. 2d 1179 (7th Cir. 1978). I wrote about the case in *Nazis in Skokie: Freedom, Community, and the First Amendment* (Notre Dame, IN: University of Notre Dame Press, 1985). There I termed the proposed Nazi speech a "verbal assault." See also Aryeh Neier, *Defending My Enemy: The Skokie Case, American*

Nazis, and the Risks of Freedom (New York: Dutton, 1979). Neier was the national director of the ACLU during the Skokie litigation.

47. For a smart conservative critique of the Skokie decisions, see, e.g., Hadley Arkes, *The Philosopher in the City: The Moral Dimensions of Urban Politics* (Princeton, NJ: Princeton University Press, 1981), pp. 30–31, 81–82. For a history of the ACLU that includes a chapter on Skokie and the reaction to it, see Samuel Walker, *In Defense of American Liberties: A History of the ACLU* (New York: Oxford University Press, 1990), chap. 15.

48. *American Booksellers Association v. Hudnut*, 771 F.2d 323 (7th Cir. 1985), aff'd. mem., 475 U.S. 1001 (1986); Catharine A. MacKinnon, "Pornography, Civil Rights, and Speech," *Harvard Civil Rights–Civil Liberties Law Review* 20, no. 1 (1984): 42. See also MacKinnon, *Only Words* (Cambridge, MA: Harvard University Press, 1993); Donald A. Downs, *The New Politics of Pornography* (Chicago: University of Chicago Press, 1989).

49. See, e.g., Alan Charles Kors and Harvey A. Silverglate, *The Shadow University: The Betrayal of Liberty on America's Campuses* (New York: Free Press, 1998); Donald A. Downs, *Restoring Free Speech and Liberty on Campus* (Cambridge: Cambridge University Press, 2005).

50. *R.A.V. v. St. Paul*, 505 U.S. 377 (1992), pp. 391–92; Edward J. Cleary, *Beyond the Burning Cross: A Landmark Case of Race, Law, and the First Amendment* (New York: Vintage, 1994).

51. On the campus resistance to R.A.V., see Jon B. Gould, *Speak No Evil: The Triumph of Speech Code Regulation* (Chicago: University of Chicago Press, 2005); Martin J. Sweet, *Merely Judgment: Ignoring, Evading, and Trumping the Supreme Court* (Charlottesville, VA: University of Virginia Press, 2010); Gerald N. Rosenberg, *The Hollow Hope: Can Courts Bring About Social Change?* 2nd ed. (Chicago: University of Chicago Press, 2008).

52. FIRE, *Spotlight on Speech Codes 2017: The State of Free Speech on Our Nation's Campuses.*

53. Frederick M. Hess and Grant Addison, "Colleges Should Protect Speech—Or Lose Funds," *Wall Street Journal*, October 30, 2017, p. A17.

CHAPTER 5

1. Franklin Foer, "The Death of the Public Square," *Atlantic Monthly*, July 6, 2018. See also Franklin Foer, *World Without Mind: The Existential Threat of Big Tech* (New York: Penguin, 2017).

2. Hannah Arendt, "Truth and Politics," *New Yorker*, February 25, 1967.

3. See, e.g., Jennifer Kavanagh and Michael D. Rich, *Truth Decay: An Initial Exploration of the Diminishing Role of Facts and Analysis in American Public Life* (Santa Monica, CA: RAND Corporation, 2018).

4. Jeremi Suri, *The Impossible Presidency: The Rise and Fall of America's Highest Office* (New York: Basic Books, 2017); Alan I. Marcus, ed., *Service as Mandate: How American Land-Grant Universities Shaped the Modern World, 1920–2015* (Tuscaloosa, AL: University of Alabama Press, 2015); Richard K. Vedder questions the significance of the Morrill Act in *Restoring the Promise: Higher Education in America* (Oakland, CA: Independent Institute, 2019).

5. See AAUP, *Higher Education at a Crossroads: The Annual Report on the Economic Status of the Profession, 2015–16.*

6. Michael Horn, "Will Half of All Colleges Really Disappear in the Next Decade?" *Forbes*, December 13, 2018; Clayton M. Christensen and Michael B. Horn, "Innovation Imperative: Change Everything," *New York Times*, November 1, 2013.

7. Herb Childress, *The Adjunct Underclass: How America's Colleges Betrayed Their Faculty, Their Students, and Their Missions* (Chicago: University of Chicago Press, 2019).

8. Milton Sanford Mayer, *Robert Maynard Hutchins: A Memoir* (Berkeley, CA: University of California Press, 1993), p. 135.

9. See Larry G. Gerber, *The Rise and Decline of Faculty Governance: Professionalism and the Modern American University* (Baltimore: Johns Hopkins University Press, 2014).

10. James Madison, *Federalist No. 51*; Mayer, *Robert Maynard Hutchins*, p. 135; Benjamin Ginsberg, *The Fall of the Faculty: The Rise of the All-Administrative University and Why It Matters* (New York: Oxford University Press, 2011).

11. See Katherine Mangan, "New Disclosures About an NYU Professor Reignite a War Over Gender and Harassment," *Chronicle of Higher Education*, August 15, 2018.

12. The legal academic freedom status of course exams tends to favor the instructor, but this is not abundantly clear. However, the normative point is.

13. On how law and policy had not dealt forthrightly with sexual assault, see Stephen J. Schulhofer, *Unwanted Sex: The Culture of Intimidation and the Failure of Law* (Cambridge, MA: Harvard University Press, 1998).

14. R. Shep Melnick, "The Strange Evolution of Title IX," *National Affairs*, Summer 2018; Jacob Gersen and Jeannie Suk, "The Sex Bureaucracy," *California Law Review* 881 (2016); More broadly, see Philip Hamburger, *Is Administrative Law Unlawful?* (Chicago: University of Chicago Press, 2014).

15. *Doe v. University of Michigan*, 721 F. Supp. 852 (E.D. Mich. 1989).

16. David Jesse, "University of Michigan to Invest $85 Million in Diversity Programs," *Detroit Free Press*, October 6, 2016.

17. American Council of Trustees and Alumni, *A Crisis in Civic Education* (January 2016).

18. Holmes' dissent in *Abrams v. United States*, 250 U.S. 616 (1919), p. 630; Haidt, *The Righteous Mind: Why Good People Are Divided by Politics and Religion* (New York: Pantheon Books, 2012), p. 283 and elsewhere.

19. Paul Ricoeur, *Freud and Philosophy: An Essay on Interpretation* (New Haven, CT: Yale University Press, 1970).

20. For a probing and controversial exegesis of the relationship between "moral anger" and justice, see Walter Berns, *For Capital Punishment* (New York: Basic Books, 1979). See also Simon Wiesenthal, *The Sunflower: On the Possibilities and Limits of Forgiveness* (New York: Schoken Books, 1997).

21. Francisco José Moreno, *Between Faith and Reason: An Approach to Individual and Social Psychology* (New York: New York University Press, 1977). Moreno also discusses Søren Kierkegaard's philosophy of fear and dread. Like Moreno, Kierkegaard distinguished specific reasons for fear from the more general states of anxiety and dread. See, e.g., Søren Kierkegaard, *Fear and Trembling* (New York: Penguin Classics, 1985), as well as "On Anxiety," in *The Essential Kierkegaard*, Howard V. Hong and Edna H. Hong, ed. (Princeton, NJ: Princeton University Press, 1990).

22. Philip Jenkins, "Failure to Launch: Why Do Some Social Issues Fail to Detonate Moral Panics?" *British Journal of Criminology* 49, no. 1 (January 2009): 35–47. See also Joanna Bourke, *Fear: A Cultural History* (Berkeley, CA: Shoemaker Hoard, 2005).

23. See, e.g., Debbie Nathan and Michael Snedeker, *Satan's Silence: Ritual Abuse and the Making of a Modern American Witch Hunt* (New York: Basic Books, 1995); Dorothy Rabinowitz, *No Crueler Tyrannies: Accusation, False Witness, and Other Terrors of Our Times* (New York: Free Press, 2003); and Neil Hamilton, *Zealotry and Academic Freedom: A Legal and Historical Perspective* (Piscataway, NJ: Transaction Books, 1995).

24. Richard S. Randall, *Freedom and Taboo: Pornography and the Politics of a Self Divided* (Berkeley, CA: University of California Press 1989), pp. 5–6. For a philosophic and literary analysis of the universal desire to limit "forbidden knowledge," beginning with the story of Adam and Eve, see Roger Shattuck, *Forbidden Knowledge: From Prometheus to Pornography* (New York: Harcourt Brace & Co., 1996).

25. On Berlin, see John Lewis Gaddis, *On Grand Strategy* (New York: Penguin Books, 2018), esp. chap. 10. See, e.g., Isaiah Berlin, *The Hedgehog and the Fox: An Essay on Tolstoy's View of History* (Princeton, NJ: Princeton University Press, 2013); Isaiah Berlin, *The Crooked Timber of Humanity* (New York: Knopf, 1991). On social and political bi-formities, see Michael G. Kammen, *People of Paradox: An Inquiry Concerning the Origins of American Civilization* (New York: Knopf, 1972). On the paradox of freedom, see Erich Fromm, *Escape from Freedom* (New York:

Avon Books, 1969). On depth psychology, the "double," and related matters, see Henri F. Ellenberger's magisterial book, *The Discovery of the Unconscious: The History and Evolution of Dynamic Psychiatry* (New York: Basic Books, 1970).

26. Jon A. Shields and Joshua M. Dunn Sr., *Passing on the Right: Conservative Professors in the Progressive University* (New York: Oxford University Press, 2016); Paul Horwitz, *First Amendment Institutions* (Cambridge, MA: Harvard University Press, 2013).

27. As Roberto Unger wrote in *Law in Modern Society* about rule of law as a moral compromise, "For all parties concerned, the rule of law, like life insurance, and liberalism itself, was an attempt to make the best of a bad situation." Roberto Unger, *Law in Modern Society: Toward a Criticism of Social Theory* (New York: Free Press, 1977), p. 76.

28. See Donald A. Downs, "Whose Ox Is Gored? Free Speech, the War on Terror, and the Indivisibility of Rights," *The Good Society* 14, no. 1–2 (2005): 72–79.

29. In addition to Mill, see, e.g., Charlan Nemeth, *In Defense of Troublemakers: The Power of Dissent in Life and Business* (New York: Basic Books, 2018).

30. See, e.g., John M. Ellis, "Higher Education's Deeper Sickness," *Wall Street Journal*, November 13, 2017.

31. Students quoted in David Wienir and Marc Berley, eds., *The Diversity Hoax: Law Students Report from Berkeley* (Foundation for Academic Standards and Tradition, 1999), pp. 52–53, 155. See also Donald A. Downs, *Restoring Free Speech and Liberty on Campus* (Cambridge: Cambridge University Press, 2006), chap. 4.

32. Sandra Y. L. Korn, "The Doctrine of Academic Freedom: Let's Give Up on Academic Freedom in Favor of Justice," *Harvard Crimson*, February 18, 2014.

33. See, e.g., Center for Responsive Politics, OpenSecret.org, "Education," https://www.opensecrets.org/industries/indus.php?ind=W04.

34. Mitchell Langbert, Anthony J. Quain, and Daniel B. Klein. "Faculty Voter Registration in Economics, History, Journalism, Law, and Psychology," *Econ Journal Watch* 13, no. 3 (2016).

35. Neil Gross, *Why Are Professors Liberal and Why Do Conservatives Care?* (Cambridge, MA: Harvard University Press, 2013).

36. In *Why Liberalism Failed*, Patrick J. Deneen distinguished the more classical type of liberal who emerged out of the Enlightenment and who prioritized liberty and a more limited state, as well as second stage liberals who seek equality and complete freedom for the self under the aegis of strong state support. (New Haven, CT: Yale University Press, 2018), chap. 2.

37. Shields and Dunn, *Passing on the Right*, pp. 4, 79, 185, chap. 4 generally.

38. See, e.g., Brooke Sopelsa, "Brown Criticized for Removing an Article on Transgender Study," *NBC News*, September 5, 2018.

CHAPTER 6

1. Sally Carpenter, "The mystery of the Peanuts' parents," Ladies of Mystery (website), https://ladiesofmystery.com/2017/02/06/the-mystery-of-the-peanuts-parents/.

2. On this distinction, see John Villasenor, "Views Among College Students Regarding the First Amendment: Results from a New Survey," *FixGov* (blog), Brookings Institution, September 18, 2017.

3. Samuel J. Abrams, "Professors Support Free Speech," *The American Interest*, April 18, 2018.

4. See, e.g., Samuel A. Stouffer, *Communism, Conformity, and Civil Liberties: A Cross-Section of the Nation Speaks Its Mind* (New York: John Wiley & Sons, 1955); Herbert McClosky and Alida Brill, *Dimensions of Tolerance: What Americans Believe about Civil Liberties* (New York: Russell Sage Foundation, 1983).

5. On how broader attitudes about the implications of administrative regulation are linked to positions on campus speech and harassment policies, see J. K. Miles, "Skepticism About Title IX Culture," in *The Value and Limits of Academic Speech*, ed. Donald A. Downs and Chris W. Surprenant. (Abingdon, UK, and New York, NY: Routledge, 2018).

6. Timur Kuran, *Private Truths, Public Lies: The Social Consequences of Preference Falsification* (Cambridge, MA: Harvard University Press, 1995).

7. Quoted in George Will, "A Red Flag on Campus Free Speech," *Washington Post*, May 18, 2018.

8. Lorelle L. Espinosa, Jennifer R. Crandall, and Philip Wilkinson, "Free Speech and Campus Inclusion: A Survey of College Presidents," *HigherEducationToday* (blog), American Council on Education, April 9, 2018.

9. Samuel J. Abrams, "Think Professors Are Liberal? Try School Administrators," *New York Times*, October 16, 2018.

10. Knight Foundation, *Free Expression on Campus: A Survey of U.S. College Students and U.S. Adults*, with Gallup and Newseum Institute (2016). On the General Social Survey, see JustinMurphy.net (blog), "Who Is Afraid of Free Speech in the United States?," February 16, 2018.

11. Knight Foundation and Gallup, *Free Expression on Campus: What College Students Think About First Amendment Issues*, (2018).

12. Jeremy Waldron, *The Harm in Hate Speech* (Cambridge, MA: Harvard University Press, 2012).

13. See, e.g., Jonathan Rauch, *Kindly Inquisitors: The New Attacks on Free Thought* (Chicago: University of Chicago Press, 1993).

14. McLaughlin and Associates, *National Undergraduate Study*, sponsored by the William F. Buckley Jr. Program at Yale, http://docs.wixstatic.com/ugd/b0cbbd_505c6b0d1a424195847da6955ba42e4b.pdf.

15. John Merigliano, presentation, *Speaking Freely: What Students Think about Expression at American Colleges*, FIRE, October 11, 2017.

16. Cato Institute and YouGov, 2017 Free Speech and Tolerance Survey, August 15–23, 2017.

17. *Texas v. Johnson*, 491 U.S. 397 (1989).

18. See, e.g., *Afroyim v. Rusk*, 387 U.S. 253 (1967); *Maslenjuk v. United States*, 137 S. CT. 1918 (2017).

19. See, e.g., the American Political Science Association report by a panel of experts on civic understanding and involvement in, Stephen Macedo, ed., *Democracy at Risk: How Political Choices Undermine Citizen Participation, and What to Do About It* (Washington, DC: Brookings Institution, 2005). A recent survey by the American Council of Trustees and Alumni (ACTA) has shown at least one reason for this dearth: the disappearance of college courses in American and constitutional history. ACTA, *No U.S. History? How College History Departments Leave American History Out of the Major*, July 2016.

20. E. D. Hirsch Jr., *Cultural Literacy: What Every American Needs to Know* (New York: Vintage Random House, 1988).

21. Monitoring the Future has asked more than 1,000 questions of 12th graders each since 1976 and 8th and 10th graders since 1991, the Youth Risk Behavior Surveillance System has surveyed high school students since 1991 with the assistance of the Centers for Disease Control and Prevention, the CIRP Freshman Survey has interviewed students entering four-year colleges and universities beginning in 1966 and is administered by the Higher Education Research Institute, and the General Social Survey has questioned adults aged 18 and higher since 1972. Jean M. Twenge, *iGen: Why Today's Super-Connected Kids Are Growing Up Less Rebellious, More Tolerant, Less Happy—and Completely Unprepared for Adulthood* (New York: Atria Books, 2017), pp. 6, 9, 1–13.

22. Jean M. Twenge, *iGen*, pp. 154–56 and, generally, chap. 9.

23. Greg Lukianoff and Jonathan Haidt, *The Coddling of the American Mind: How Good Intentions and Bad Ideas Are Setting Up a Generation for Failure* (New York: Penguin Press, 2018).

24. Twenge, *iGen*, pp. 255, 251.

25. Twenge, *iGen*, pp. 76–78.

26. Hannah Arendt, *The Human Condition* (Chicago: University of Chicago Press, 1958), parts V & VI, esp. section 39 titled "Introspection and the Loss of Common Sense."

27. For an insightful firsthand portrayal of the freedom-inhibiting omnipresence of helicoptering parenting, see Hanna Rosin, "The Overprotected Kid: A Preoccupation with Safety Has Robbed Children of Independence, Risk Taking, and Discovery—Without Making It Safer. A New Kind of Playground Points to a Better Solution," *Atlantic Monthly*, April 2014.

28. F. A. Hayek, *Individualism and Economic Order* (University of Chicago Press, 1948); Michael Polanyi, *The Logic of Liberty: Reflections and Rejoinders* (Indianapolis, IN: Liberty Fund, 1998).

1. George P. Fletcher, *A Crime of Self-Defense: Bernard Goetz and the Law* (University of Chicago Press, 1988), chap. 2, "Passion and Reason in Self-Defense."

2. See, e.g., Jack Donnelly, *Universal Human Rights in Theory and Practice* (New York: Cornell University Press, 2013); Donald A. Downs, "Civil Liberties and Human Rights," in *International Encyclopedia of the Social and Behavioral Sciences*, 2nd ed., ed. James Wright (Oxford: Pergamon, 2015).

3. See, e.g., Allen C. Guelzo, *Reconstruction: A Concise History* (New York: Oxford University Press, 2018). On the genius of constitutionalism lying in creating power to protect liberty as well as the means to limit such government so it will not violate liberty itself, see Stephen Holmes, *Passions and Constraint: On the Theory of Liberal Democracy* (Chicago: University of Chicago Press, 1995).

4. *Korematsu v. United States*, 323 U.S. 214 (1944), p. 243, Jackson dissenting opinion.

5. Lin Zhao, quoted in Lian Xi, "The Chinese Dissident Who Wrote in Blood," *The Wall Street Journal*, April 14–15, 2018. See Lian Xi, *Blood Letters: The Untold Story of Lin Zhao, a Martyr in Mao's China* (New York: Basic Books, 2018).

6. Immanuel Kant, *Metaphysics of Morals*, trans. Mary Gregor, ed. Laura Denis (Cambridge: Cambridge University Press, 2017).

7. See, e.g., Frank Dobbin and Alexandra Kalev, "Why Diversity Programs Fail," *Harvard Business Review*, July–August 2016.

8. *West Virginia Board of Education v. Barnette*, 319 U.S. 624 (1943).

9. *Whitney v. California*, 274 U.S. 357 (1927), p. 375.

10. *Whitney v. California,* p. 376.

11. Alexander Meiklejohn considered the rights of listeners as free citizens to be the preeminent justification for free speech under the First Amendment. See his "Free Speech and Its Relationship to Self-Government," in *Political Freedom: The Constitutional Powers of the People* (New York: Oxford University Press, 1965).

12. See, e.g., Nurit Tal-Or, Yariv Tsfati, and Albert C. Gunther, "The Influence of Presumed Media Influence: Origins and Implications of the Third-Person Perception," in *The Sage Handbook of Media Processes and Effects*, ed. Robin L. Nabi and Mary Beth Oliver (Thousand Oaks, CA: Sage Publications, 2009).

13. Similarly, see the Court's "variable obscenity" cases in which the court has held that laws may prohibit access to nonobscene pornography by minors but not by adults. The state may not "burn the house to roast the pig." See, e.g., *Butler v. Michigan*, 352 U.S. 380 (1957).

14. John Locke, *A Letter Concerning Toleration and Other Writings*, ed. Mark Goldie (Indianapolis, IN: Liberty Fund, 2010). On religious conviction as an internal sense of calling that constitutes a kind of inner necessity, see Dietrich Bonhoeffer, *The Cost of Discipleship* (London: SCM Press, 1959).

15. On the tension between constructive and destructive conflict, see, e.g., José Ortega y Gasset, *Concord and Liberty*, trans. Helene Weyl (New York: W. W. Norton & Co., 1946), pp. 14–15.

16. See Madison, *Federalist No. 10*, in Hamilton, Madison, and Jay, *The Federalist Papers*, ed. Clinton Rossiter (New York: New American Library, 1961).

17. Jonathan Haidt, "The Age of Outrage," speech, Manhattan Institute's Wriston Lecture, November 15, 2017. The quotation is from E. D. Hirsch.

18. Nat Hentoff, *Free Speech for Me—But Not for Thee: How the American Left and Right Relentlessly Censor Each Other* (New York: Harper Collins, 1992).

19. See, e.g., Juliana Geran Pilon, *The Utopian Conceit and the War on Freedom* Washington: Academica Press, 2019).

20. Hamilton, *Federalist No. 6*, in Hamilton, Madison, and Jay, ed. Rossiter, *The Federalist Papers*.

21. John Milton, *Areopagitica*, in *The Portable Milton* (New York: Penguin, 1976), p. 166; Goethe, *Faust*, Part I (London: Harmondsworth, 1949), p. 175.

22. On *actus reus*, see, e.g., the insightful materials on the *actus reus* principle in Sanford H. Kadish, Stephen J. Schulhofer, and Rachel E. Barkow, *Criminal Law and Its Processes* (Philadelphia: Wolters Kluwer Law and Business, 2016). See also "Character Evidence; Crimes of Other Acts," *Federal Rules of Evidence*, https://www.rulesofevidence.org/article-iv/rule-404/. In a similar vein, *Robinson v. California* held that the state may not punish a person simply on the basis of his *status* as an addict of illegal drugs. See *Robinson v. California,* 370 U.S. 660 (1962).

23. *Whitney v. California,* p. 376.

24. United States Constitution, Article I, Section 6, Clause 1; Meiklejohn, "Free Speech and Its Relation to Self-Government."

25. On voters' ignorance and irrationality, see, e.g., Bryan Caplan, *The Myth of the Rational Voter: Why Democracies Choose Bad Policies* (Princeton, NJ: Princeton University Press, 2007), and Walter Lippmann's classic, *Public Opinion* (New York: Macmillan, 1922).

26. See Vincent Blasi, "The Checking Function in First Amendment Theory," *Law and Social Inquiry* 2, no. 3 (1977): 521–649.

27. *New York Times v. Sullivan*, 376 U.S. 254 (1964), p. 270. On the crucial practical extension of principle in *Sullivan*, see Lillian BeVier, "The First Amendment and Political Speech: An Inquiry into the Substance and Limits of Principle," *Stanford Law Review* 30, no. 2 (1978): 299–358. See also *Cohen v. California*, 403 U.S. 21 (1971), p. 25, about the importance of "verbal cacophony" to self-government.

28. Harry Kalven Jr., "The *New York Times* Case: A Note on 'The Central Meaning of the First Amendment,'" *The Supreme Court Review* 1964 (Chicago: University of Chicago Press, 1964), pp. 191–221, n. 125, quoting Alexander Meiklejohn.

See also Justice William Brennan, "The Supreme Court and the Meiklejohn Interpretation of the First Amendment," *Harvard Law Review* 79, no. 1 (November 1965).

29. Ronald Dworkin, "Even Bigots and Holocaust Deniers Must Have Their Say," *The Guardian*, February 13, 2006.

30. See Alexander M. Bickel, *The Morality of Consent* (New Haven, CT: Yale University Press, 1975).

31. Mill, *On Liberty*. A more contemporary update of Mill in this regard that takes into consideration new challenges to the pursuit truth from the progressive and "humanitarian" left is Jonathan Rauch's *Kindly Inquisitors: The New Attacks on Free Thought* (Chicago: University of Chicago Press, 1993). Thomas Kuhn, *The Structure of Scientific Revolutions* (Chicago: University of Chicago Press, 1967).

32. Rauch, *Kindly Inquisitors,* pp. 27–28. Rauch's model is indebted to theorists such as Karl Popper and Charles Peirce.

33. Natalie Wolchover, "Evidence Found for a New Fundamental Particle," *Quanta Magazine*, June 1, 2018. Quoting Scott Dodelson on Carnegie Mellon University.

34. See Hannah Arendt, *The Human Condition*, 2nd ed. (Chicago: University of Chicago Press, 1958), Section V. "Action," esp. pp. 243–47.

35. Thomas Nagel, *Mind and Cosmos: Why the Materialist Neo-Darwinian Conception of Nature Is Almost Certainly False* (New York: Oxford University Press, 2012); Michael S. Gazzaniga, *The Consciousness Instinct: Unraveling the Mystery of How the Brain Makes the Mind* (New York: Farrar, Strays and Giroux, 2018), p. 5. Psychiatry treats the difference between "mind" and "brain" in terms of the distinction between "form" and "function." See Paul R. McHugh and Phillip R. Slavney, *The Perspectives of Psychiatry* (Baltimore: Johns Hopkins University Press, 1986), p. 23.

36. See, e.g., Jeffrey Rosen, "The Brain on the Stand," *New York Times Magazine*, March 11, 2007.

37. See, e.g., Karl Popper, *The Open Society and Its Enemies* (Abingdon, UK, and New York: Routledge, 2011).

38. Meiklejohn, "Free Speech and Its Relation to Self-Government," p. 12; Roger Scruton, *The Soul of the World* (Princeton, NJ: Princeton University Press, 2014); Nagel, *Mind and Cosmos*.

39. On the critical role of feminism in fathoming new truths about domestic violence, see Donald A. Downs, *More than Victims: Battered Women, the Syndrome Society, and the Law* (Chicago: University of Chicago Press, 1996).

40. See, e.g., Sara Evans, *Personal Politics: The Roots of Women's Liberation in the Civil Rights Movement and the New Left* (New York: Random House, 1979).

41. Drawing on his intellectual debt to Niebuhr as well as his own experience, Martin Luther King Jr. premised his theory of civil disobedience on

his understanding of the need to sometimes take pointed action to challenge interests and prejudices deeply entrenched in the social order. He also understood the need to pay due respect to the general system of laws in a democratic order. Civil disobedience embodies this tension. See "Letter from the Birmingham Jail," in *Civil Disobedience: Theory and Practice* ed. Hugo Adam Bedau (New York: Pegasus, 1969).

42. Reinhold Niebuhr, *Moral Man and Immoral Society* (New York: Scribner, 1932). Realism in international relations (IR) theory is similar as applied to the international realm. Hans Morgenthau was also a moral realist like Niebuhr. IR theorist Kenneth Waltz maintains that the structural aspects of IR, which include the absence of a true international sovereign, unavoidably lead to a system in which competition, power, and national interest must rule the day. See his *Theory of International Politics* (New York: McGraw Hill, 1979).

43. *Whitney v. California,* p. 375.

44. Jennifer A. Doudna and Samuel H. Sternberg, *A Crack in Creation: Gene Editing and the Unthinkable Power of Controlling Evolution* (New York: Houghton Mifflin Harcourt, 2017). On Doudna's dream, see Michael Hiltzik, "CRISPR Pioneer Jennifer Doudna Struggles with the Ethical Implications of What She Has Wrought," *Los Angeles Times,* July 21, 2017.

45. Leon Kass, "Preventing a Brave New World," *The New Republic,* June 21, 2001. See also Roger Shattuck, *Forbidden Knowledge: From Prometheus to Pornography* (New York: Harcourt, Brace and Co., 1996); Philip Rieff, *My Life Among the Deathworks: Illustrations of the Aesthetics of Authority* (Charlottesville: University of Virginia Press, 2006); Patrick Deneen, *Why Liberalism Failed* (New Haven, CT: Yale University Press, 2018).

46. See, e.g., *Central Hudson Gas and Electric Corp. v. Public Service Corp. of New York,* 447 U.S. 557 (1980) (special test for commercial speech). See also *44 Liquormart, Inc. v. Rhode Island,* 517 U.S. 484 (1996) (truthful advertising information entitled to strong First Amendment protection vs. state paternalism claims).

47. In *What's Happened to the University?* (Abingdon, UK, and New York: Routledge, 2016), Frank Furedi draws on Arendt in his discussion of the importance of judgment, and how contemporary therapeutic and identity politics on campus have marginalized judgment in favor of sensitivity.

48. George F. Kennan, *Democracy and the Student Left* (New York: Bantam Books, 1968), pp. 10–11. Meiklejohn, "Free Speech and Its Relation to Self-Government," p. 9.

49. *Whitney v. California,* p. 377. Hannah Arendt, *The Human Condition* (Chicago: University of Chicago Press, 1958), p. 36.

50. *Tinker v. Des Moines Sch. Dist.,* 393 U.S. 503 (1969).

51. *Dennis v. United States,* 341 U.S. 494 (1951), p. 581.

52. For the changes and common understandings of courage as a concept over time, see Richard Avramenko, *Courage: The Politics of Life and Limb* (Notre Dame, IL: University of Notre Dame Press, 2011).

53. Aristotle, *Nicomachean Ethics*, 1116b17–19, book 3.6–9.

54. *Brandenburg v. Ohio*, 395 U.S. 444 (1969), p. 447.

55. For a critique of expecting reason in such emotional cases as self-defense, see Richard Restak's critique of the expectation of reason in the Bernhard Goetz case in the 1980s, "The Law: The Fiction of the 'Reasonable Man.'" *Washington Post*, May 17, 1987. Restak's take is that of a neuroscientist, which runs counter to the normative demand of reason in law and citizenship.

56. See George Fletcher's insightful analysis of the imminence standard and other aspects of self-defense law in *A Crime of Self-Defense*, chaps. 2 and 3.

57. Bruno Bettelheim, *The Uses of Enchantment: The Meaning and Importance of Fairy Tales* (New York: Vintage, 1975). Bettelheim won the National Book Award and the National Book Critics Circle Award for this book. Some aspects of Bettelheim's work have been challenged, such as its Freudian roots and the deeply unfair way he wrongly blamed mothers for the autism of their children. These critiques ring true. That said, Bettelheim's understanding of the uses of scary children's stories is widely respected and convincing. See also Bettelheim, "Surviving," in *Surviving and Other Essays* (New York: Vintage, 1979), where Bettelheim shows how self-reliant and politically knowledgeable concentration camp inmates were the most suited to maintain mental toughness in the camps. On the ethical basis of psychoanalysis properly pursued, see Philip Rieff, *Freud: The Mind of the Moralist* (Chicago: University of Chicago Press, 1959).

58. Walter Isaacson, *Leonardo Da Vinci* (New York: Simon and Schuster, 2017). See also Steven H. Shiffrin, *The First Amendment, Democracy, and Romance* (Cambridge, MA: Harvard University Press, 1990).

59. Jung depicts the "shadow" as a dark, unconscious force that has sinister aspects for the personality. But encountering its difficult to access and to process aspects contributes to self-knowledge and growth. "To become conscious of it involves recognizing the dark aspects of the personality as present and real. This act is the essential condition for any kind of self-knowledge, and it therefore, as a rule, meets with considerable resistance." Joseph Campbell, ed., *The Portable Jung* (New York: Viking Press, 1971), p. 145.

60. Bettelheim, *The Uses of Enchantment*, pp. 3–8.

61. On cognitive-behavioral therapy as a tool for dealing with anxiety, depression, phobias, etc., see Robert L. Leahy and Stephen J. Holland, *Treatment Plans and Interventions for Depression and Anxiety Disorders* (New York: Guilford, 2000). Greg Haidt and Jonathan Lukianoff, "The Coddling of the American Mind," *Atlantic Monthly*, September 2015.

62. See Madeline J. Bruce, "Does Trauma Centrality Predict Trigger Warning Use? Physiological Responses to Using a Trigger Warning," ResearchGate (website), May 2017. See also Craig Harper, "It's Official—Trigger Warnings Might Actually Be Harmful," *Medium* (website), July 28, 2018.

63. This type of integration is a theme of classic literature and mythology, as well as depth psychology. A good example of the latter is Erik Erikson, *Insight and Responsibility: Lectures on the Ethical Implications of Psychoanalytic Insight* (New York: W. W. Norton, 1964).

64. Joshua Wolf Shenk, *Lincoln's Melancholy: How Depression Challenged a President and Fueled His Greatness* (New York: Houghton Mifflin, 2005).

65. See, e.g., Pascal Bruckner, *Tyranny of Guilt: An Essay on Western Masochism* (Princeton, NJ: Princeton University Press, 2006).

66. Rauch, *Kindly Inquisitors*, p. 68.

67. *Abrams v. United States*, 250 U.S. 616 (1919), p. 630. For a fascinating account of Holmes's famous changing of his mind, see Thomas Healy, *The Great Dissent: How Oliver Wendell Holmes Changed His Mind—and Changed the History of Free Speech in America* (New York: Henry Holt & Co., 2013). Judge Learned Hand presented a strong version of the incitement test two years before Holmes in a lower federal court case. See *Masses Publishing Co. v. Patten,* 244 Fed. 535 (1917).

68. See also Jonathan Zimmerman and Emily Robertson, *The Case for Contention: Teaching Controversial Issues in American Schools* (Chicago: University of Chicago Press, 2017), p. 61: "Developing the capacities for deliberation requires a focus on a particular set of skills and dispositions. Effective deliberators should be able to construct sound arguments for their positions but should also be open to changing their views when confronted with better arguments." See also Diana E. Hess, *Controversy in the Classroom: The Democratic Power of Discussion* (Abingdon, UK, and New York: Routledge, 2009).

69. Lee C. Bollinger, *The Tolerant Society: Freedom of Speech and Extremist Speech in America* (New York: Oxford University Press, 1986).

70. See, e.g., Jeffrey Abramson, *We, the Jury: The Jury System and the Ideal of Democracy* (New York: Basic Books, 1994).

71. John Gaddis, *On Grand Strategy* (New York: Penguin Random House, 2018). Gaddis's political theory model of this way of thinking is Isaiah Berlin. I also discuss this aspect of jury deliberation in *More than Victims: Battered Women, the Syndrome Society, and the Law* (Chicago: University of Chicago Press, 1996).

72. George F. Kennan, *Memoirs 1950–1963* (New York: Pantheon Books, 1972), pp. 199–200. The internal quotations are from a letter he wrote to a friend about McCarthyism. See also Frank Furedi's discussion of Hannah Arendt's conception of "judgment" as an enlarged way of thinking, which is "judgment knows how to transcend its own individual limitations," in Furedi's *What's Happened to the University?* pp. 74–80; Hannah Arendt, *The Life of the Mind* (New York: Harcourt, 1978), p. 39.

73. *Palko v. Connecticut*, 302 U.S. 319 (1937), p. 327.

CHAPTER 8

1. Alexander Hamilton, *Federalist No. 84*, in *The Federalist Papers*, ed. Clinton Rossiter, (New American Library, 1961). See also H. L. A. Hart, *The Concept of Law* (New York: Oxford University Press, 1961), pp. 27–42, 85–88, in which citizens are more law-abiding when they agree with law's moral or practical justification; that is, when they feel an "obligation" to it above and beyond simply feeling "obliged" to it. One is "obliged" to give a gunman one's wallet, but not "obligated."

2. I testified on McAdams's behalf in the case, but my testimony did acknowledge the other side of the coin and the harm done to the instructor, thereby making my testimony ambivalent. On the case, see FIRE, "Opinion of the Supreme Court of Wisconsin in McAdams v. Marquette University," July 6, 2018.

3. See, e.g., Grant McConnell, *Private Power and American Democracy* (New York: Knopf, 1966). See also Richard A. Primus, *The American Language of Rights* (Cambridge: Cambridge University Press, 1996).

4. See FIRE report, "Chicago Statement: University and Faculty Body Support," July 12, 2019.

5. Jason Brennan, "Outside Funding for Centers: A Challenge to Institutional Mission?" in *The Value and Limits of Academic Speech*, ed. Donald A. Downs and Chris W. Surprenant (Abingdon, UK, and New York: Routledge, 2018), chap. 6.

6. See, e.g., Institute for Humane Studies, "Free Speech and Open Inquiry Initiative," https://theihs.org/academics/free-speech-open-inquiry-initiative/; the ACLU, https://www.aclu.org; ACTA, https://www.goacta.org; the National Association of Scholars, "We Uphold the Standards of a Liberal Arts Education, https://www.nas.org; Heterodox Academy, https://heterodoxacademy.org; and "PEN America Principles on Campus Free Speech," October 17, 2016, https://pen .org/advocacy-campaign/campus-speech/; numerous articles from the Cato Institute at https://www.cato.org; Speech First, "Overview," https://speechfirst.org /about; *spiked* at https://www.spiked-online.com; and the American Association of University Professors, https://www.aaup.org.

7. See Bill Rickards, "Georgetown University Adopts 'Chicago Statement,'" FIRE, June 15, 2017. See also John Hasnas's presentations at IHS events attended by the author, and email correspondence with Hasnas.

8. See, e.g., Alan Charles Kors and Harvey A. Silverglate, *The Shadow University: The Betrayal of Liberty on America's Campuses* (New York: Free Press, 1998).

9. See, e.g., Alex Morey, "Faculty Focus: How Three Professors Banded Together to Beat Back a Free Speech Threat at Clemson," FIRE, December 28, 2015. I also had personal and email correspondence with Brad Thompson about this issue.

10. AAUP, "Threats to the Independence of Student Media," December 2016. See also Donald A. Downs, "On Threats to Student Press Freedom and

the Indispensability of Student Journalism: Reflections on the AAUP Report on Student Media," *Free Speech and Open Inquiry Project* (blog), December 12, 2016.

11. Email correspondence and private conversations with Mitch Pickerill, June 2018.

12. See, e.g., Primus, *The American Language of Rights.*

13. See Jon A. Shields and Joshua M. Dunn Sr., *Passing on the Right: Conservatives in the Progressive University* (New York: Oxford University Press, 2016).

14. Linda S. Frey, University of Montana, email, October 2017, and conversation with author.

15. "Academic Freedom at Johns Hopkins," https://provost.jhu.edu/wp-content/uploads/sites/4/2017/08/AcademicFreedomatJohnsHopkins.pdf; HUB Staff Report, "Johns Hopkins Adopts Statement on Academic Freedom Principles, Philosophy," Johns Hopkins University, https://hub.jhu.edu/2015/09/11/johns-hopkins-statement-academic-freedom/. I also had several conversations with Grossman about this movement.

16. The signees were economist Richard T. Ely and education professor Edward C. Eliott. AAUP, "Appendix I: 1915 Declaration of Principles on Academic Freedom and Tenure"; Official Statement of Board of Regents, University of Wisconsin, 1894, http://digicoll.library.wisc.edu/WIReader/WER1035-Chpt6.html. See also Theodore Herfurth, "Sifting and Winnowing: A Chapter in the History of Academic Freedom at the University of Wisconsin," in *Academic Freedom on Trial: 100 Years of Sifting and Winnowing at the University of Wisconsin*, ed. W. Lee Hansen (Office of University Publications, University of Wisconsin–Madison, 1998), pp. 58–89.

17. See the equation of liberalism to an "insurance policy" aspect in Roberto Unger, *Law in Modern Society: Toward a Criticism of Social Theory* (New York: Free Press, 1977), p. 76.

18. See FIRE, "Victory at UW–Stout: Chancellor Folds after Censorship of 'Firefly' and Anti-Fascism Posters," October 4, 2011. Discussions and interactions with Timothy Shiell.

19. See "Fired for Profane Language," *AAUP Updates*, May 7, 2018, Discussions with political scientist James Stoner, LSU.

20. AAUP, "On Collegiality as a Criterion for Faculty Evaluation," 2016 Revision.

21. See Susan Kruth, "UW–Madison Must Remain Faithful to Speech-Protective Language of Anti-Bullying Policy," FIRE, January 8, 2015.

22. FIRE, "Office for Civil Rights and the First Amendment," August 12, 2003.

23. See Tyler Coward, "Louisiana Governor Signs Imperfect Campus Free Speech Bill," FIRE Newsdesk, June 6, 2018.

24. Jim Manley, "Campus Free Speech: A Legislative Proposal," Goldwater Institute, January 30, 2017.

25. Stanley Kurtz, "Georgia Passes Goldwater-Based Campus Free Speech Bill," *National Review*, May 15, 2018. Kurtz is the main author of the Goldwater model bill.

26. Teri Lyn Hinds, "Untangling the Threads: 2018 State Legislation Addressing Campus Speech Concerns," May 31, 2018.

27. John Hardin, "You Can't Legislate Free Inquiry on Campus," *New York Times*, May 21, 2018.

28. Sigal R. Ben-Porath, *Free Speech on Campus* (Philadelphia: University of Pennsylvania Press, 2017), p. 10; Frank Furedi, *What's Happened to the University?* (Abingdon, UK, and New York: Routledge, 2016).

29. Nadine Strossen, *Hate: Why We Should Resist It with Free Speech, Not Censorship* (New York: Oxford University Press, 2018), chap. 8; Donald A. Downs, *Nazis in Skokie: Freedom, Community, and the First Amendment* (Notre Dame, IN: University of Notre Dame Press, 1985).

30. Donald A. Downs, George Waldner, and Emily Chamlee-Wright, *A Framework for Campus Free Speech Policy*, Institute for Humane Studies (2016). On "priming," see Daniel Kahneman, *Thinking, Fast and Slow* (New York: Farrar, Straus, & Giroux, 2011), pp. 52–58.

31. Donald A. Downs, Kristin Roman, George Waldner, and Emily Chamlee-Wright, "A Framework for Campus Crisis Management," Institute for Human Studies Report, 2018, p. 9.

32. University of Wisconsin, *Commitment to Academic Freedom and Freedom of Expression* (Regent Policy Document 4-21), adopted October 6, 2017.

33. This wording is from the text that the dean of students' office accepted and provided to students. Unfortunately, the university did not provide the primer with an online link, which seemed in my mind to give it less status in orientation than the other programs regarding diversity and the like. If this is so, the use of the primer would have to have been construed as a quasi-victory for academic free speech. I have a copy of the text in my personal possession.

34. American Council of Trustees and Alumni, *A Crisis in Civic Education* (January 2016).

35. Peter H. Schuck, *Diversity in America: Keeping Government at a Safe Distance* (Cambridge, MA: Harvard University Press, 2003).

36. Frank Dobbin and Alexandra Kalev, "Why Diversity Programs Fail," *Harvard Business Review*, July–August 2016.

37. Dana Villa, *Socratic Citizenship* (Princeton, NJ: Princeton University Press, 2001), p. 23.

38. In his book on privacy and harassment, Jeffrey Rosen presents a similar approach to the more universalist reframing of harassment law and policy.

The Unwanted Gaze: The Destruction of Privacy in America (New York: Random House, 2000), pp. 117–18, 165, and 192–93.

39. University of Chicago, *Report of the Committee on Freedom of Expression*, Geoffrey Stone, Chair (2015).

40. *Davis v. Monroe County Board of Education*, 526 U.S. 629, p. 651.

41. For a balanced and sensible essay on how to think about the line between allowable and improper offensive speech in classroom discussion, see Christina Easton, "Words That Wound in the Classroom: Should They Be Silenced or Discussed?" in *The Value and Limits of Academic Speech*, ed. Downs and Surprenant.

42. UW–Madison, ASA Document 275; "Prohibited Harassment: Definitions and Rules Governing the Conduct of UW–Madison Faculty and Academic Staff, Part III, Expression in Instructional Settings," FIRE.

43. Andrew Duehren and Cameron McWhirter, "White Nationalist Rally Musters Little Enthusiasm," *Wall Street Journal*, August 12, 2018.

44. I portray the almost unprecedented problems attendant upon the Skokie confrontation in *Nazis in Skokie*.

45. *New York Times v. United States*, 403 U.S. 713 (1971). Over time, presidential parties and major press organizations developed the ritual of informal negotiations to avoid overt government suppression in exchange for self-imposed limits on the part of the press. See Jack Goldsmith, *Power and Constraint: The Accountable Presidency after 9/11* (W. W. Norton & Co., 2012).

46. Prudence Carter and R. Jay Wallace, letter with "Report of the Chancellor's Commission on Free Speech, UC–Berkeley," April 9, 2018.

47. Emily Chamlee-Wright, IHS president and chief executive officer, correspondence with *Open Inquiry Project of the Institute for Humane Studies' Free Speech and Open Inquiry Initiative*, April 2018.

48. See https://freespeech.berkeley.edu. Private correspondence of author with Gilman.

49. Conor Friedersdorf, "The Damage That Harvard Has Done," *The Atlantic*, May 14, 2019.

50. Scott Jaschik, "University Rejects Calls to Fire Camille Paglia," *Inside Higher Ed*, April 17, 2019.

INDEX

Index to *Free Speech and Liberal Education* by Donald Alexander Downs

Note: Information in notes is indicated by n.

Brennan, John, 13–14
Brennan, William, 57, 160
Brinton, Crane, 34, 35
brow-beating, 209
Brown University, 123–24
BRTs. *See* bias response teams (BRTs)
Buchanan, Teresa, 196
Buckley Survey, 136–38
bullying, 151, 197, 208
bureaucratic pressures, examples of, 21–22

CAFAR. *See* Committee for Academic Freedom and Rights (CAFAR)
Calderon, Ian, 14
California Proposition 209 (Prop 209), 119, 233n28
California State University–Los Angeles, 13–14
Callanan, Keegan, 25
campus
  bureaucracy, burgeoning of, 23, 51
  governance, 49–50
  leadership, 202–3
  mobilization, 183–217
  research centers, 186–87
  sexual paranoia on, 18–19
Cardozo, Benjamin, 181
Carpenter, Sally, 125
Cato Institute, 188
Cato Institute survey, 139–43
CBT. *See* cognitive-behavioral therapy (CBT)
censorship, 115, 151
Center for Political Thought and Leadership, 186
Center for Responsive Politics (CRP), 120
Center for the Study of Institutions and Innovation (UW–Stout), 186, 196
Center for the Study of Liberal Democracy, 186
Centers for Disease Control and Prevention, 244n20
Chamlee-Wright, Emily, 214
Chapman University, 189
Charles Koch Foundation, 200
Charles Koch Institute, 132–33
Charney, Evan, 11
checking function, 160
checks and balances, 108, 230n47
Chemerinsky, Erwin, 66, 202–3

Chicago Statement on the Principles of Free Expression (University of Chicago), 17, 74, 186, 189, 196, 205, 210
children, fear and, 174–75, 249n57
Childress, Herb, 107
chilling effect, 15, 136
Chinese People's Daily, 151
Christensen, Clayton, 106
Chronicle of Higher Education, 18–19, 30
Churchill, Ward, 193
Churchill, Winston, 165
chutzpah, 176–81
CIRP Freshman Institute, 244n20
citizenship, revoking, 140
civic commitment, 190
civic education, 111–12
Civil Discourse 101 programs, 205
civil disobedience, 248n41
civility
  in classrooms, 211
  in higher education, 44–47
  modern conceptions of, 45
  origin and definition of, 45
  overview, 206–7, 228n27
civil rights anti-pornography ordinance, 99–100
civil rights movement, 42, 230n44
Claremont McKenna College, 14
Clark, Kenneth, 35
classical liberal model, 6, 7
"The Classic First Amendment Under Stress: Freedom of Speech and the University" speech (Post), 58
classroom limits, 211–12, 254n41
Cleary, Edward, 48, 101
Clemson University, 190
cloning, 168
The Closing of the American Mind (Bloom), 27
"Co-Curricular Educational Programming" (University of Chicago), 206
The Coddling of the American Mind (Haidt and Lukianoff), 83, 145
coercion of belief, 154
cognitive-behavioral therapy (CBT), 175–76, 249n61
Cohn, Joe, 199
colleges. *See* universities
college speech codes. *See* speech codes
collegiality, 197
commenting, to audiences, 13

deontological virtues, of free speech, 150–61
Department of Education (DOE), 19, 82, 110, 198
DeVos, Betsy, 82
Dickenson, Matthew, 25, 35
discontinuities, 116
disinvitations, of speakers, 15–16, 25–26, 88–91
distancing, of people, 46
diversity
  intensity of drive for, 22–23
  training in, 208–10
  uniting through, 43
"diversity machine," 22
The Divine Comedy (Dante), 44
DOE. *See* Department of Education (DOE)
Doe v. University of Michigan, 111–12
dogmatism, 209
donations, statistics on, 120
Dostoyevsky, Fyodor, 35
Doudna, Jennifer, 168, 169
Downs, Donald Alexander
  biography of, 5
  Cornell '69, 90
  in graduate school at UC–Berkeley, 116
  Nazis in Skokie, 99, 204–5, 238n46
  reason and passion, views on, 38
  The Value and Limits of Academic Speech, 92, 187
due doubt, 176–81
due respect for limits of reason, as a Socratic virtue, 33, 34
Dunn, Joshua M. Sr., 116, 121–23, 164
Dworkin, Andrea, 99, 100
Dworkin, Ronald, 160–61, 166, 184

echo chamber problem, 31
effective deliberation, 250n68
Egalitarian Principle, 231n8
Eidelberg, Paul, 78
Einstein, Albert, 35
Elliott, Edward C., 252n16
Ellison, Ralph, 7
Ely, Richard T., 252n16
embattlement model, 18
Emerson, Thomas, 73
emotion
  balancing with reason and politics in universities, 36–44
  Haidt on, 40
emotional ambivalence, Freud on, 115
emotional correctness, 92

emotional states, 144–45
emotional teaching, 46
empirical rule, 231n8
epistemological problems, 214
epistemology, compared with ontology, 31
equality
  as an essential attribute of justice and liberal democracy, 51
  of ideas, 59–60
equal rights, 7
escape from freedom versus freedom, 115
Etchemendy, John, 1
eugenics movement, 123
Evergreen State, 14, 24–25
existential threats, 91
expression versus repression, 115
external versus local action, 183–201
extramural speech, 66–67

"factions," 155
faculty
  adjunct, 106–7
  administrative interference with, 109–10
  attitudes toward speech of, 125–30
  bias repression of, 116–17
  characteristics of great, 76
  Democrats on, 120
  "mission creep" and, 111
  political persuasion of, 116
  Republicans on, 116, 120
  survey of, 127–30
  tenured, 106–7
  type of character of, 51
  voter registration study of, 120
fallibility principle, 77, 156–57, 179, 198
The Fall of Public Man (Sennett), 228n27
The Fall of the Faculty (Ginsberg), 108
false advertising, 170
fast thinking, 37–38
Faust (Goethe), 168
fear
  basic, 114
  children and, 174–75, 249n57
  dealing with, 171–76
  human nature and, 112–16
  irrational, 172
  Moreno on, 113–14
  philosophy of, 241n21
  rational, 172
  specific, 113
  undifferentiated, 114–15, 171–72

"Free Speech and Intellectual Diversity in Higher Education" conference, 57–58

Free Speech and Open Inquiry Initiative (Institute for Humane Studies), 188

Free Speech on Campus (Chemerinsky and Gillman), 66, 202–3

free speech rights (president's survey), 130–31

free speech zone (Texas Tech University), 234n40

French, David, 192

Freud, Sigmund, 38, 115, 165, 168

Freud and Philosophy (Ricoeur), 113

Frey, Linda S., 193

Frey, Marsha, 194

Friedersdorf, Conor, 216

Furedi, Frank
alliance between student emotional regression and campus bureaucracies, views on, 224n2
Arendt's conception of judgment, views on, 248n47, 250n72
"Growing Up Disturbed," 92
recent trends in higher education, views on, 50, 144–45

Gadamer, Hans-Georg, 71

Gaddis, John, 17–18, 165, 180, 250n71

Gans, Erna, 204–5

Gazzaniga, Michael S., 163

general limits, 210–11

General Social Survey, 133, 244n20

Gen Xers, 143

Georgetown University, 22, 188

Gerstmann, Evan, 85

Gertz v. Robert Welch, 59, 61

Giddens, Anthony, 43

Gillman, Howard, 66, 202–3, 214

Ginsberg, Benjamin, 108

Goethe, Johann Wolfgang von, 168

Goffman, Erving, on "stigma signals," 122–23

Goldberger, David, 98

Goldwater Institute, 199, 200, 201, 206

governance, shared, 105–8, 111

Graham, Billy, 104

The Great Gatsby (Fitzgerald), 83

Gross, Neil, 120–21

Grossman, Joel, 194

"Growing Up Disturbed" (Furedi), 92

Grubb, Alan, 190

Haidt, Jonathan
acceptance of uncomfortable truths, views on, 47
The Coddling of the American Mind, 83, 145
human penchant for moralism and tribalism, views on, 118
identity politics, views on, 41
intersectionality, views on, 156
nature of morality and emotion, views on, 40
Plato, views on, 38
The Righteous Mind, 39, 41, 112–13
trigger warnings, views on, 176

Hamilton, Alexander, 157, 184

happiness, pursuit of, 231n4

harassment
expansive interpretations of, 91
as a general limit, 211
protection from, 86
Supreme Court's definition of, 189
UW–Madison on, 211–12

Hardin, John, 200

harm principle, 94–95, 238n41

The Harm in Hate Speech (Waldron), 61, 93–94

Harvard Business Review, 208

Harvard Crimson, 119–20

Harvard Law School, 90–91, 100

Harvard University, 216

Hasnas, John, 55, 188–89

hate speech
African Americans on, 133, 135, 138, 141
Cato Institute survey on, 141
Democrats on, 138, 141
Independents on, 141
key findings on, in Buckley Survey, 137–38
key findings on, in FIRE survey, 138
key findings on, in 2016 Knight Survey, 133
key findings on, in 2018 Knight Survey, 134–35
Latinos on, 141
limits on, 61, 212–15
overview, 93–95
Republicans on, 141
Waldron on, 232n13
whites on, 141
women on, 133, 135

intellectual freedom
respect for, 3–4
risk of, 3
as a Socratic virtue, 33, 34
tasks used to defend, 4
intellectual honesty, as a Socratic virtue, 33, 34
intellectual pluralism, 119
intellectual *polis*
commitment to, 111–12
universities as an, 36, 44, 66–72
intellectual safety, concerns for, 86
intellectual virtues, 33, 54
internal and cooperative model of action, 188
internal campus mobilization, 189–90
interpersonal relations or exchanges, university model centered on, 37
interracial marriage, reversal of opinion on, 64
irrational fear, 172
Isaacson, Walter, 175

Jackson, Robert H., 60, 151, 152
James Madison Program, 186
Jefferson, Thomas, 39
Johns Hopkins University, 194
Johnson, Edward, 90
judgment, 248n47, 250n72
Jung, Carl, 175, 249n59
juries, 180

Kahneman, Daniel, 37
Kalven, Harry Jr., 72
Kant, Immanuel, 149, 151–54, 156, 184
Kass, Leon, 168
Kennan, George F., 170, 173, 176, 180–81
Kerr, Clark, 30
Keyishian v. Board of Regents, 87
Khalid, Amna, 86–87
Kierkegaard, Søren, 241n21
Kindly Inquisitors (Rauch), 162, 247n31
King, Martin Luther Jr., 42, 74, 96, 113, 166, 247n41
"Kingdom of Ends," 152, 154
Kipnis, Laura
bureaucratic elements of shadow universities, views on, 132
bureaucratization of sexual relations, views on, 85
improper extension of Title XI investigations, views on, 70

investigated for expressing an opinion on sexual due process, 91
"netherworld" of accusation, 110
shadow university, views on, 18–23
Unwanted Advances, 20, 82–83, 114
Knight Foundation survey, 128, 132–36
knowledge
Cato Institute survey and, 141–42
compared with pursuit of truth, 31–33
cumulative, 34, 35–36
as defense of intellectual freedom, 4
limits of, 34
noncumulative, 35, 36
philosophy of, 38
pursuit of, 31–32
secular, 53
Koch Foundation, 187
Kors, Alan Charles, 12, 189, 198
Krauthammer, Charles, 9
Kuhn, Thomas, 34
Kuran, Timur, 27, 129, 191

Lamb, Brian, 17
"Language Police," 84
Latinos
flag burning, views on, 140
free speech, views on, 141
hate speech, views on, 141
knowledge of laws protecting racist statements, views on, 142
offensive speech, views on, 141, 143
political correctness, views on, 139–40
transgender identity, views on, 140
Law in Modern Society (Unger), 242n27
Learned Hand, 250n67
learning
components of, 76
informal, 69
sources of, 37
university model centered on book, 37
legal culpability, determining, 180
legislative actions, 198–201
legitimated disobedience, 233n35
Legutko, Ryszard, 25–26
Lepawsky, Albert, 1
liberal democracy
Berns on, 54
coexistence in a, 180
decline in courses teaching about, 112
Deneen on, 53–54
systems of freedom and authority in, 162
Tocqueville on, 53–54

ABOUT THE AUTHOR

Donald Alexander Downs is the Alexander Meiklejohn Professor of Political Science Emeritus and affiliate professor emeritus of law and journalism at the University of Wisconsin–Madison. He has won numerous local and national awards for scholarship, teaching, and activism in support of free speech and academic freedom. His scholarship has dealt with a wide range of issues, including academic freedom and free speech; American politics; political and legal thought and movements; citizenship; campus politics; domestic violence, psychiatry, and the criminal law; and the relationship among the military, the university, and civic education. His most recent books are *Restoring Free Speech and Liberty on Campus* (Cambridge University Press, 2005); *Arms and the University: Military Presence and the Civic Education of Non-Military Students* (Cambridge University Press, 2012), coauthored with Ilia Murtazashvili; and *The Value and Limits of Academic Speech: Philosophical, Political, and Legal Perspectives* (Routledge, 2018), coedited with Chris W. Surprenant.

Cato Institute

Founded in 1977, the Cato Institute is a public policy research foundation dedicated to broadening the parameters of policy debate to allow consideration of more options that are consistent with the principles of limited government, individual liberty, and peace. To that end, the Institute strives to achieve greater involvement of the intelligent, concerned lay public in questions of policy and the proper role of government.

The Institute is named for *Cato's Letters*, libertarian pamphlets that were widely read in the American Colonies in the early 18th century and played a major role in laying the philosophical foundation for the American Revolution.

Despite the achievement of the nation's Founders, today virtually no aspect of life is free from government encroachment. A pervasive intolerance for individual rights is shown by government's arbitrary intrusions into private economic transactions and its disregard for civil liberties. And while freedom around the globe has notably increased in the past several decades, many countries have moved in the opposite direction, and most governments still do not respect or safeguard the wide range of civil and economic liberties.

To address those issues, the Cato Institute undertakes an extensive publications program on the complete spectrum of policy issues. Books, monographs, and shorter studies are commissioned to examine the federal budget, Social Security, regulation, military spending, international trade, and myriad other issues. Major policy conferences are held throughout the year, from which papers are published thrice yearly in the *Cato Journal*. The Institute also publishes the quarterly magazine *Regulation*.

In order to maintain its independence, the Cato Institute accepts no government funding. Contributions are received from foundations, corporations, and individuals, and other revenue is generated from the sale of publications. The Institute is a nonprofit, tax-exempt, educational foundation under Section 501(c)3 of the Internal Revenue Code.

CATO INSTITUTE
1000 Massachusetts Avenue NW
Washington, DC 20001
www.cato.org